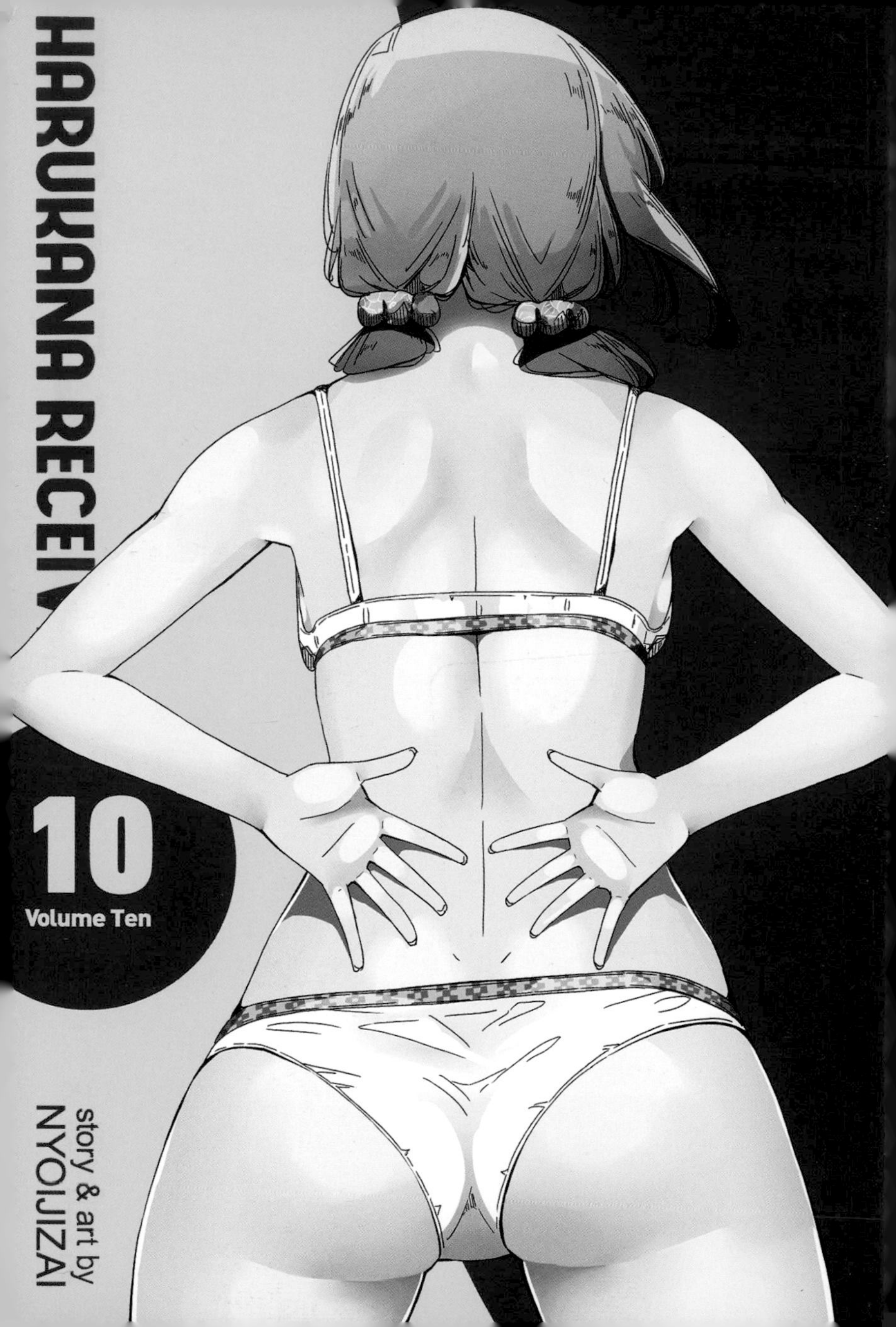
HARUKANA RECEIV
10
Volume Ten
story & art by
NYOIJIZAI

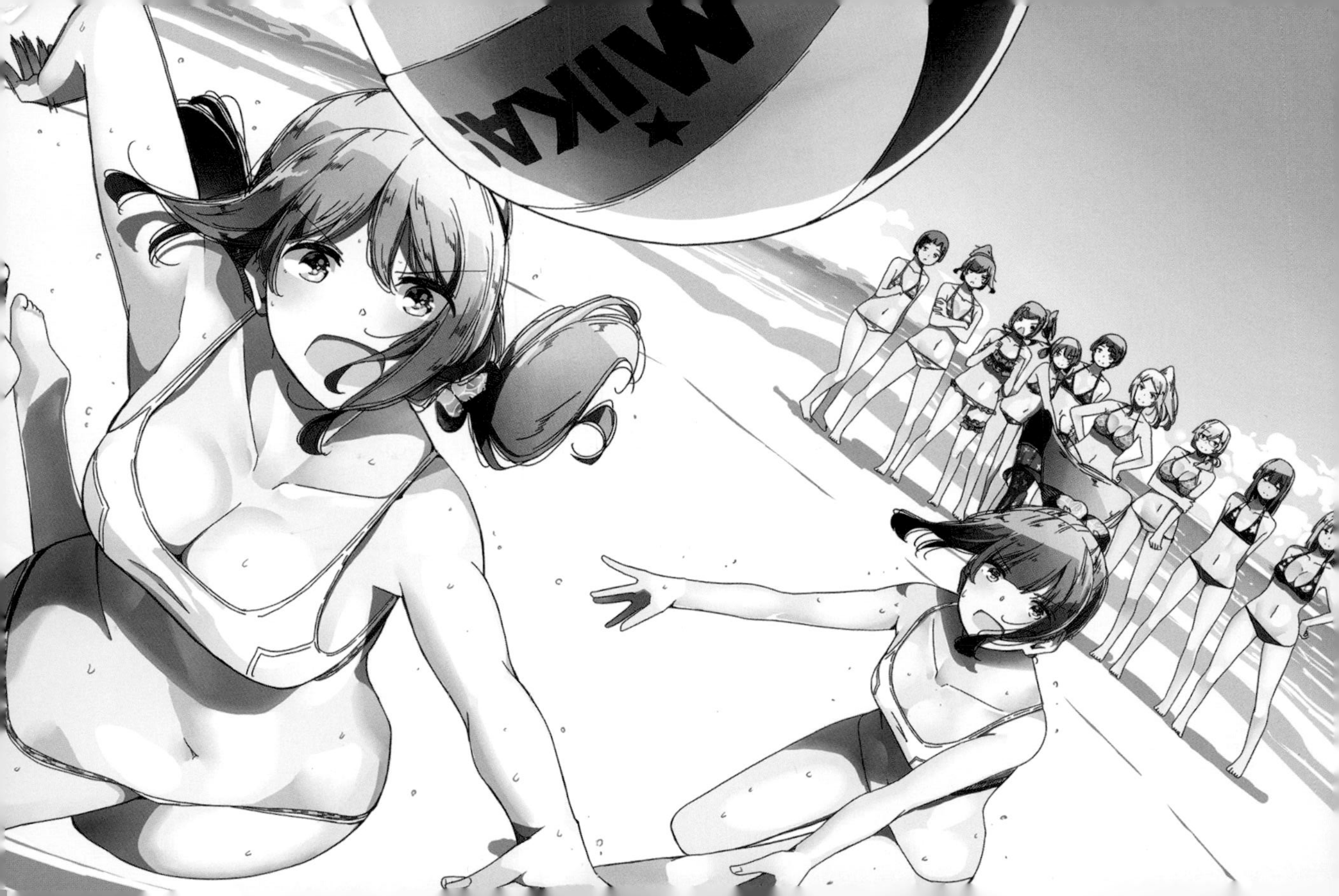
MIKA

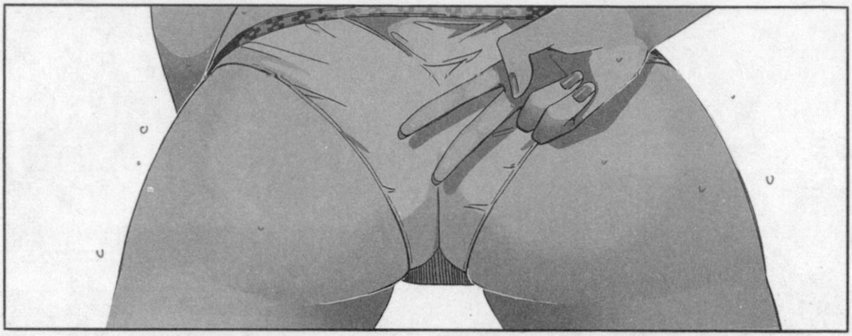
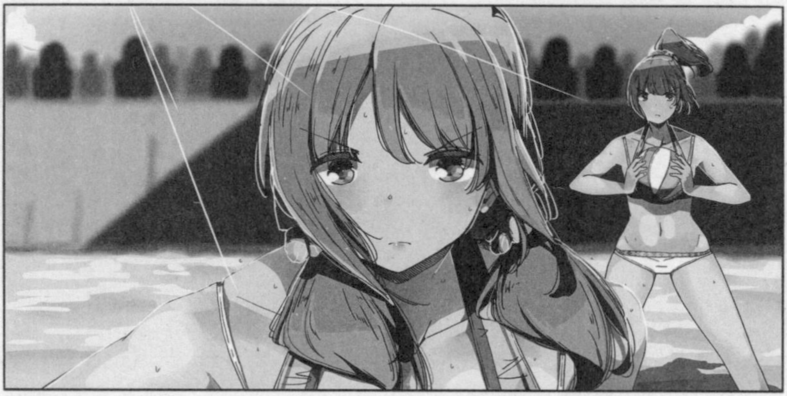
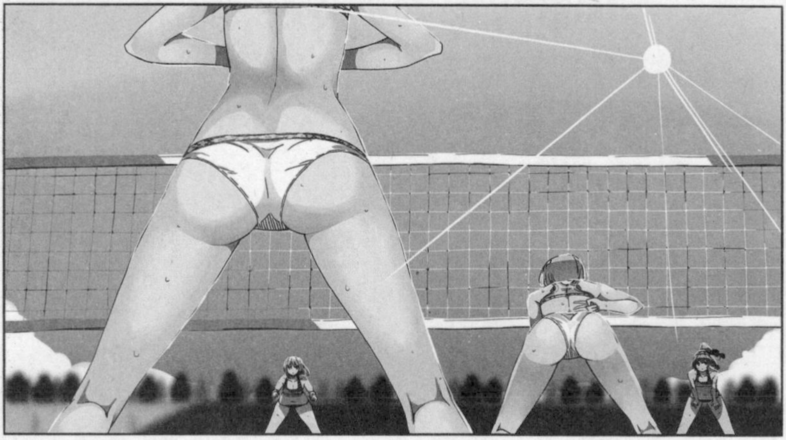

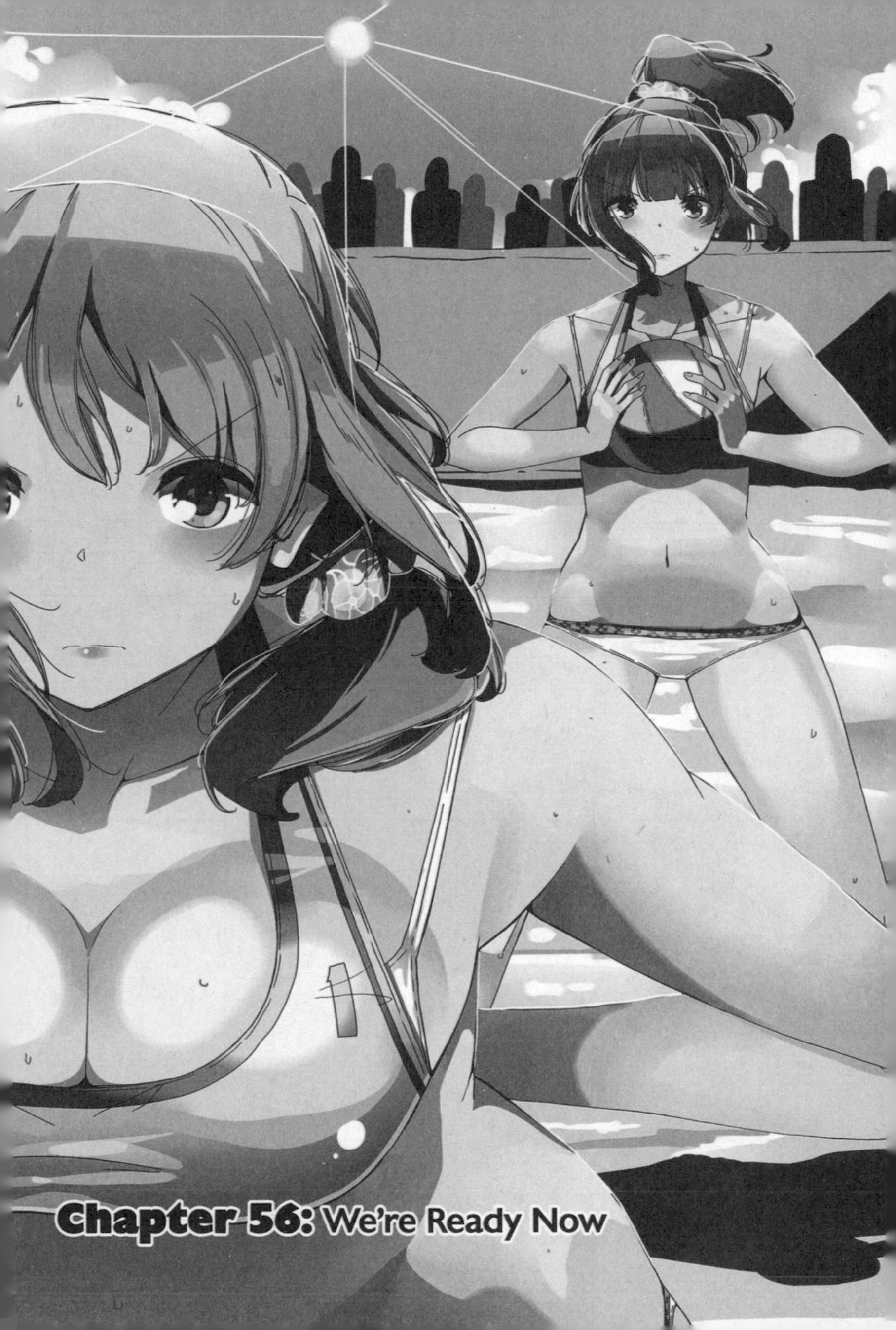
Chapter 56: We're Ready Now

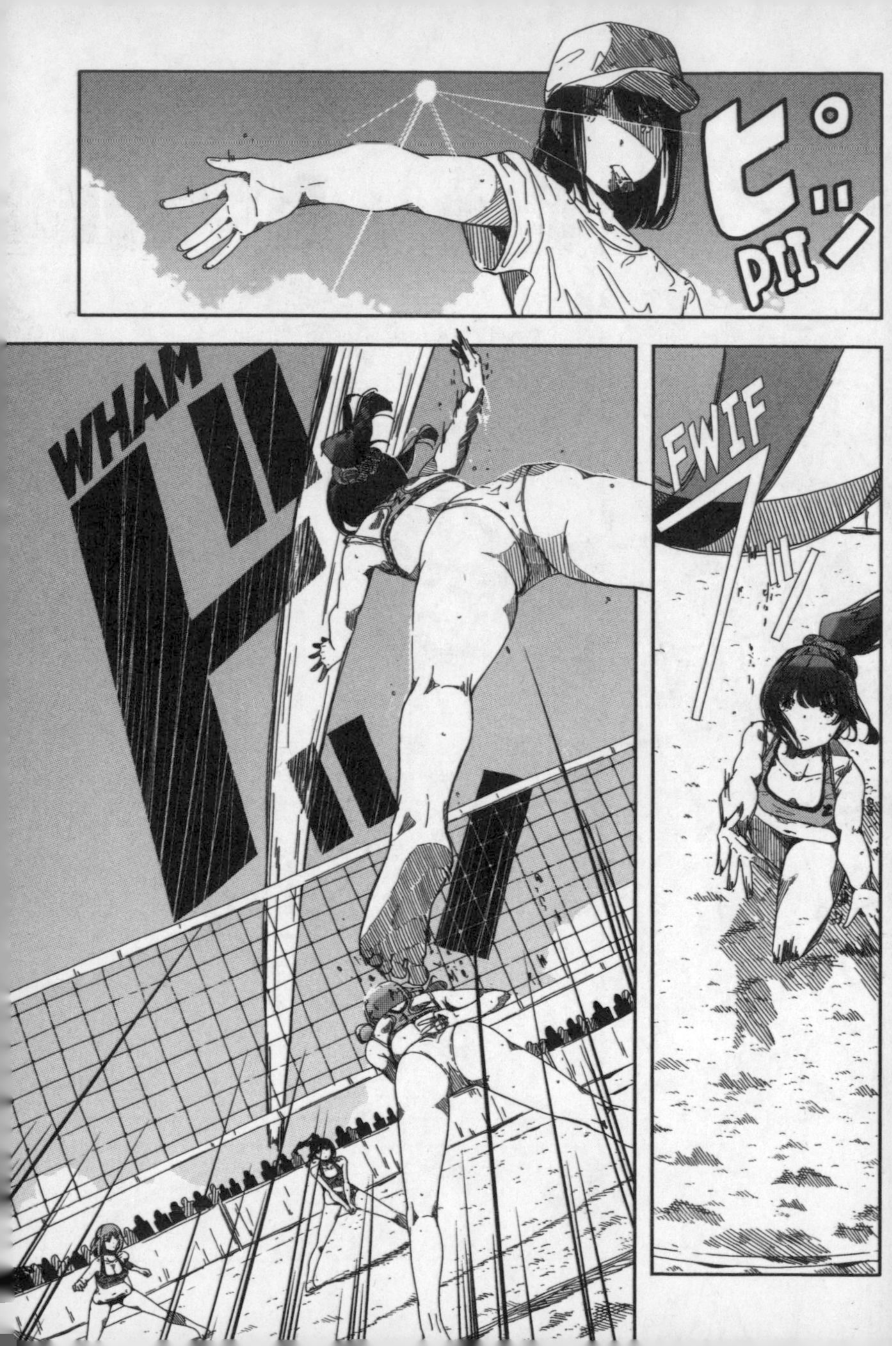
PII
FWIF
WHAM

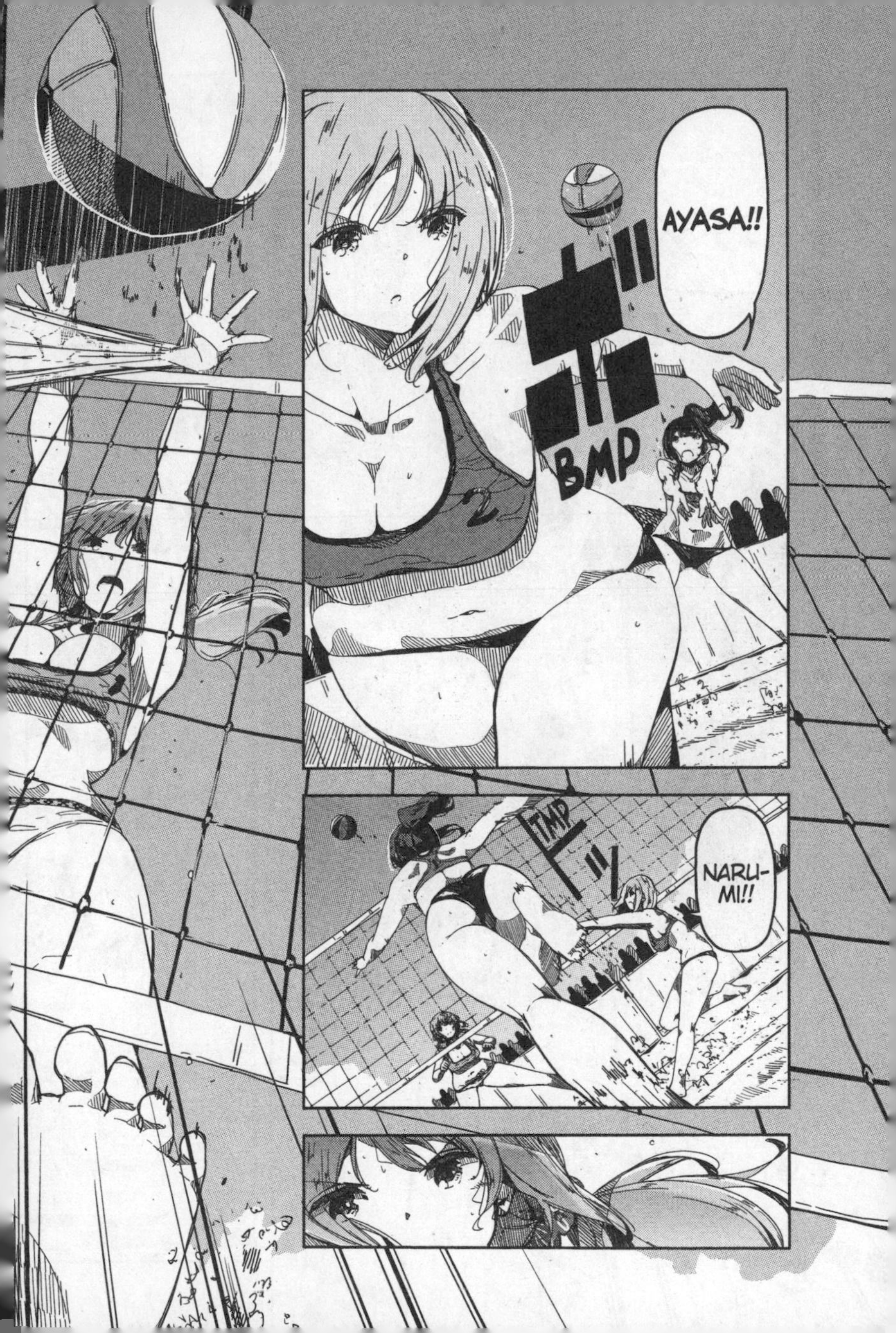
AYASA!!
BMP
TMP
NARU-
MI!!

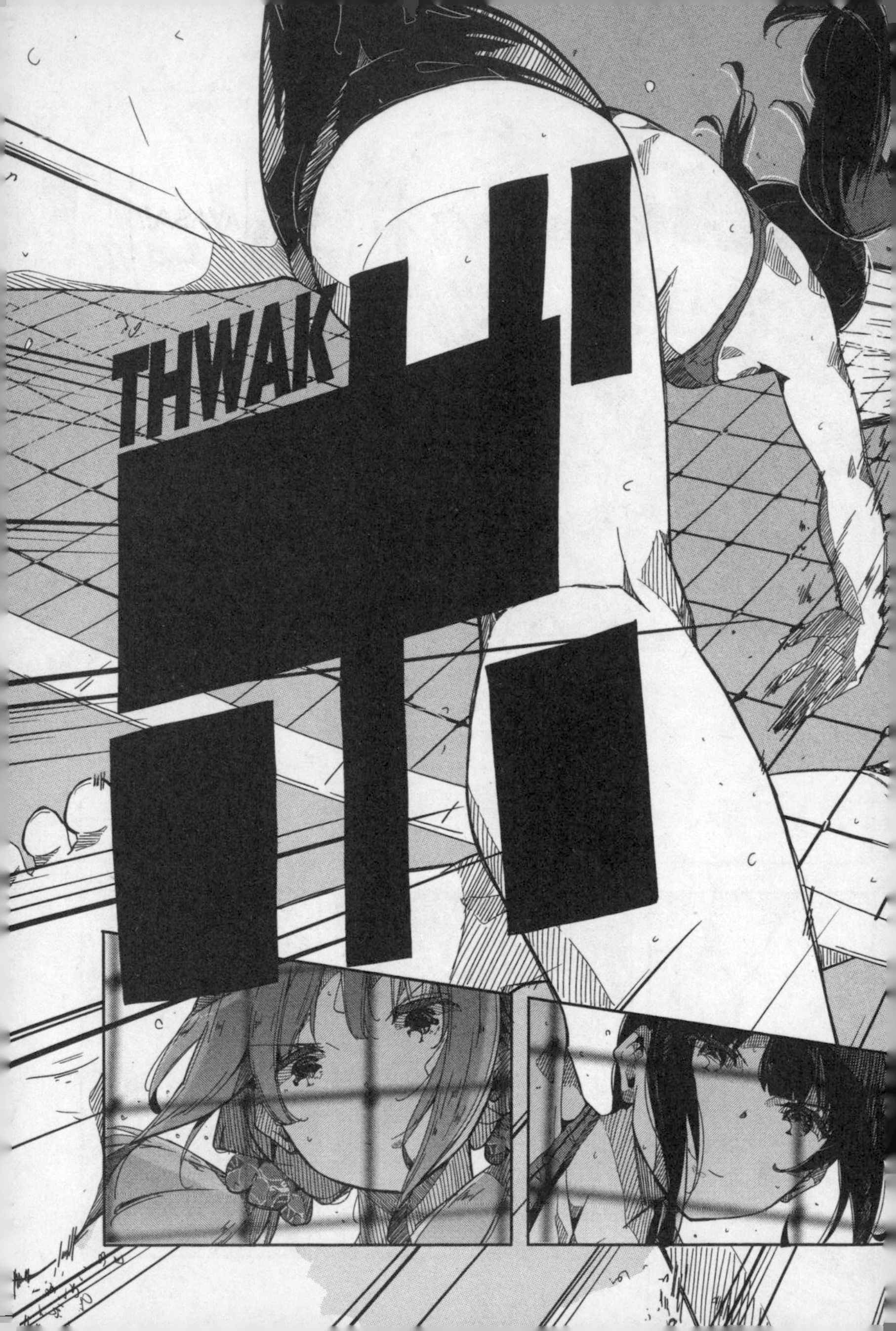
THWAK [redacted]

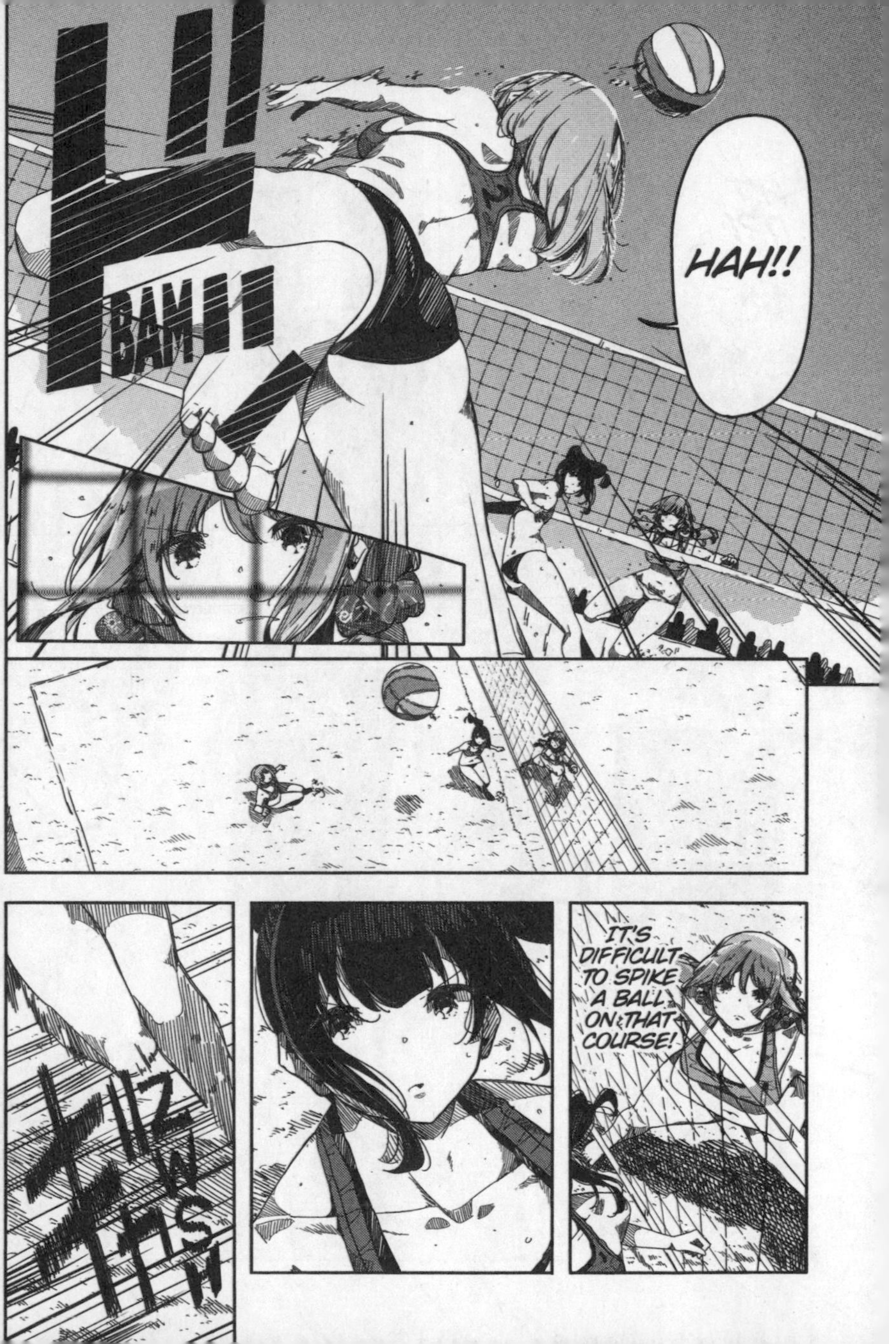
HAH!!
BAM!!
IT'S DIFFICULT TO SPIKE A BALL ON THAT COURSE!
SWISH

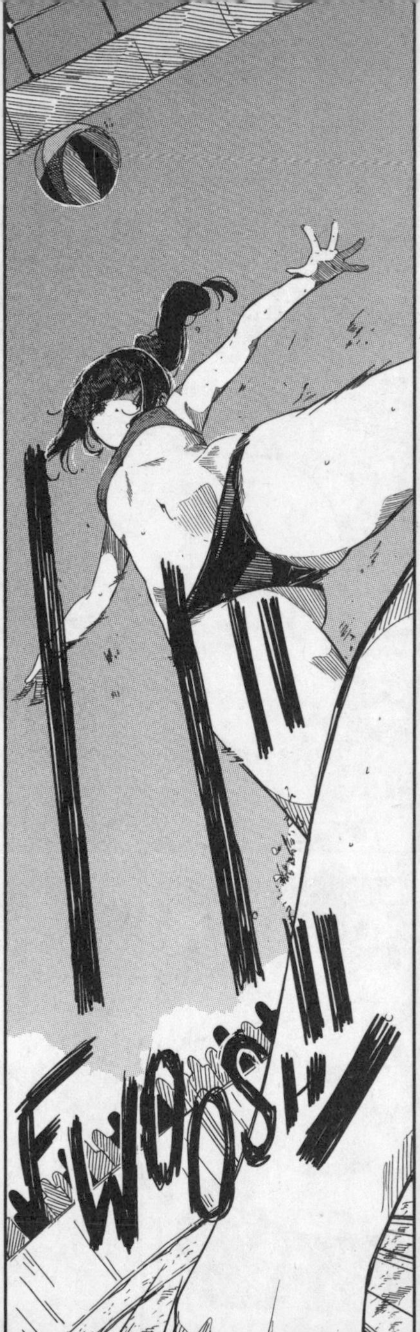
FWOOSH
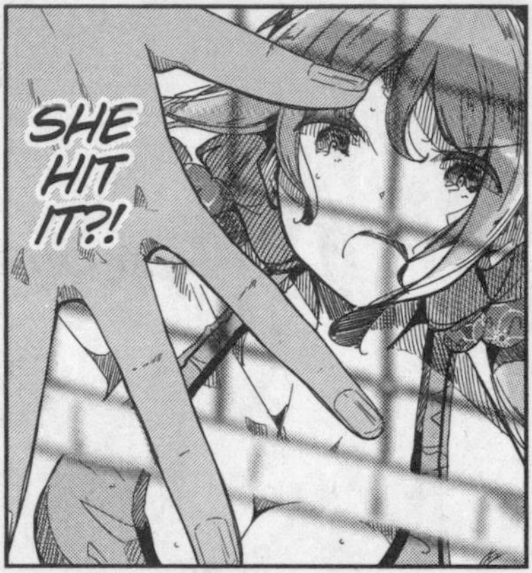
SHE HIT IT?!
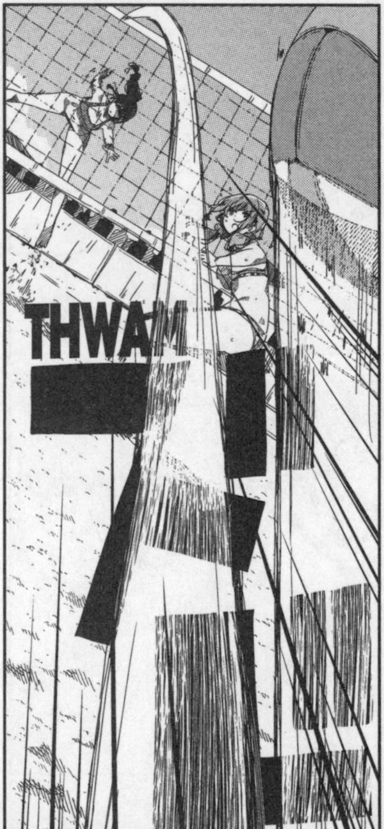
THWAM

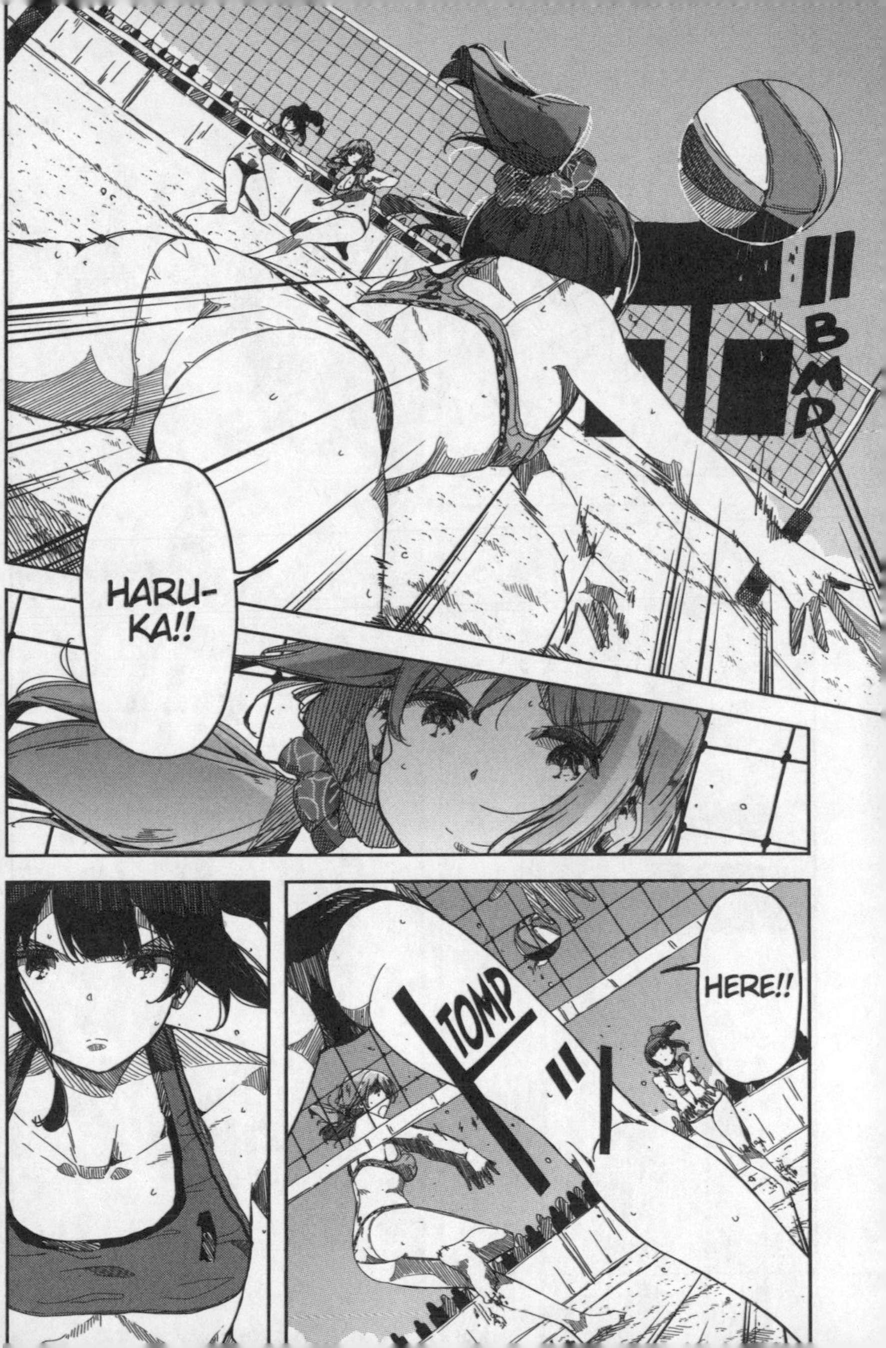
BMD!!
HARU-KA!!
HERE!!
TOMP!!

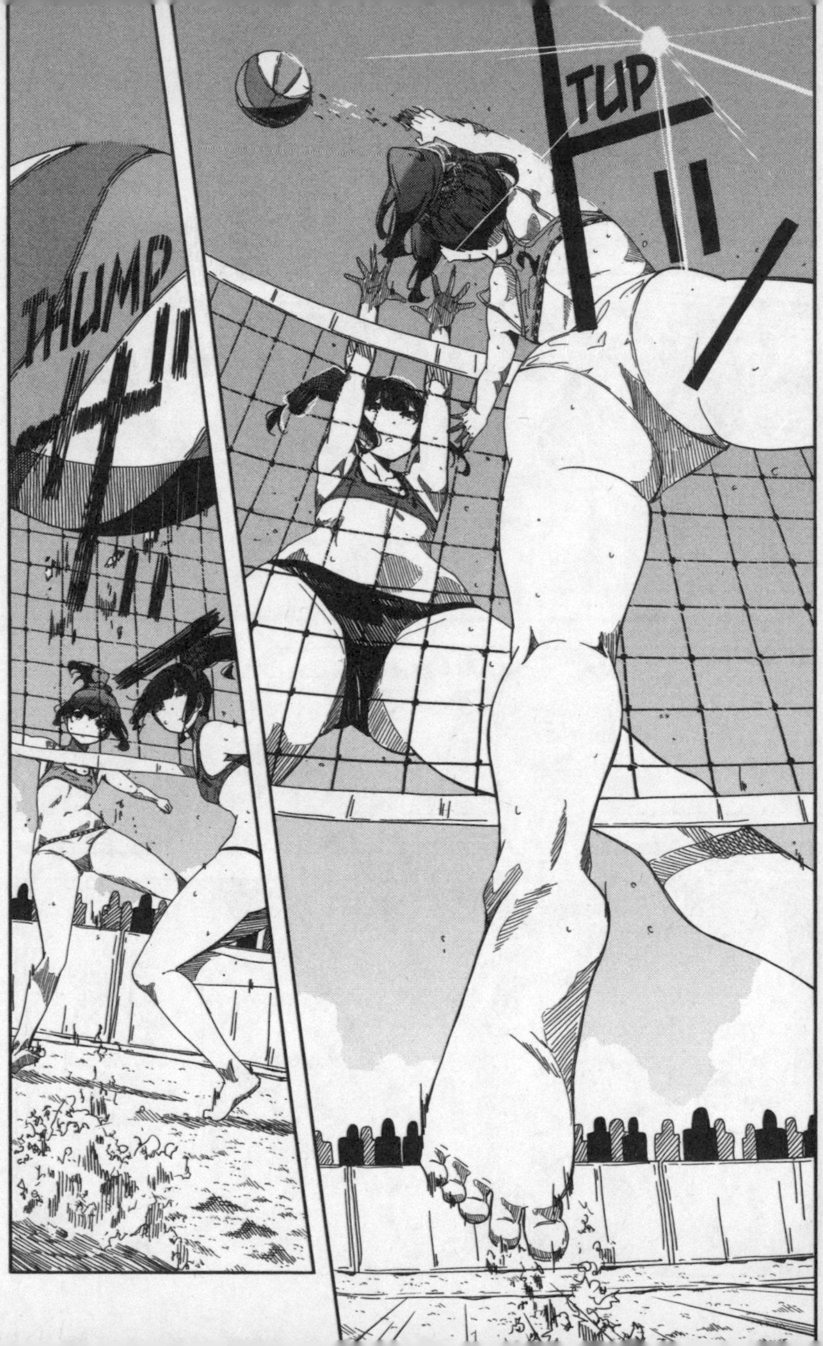
TUP
THUMP

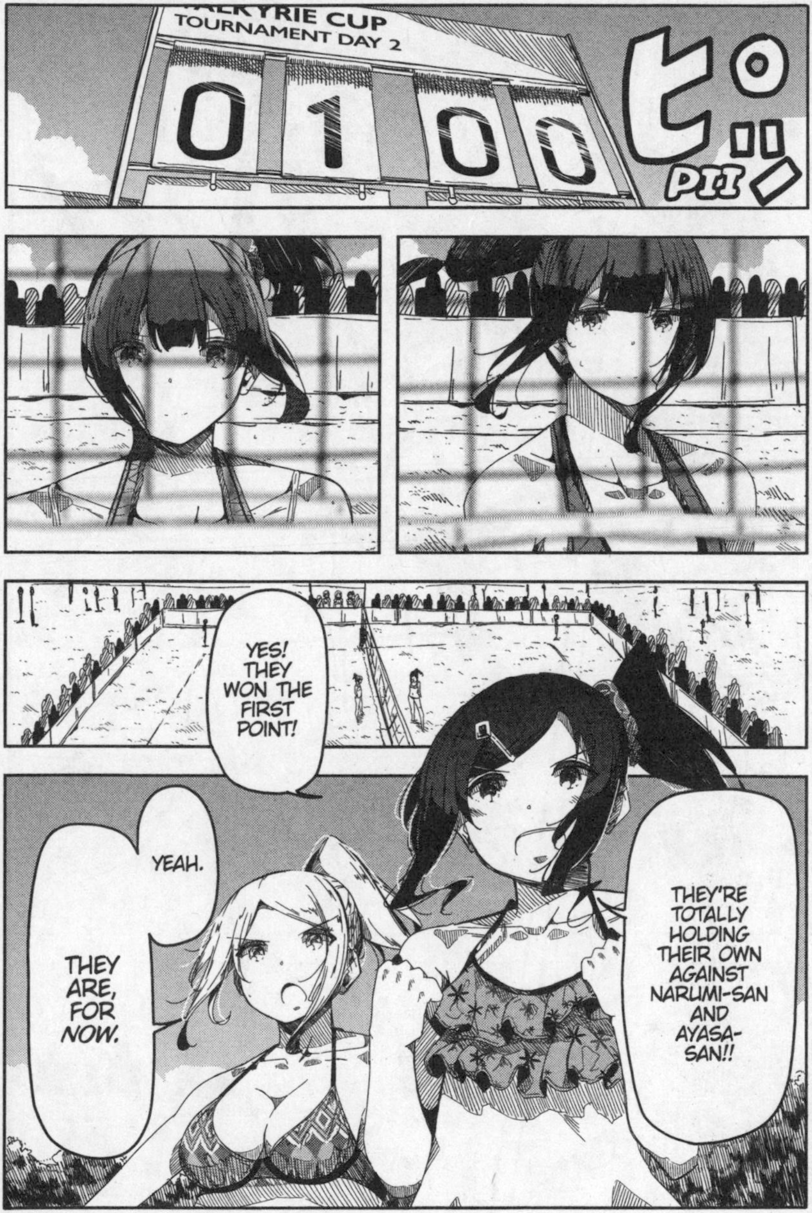
ALKYRIE CUP
TOURNAMENT DAY 2
0100
ピッ
PII
YES! THEY WON THE FIRST POINT!
THEY'RE TOTALLY HOLDING THEIR OWN AGAINST NARUMI-SAN AND AYASA-SAN!!
YEAH.
THEY ARE, FOR NOW.

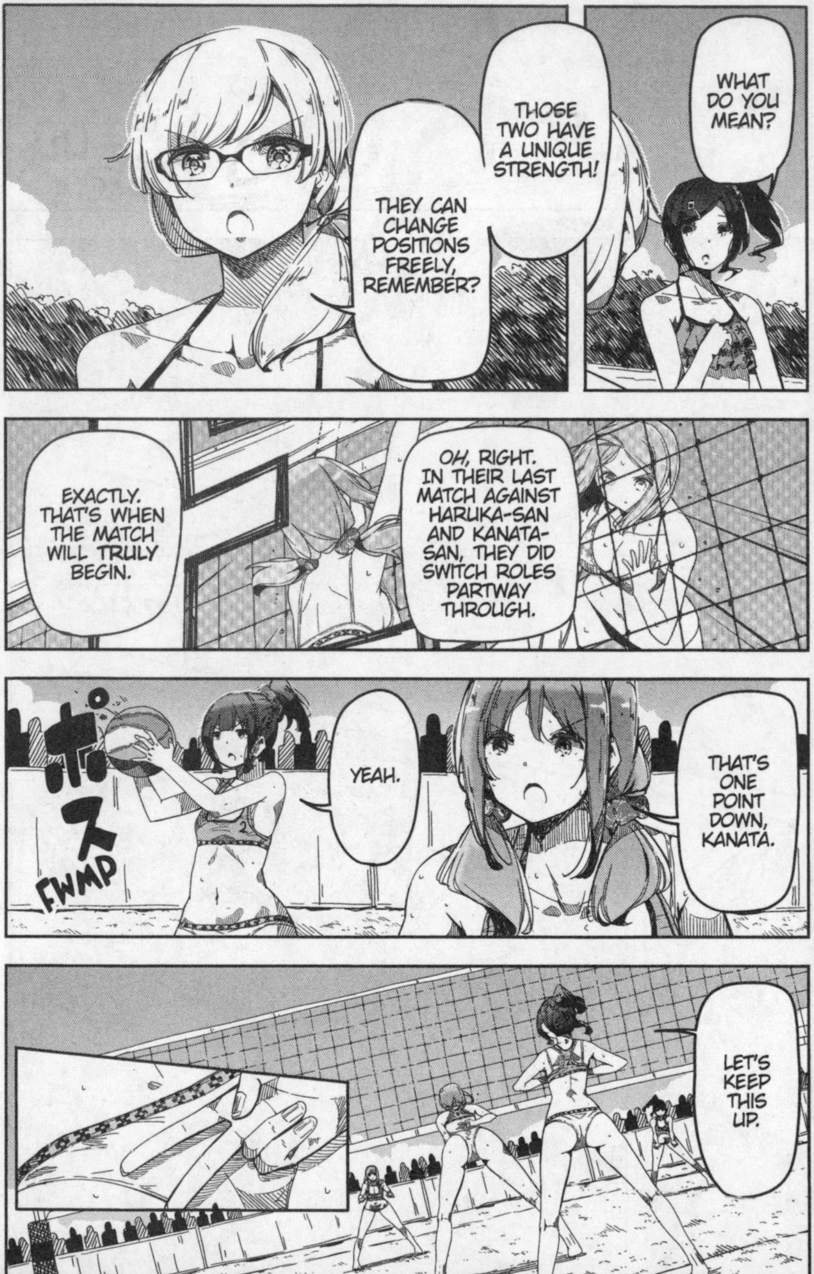
WHAT DO YOU MEAN?
THOSE TWO HAVE A UNIQUE STRENGTH!
THEY CAN CHANGE POSITIONS FREELY, REMEMBER?
OH, RIGHT. IN THEIR LAST MATCH AGAINST HARUKA-SAN AND KANATA-SAN, THEY DID SWITCH ROLES PARTWAY THROUGH.
EXACTLY. THAT'S WHEN THE MATCH WILL TRULY BEGIN.
THAT'S ONE POINT DOWN, KANATA.
YEAH.
ポス
FWMP
LET'S KEEP THIS UP.

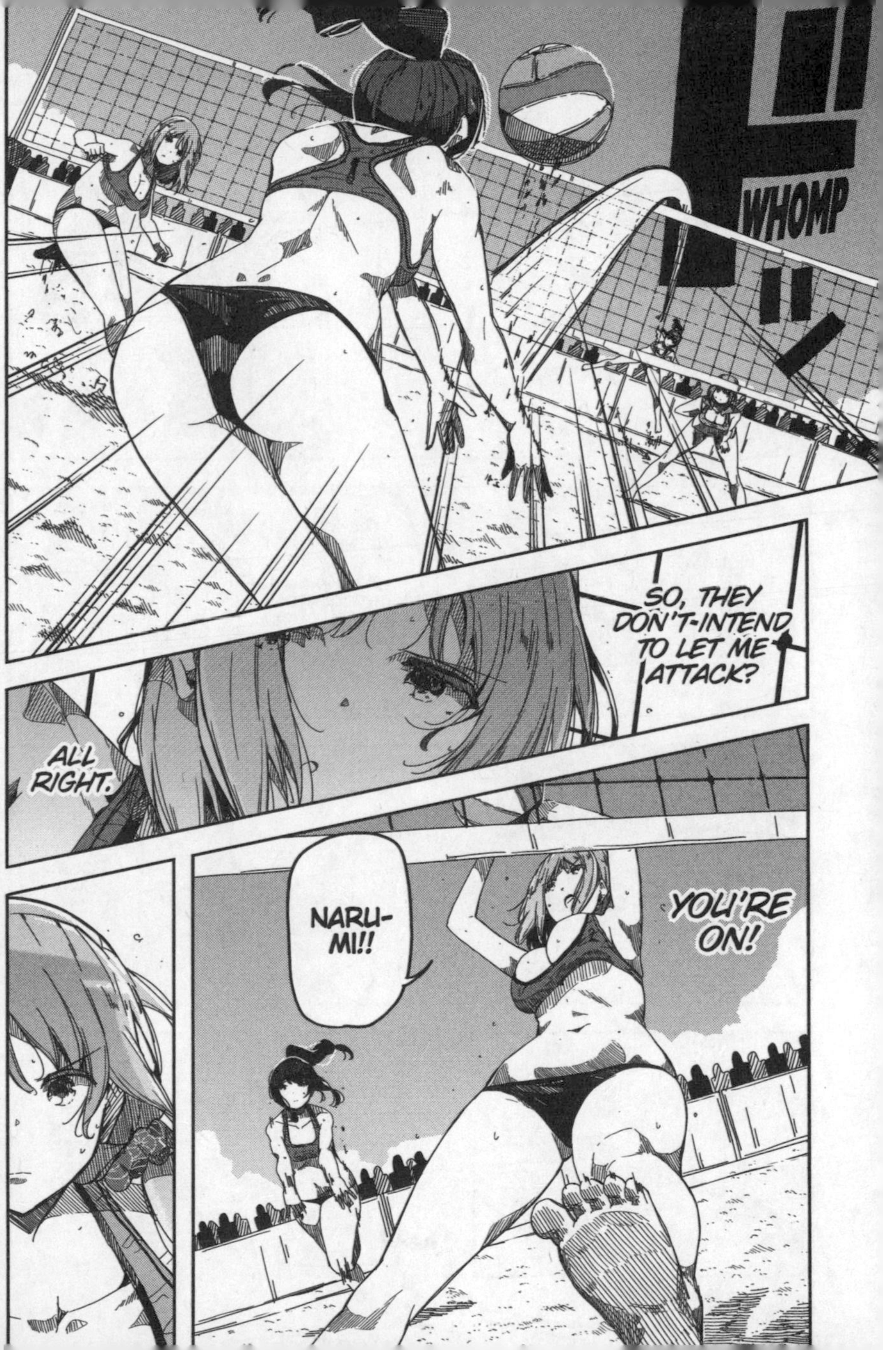
WHOMP
SO, THEY DON'T-INTEND TO LET ME ATTACK?
ALL RIGHT.
YOU'RE ON!
NARU-MI!!

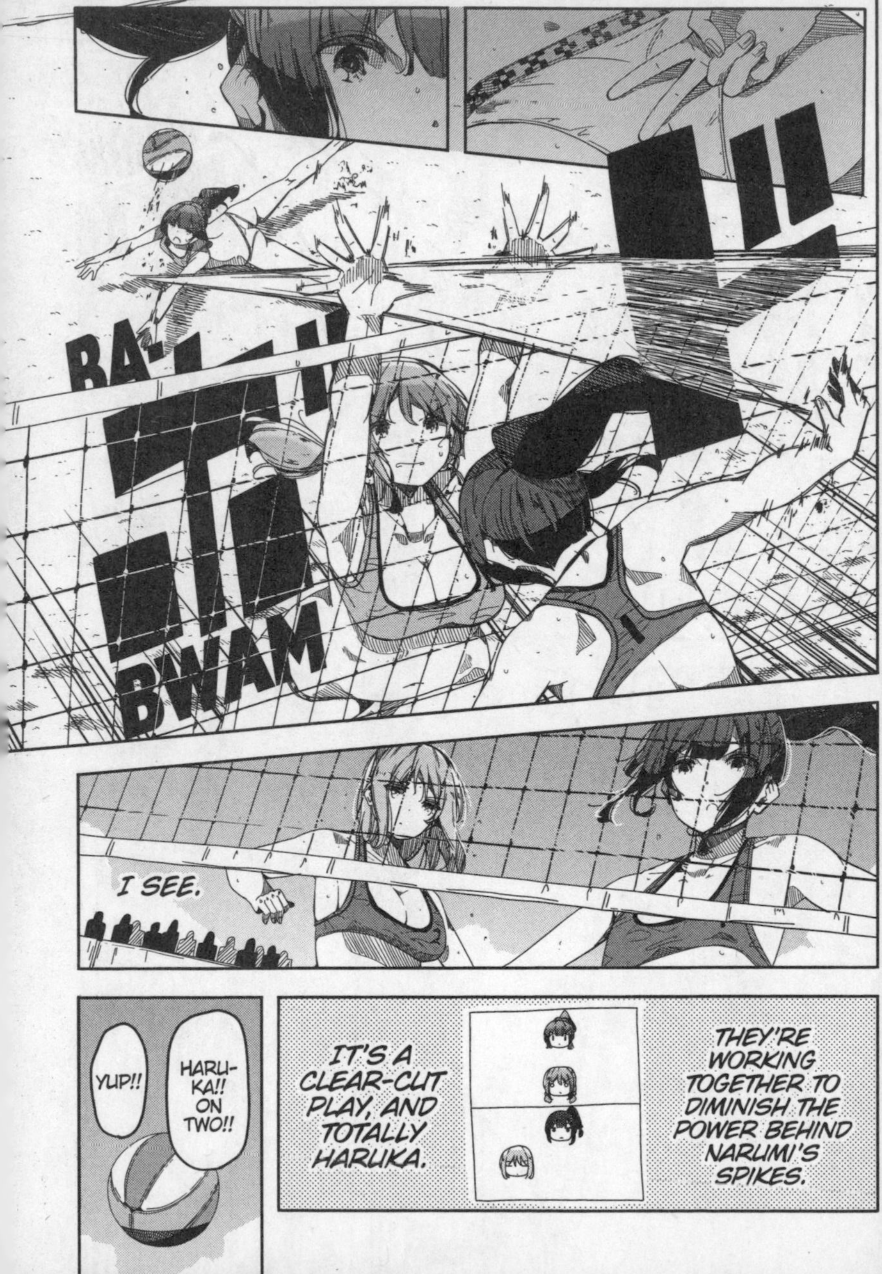
BWAM
I SEE.
THEY'RE WORKING TOGETHER TO DIMINISH THE POWER BEHIND NARUMI'S SPIKES.
IT'S A CLEAR-CUT PLAY, AND TOTALLY HARUKA.
HARU-KA!! ON TWO!!
YUP!!

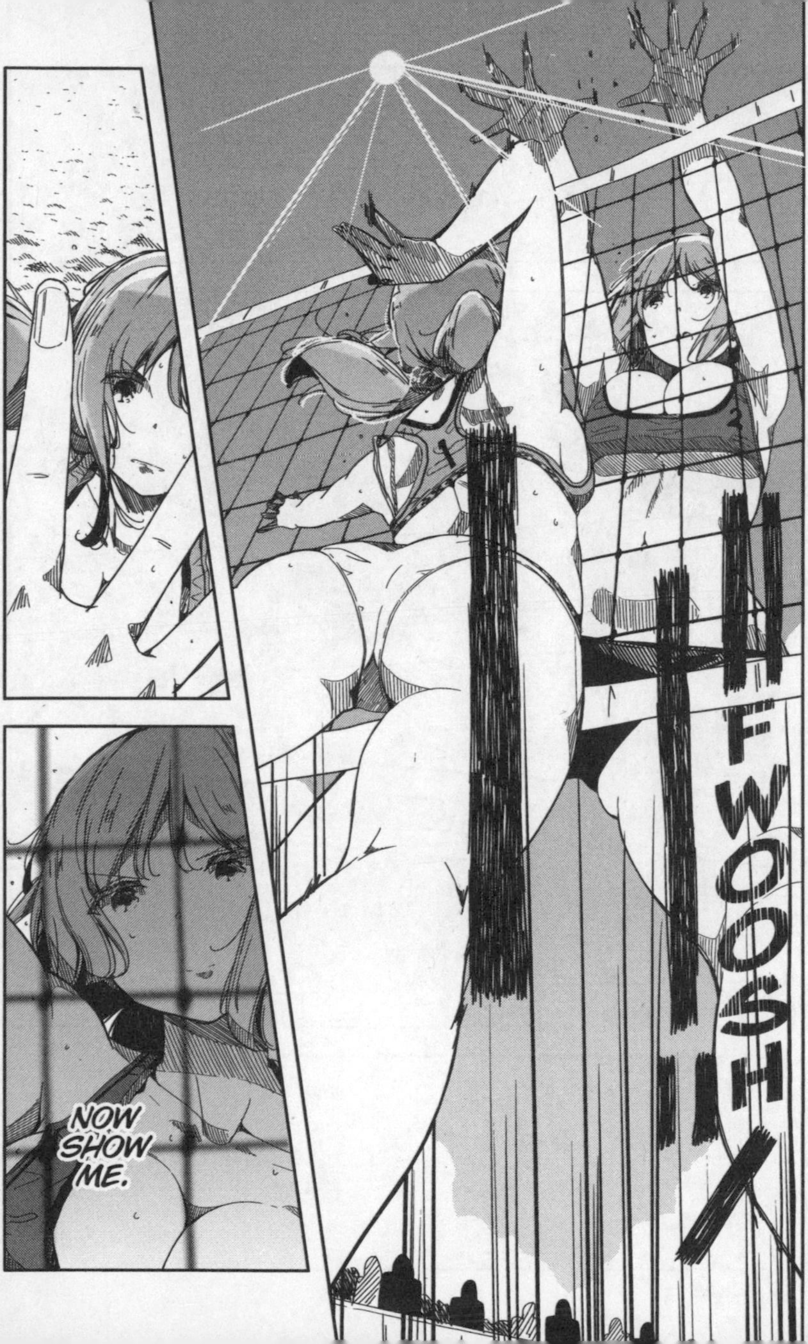
FWOOSH
NOW SHOW ME.

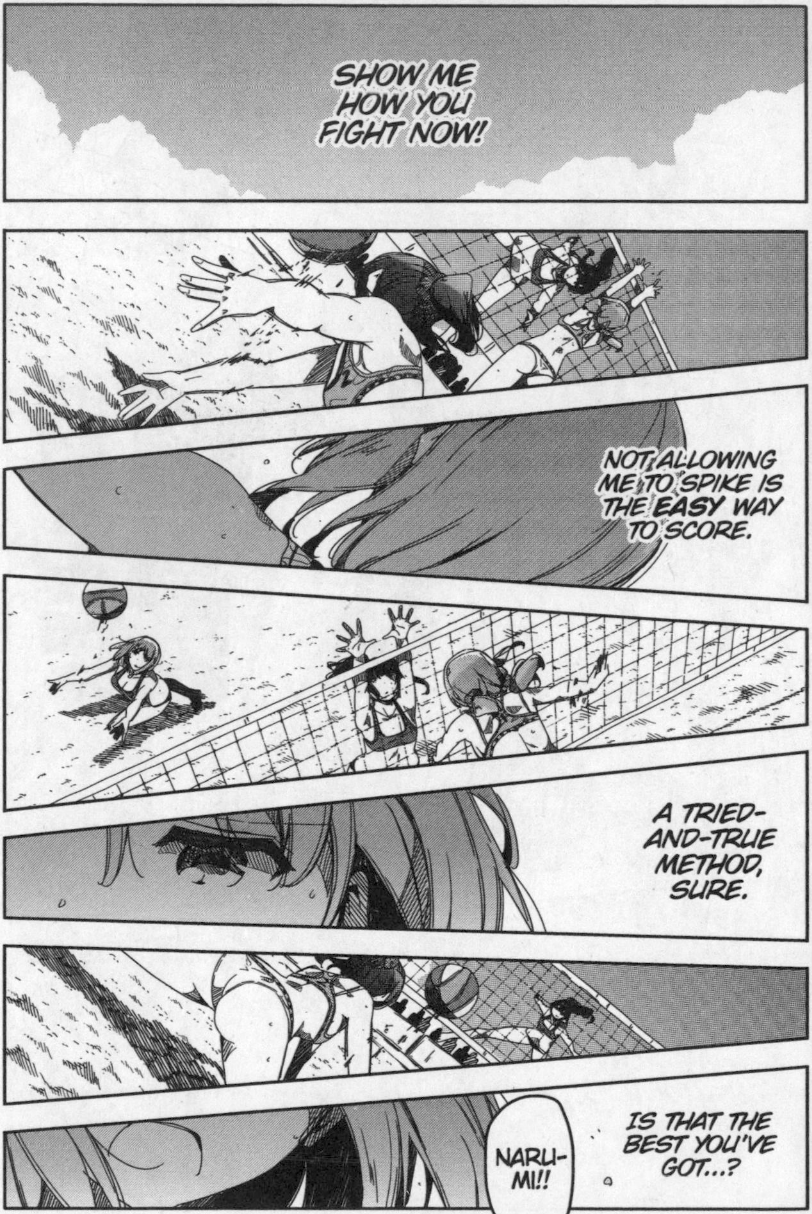
SHOW ME HOW YOU FIGHT NOW!
NOT ALLOWING ME TO SPIKE IS THE EASY WAY TO SCORE.
A TRIED-AND-TRUE METHOD, SURE.
IS THAT THE BEST YOU'VE GOT...?
NARU-MI!!

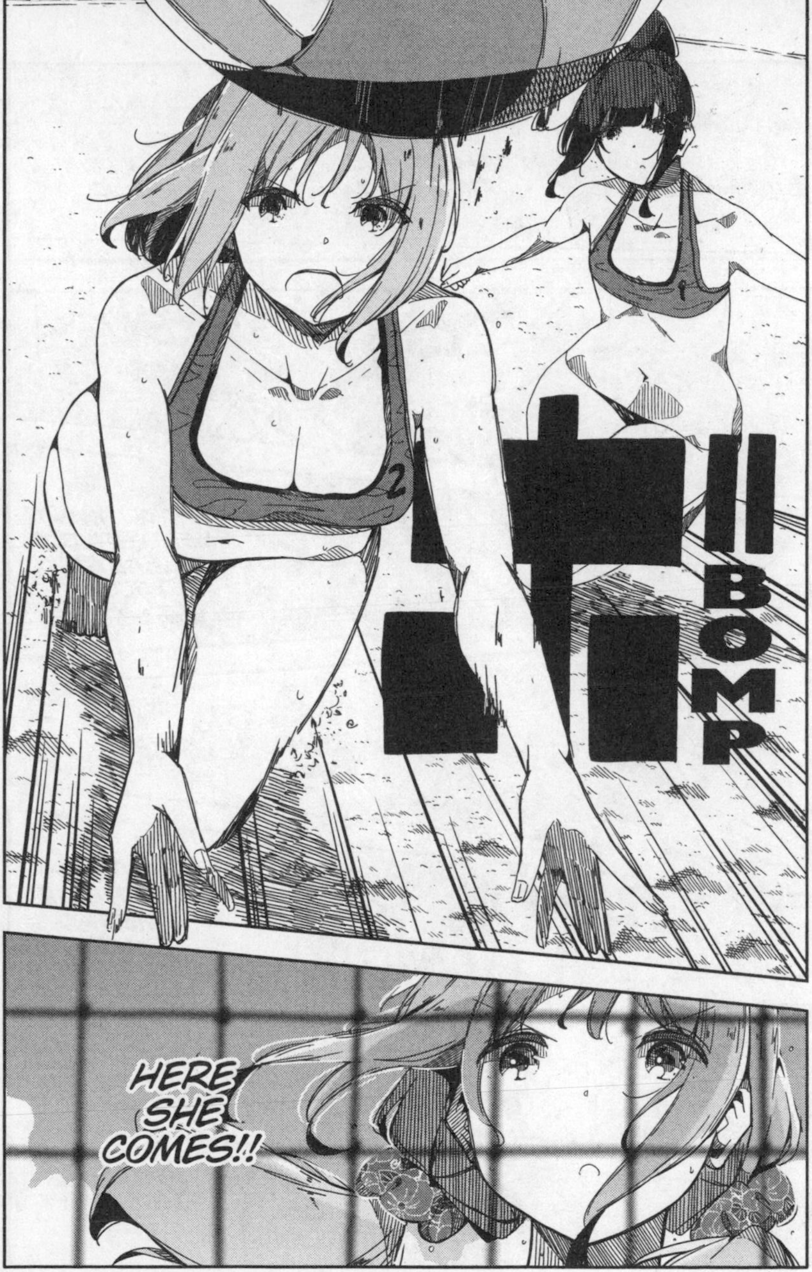
BOMP
HERE SHE COMES!!

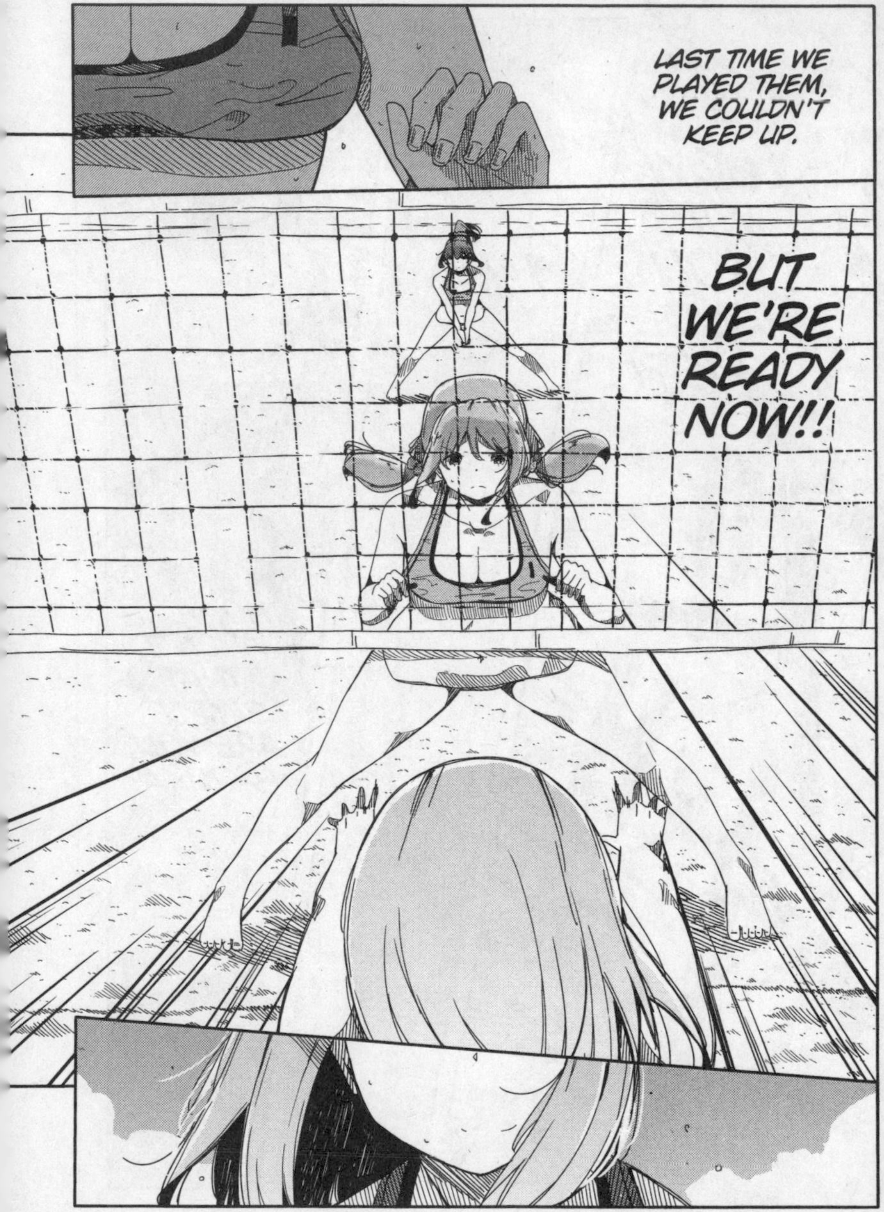
LAST TIME WE PLAYED THEM, WE COULDN'T KEEP UP.
BUT WE'RE READY NOW!!

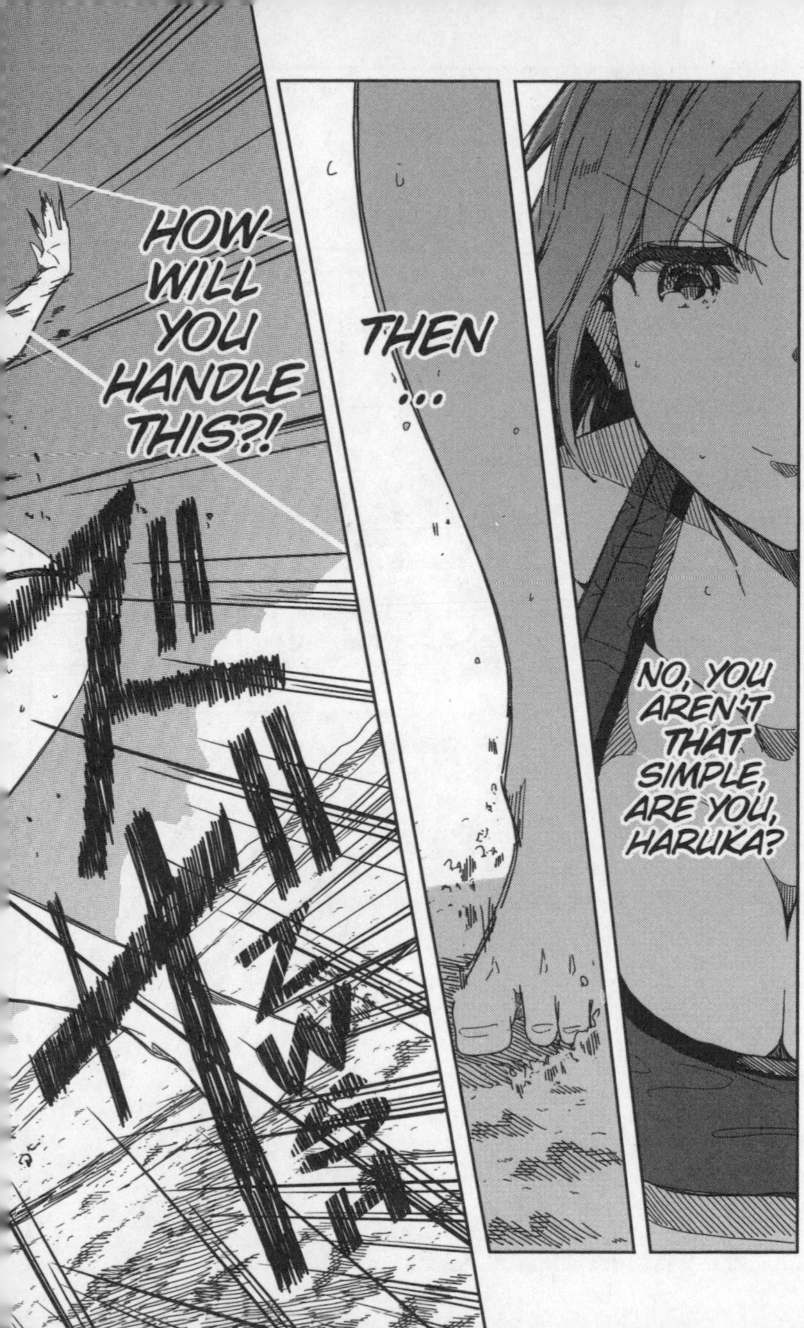
NO, YOU AREN'T THAT SIMPLE, ARE YOU, HARUKA?
THEN ...
HOW WILL YOU HANDLE THIS?!

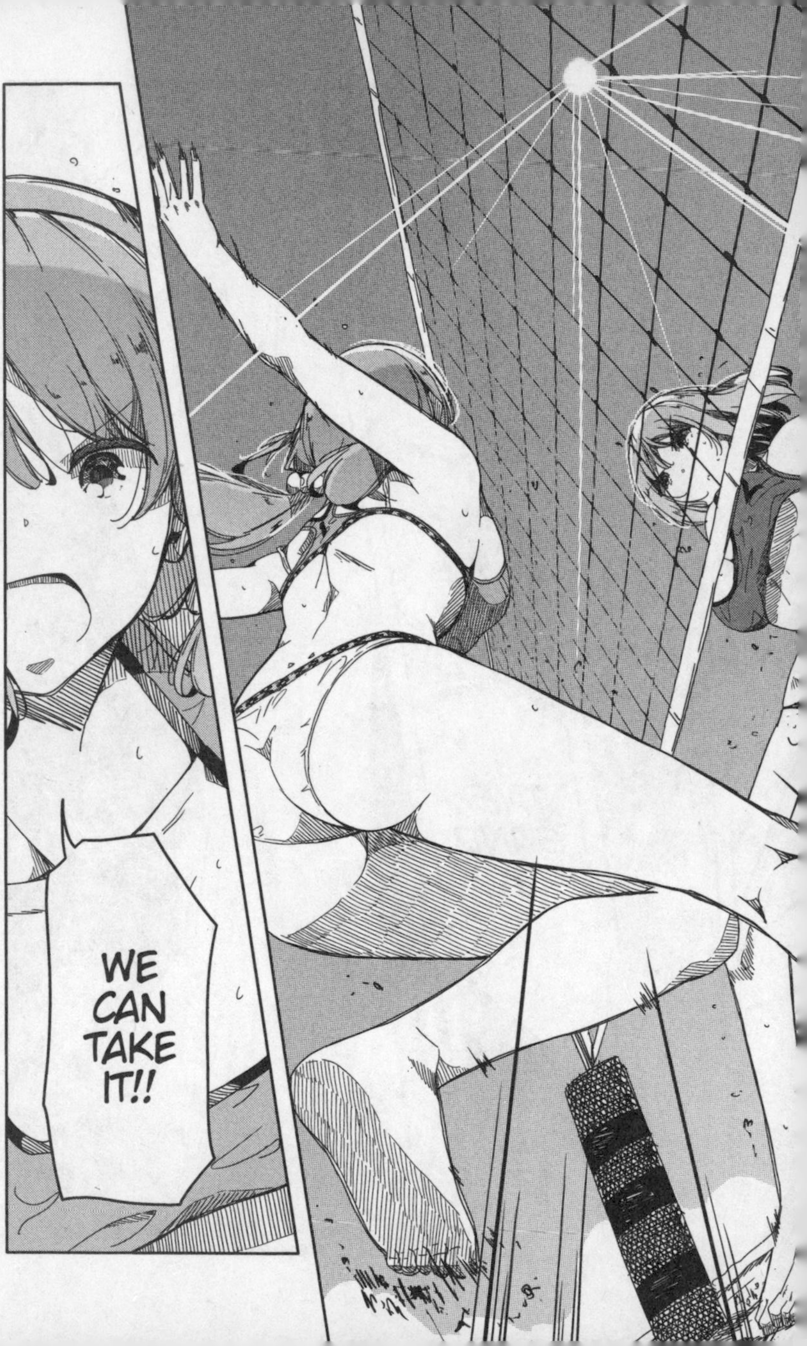
WE CAN TAKE IT!!

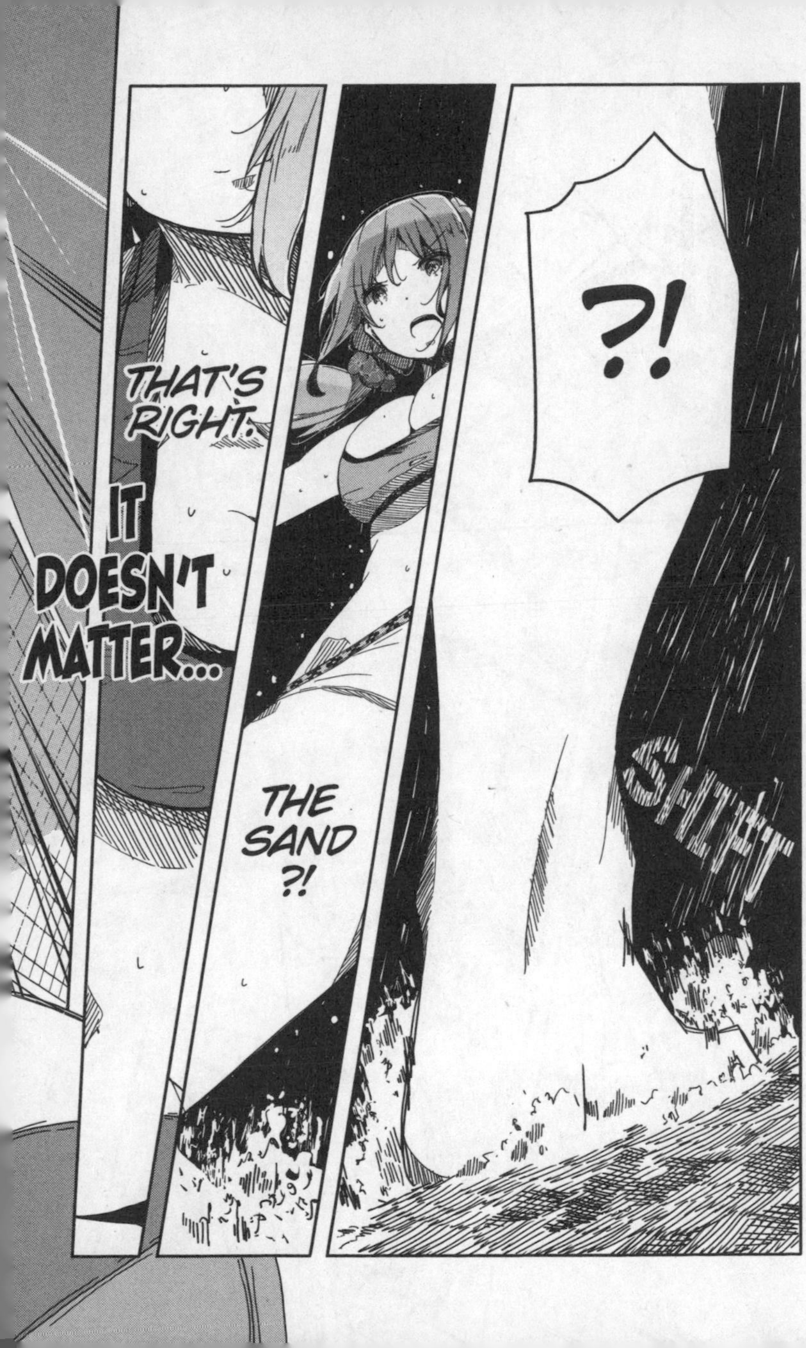
?!
SHIFT
THE SAND ?!
THAT'S RIGHT.
IT DOESN'T MATTER...

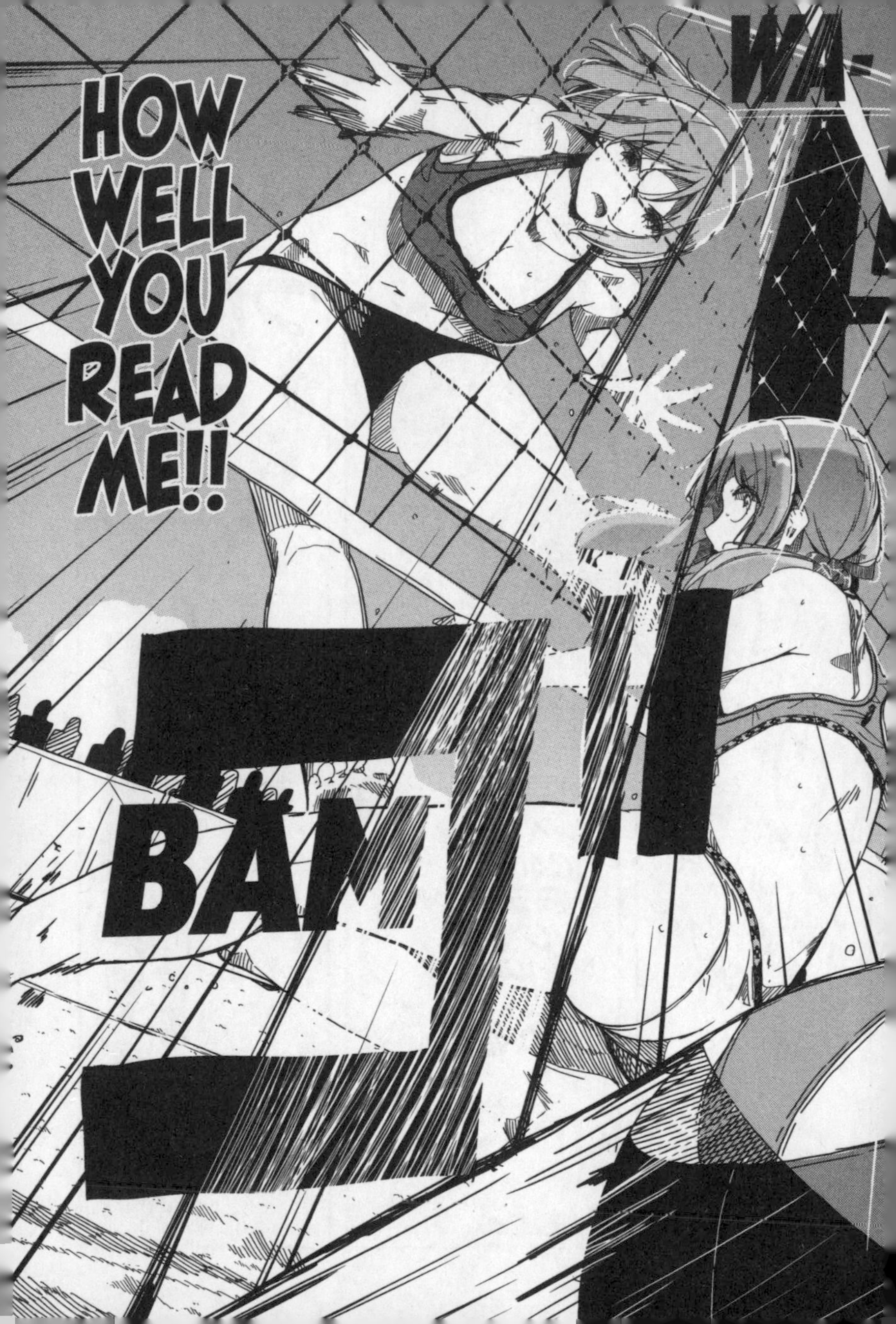
WA-
HOW WELL YOU READ ME!!
BAM

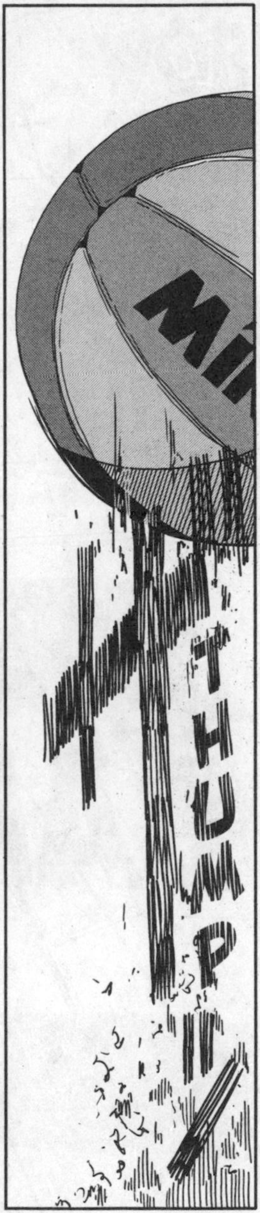
THUMP!!
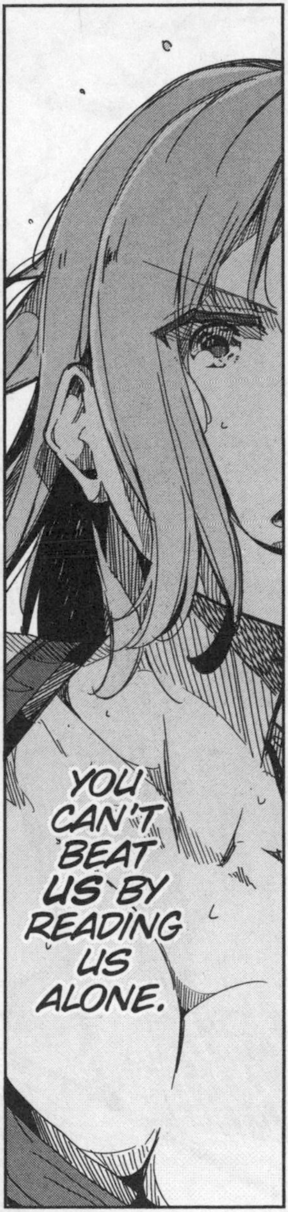
YOU CAN'T BEAT US BY READING US ALONE.
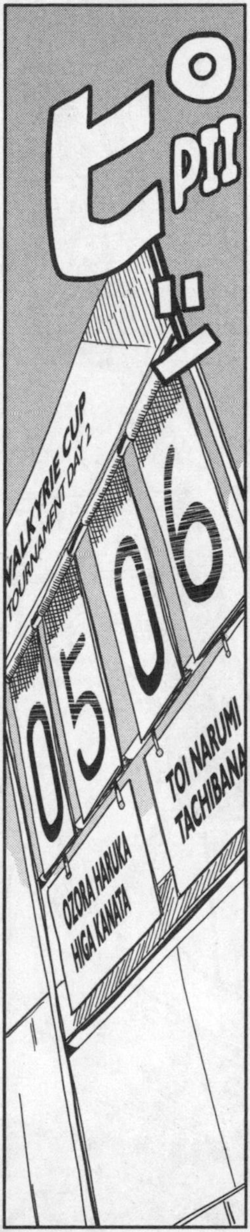
ピ
PII
VALKYRIE CUP
TOURNAMENT DAY 2
05
06
OZORA HARUKA
HIGA KANATA
TOI NARUMI
TACHIBANA

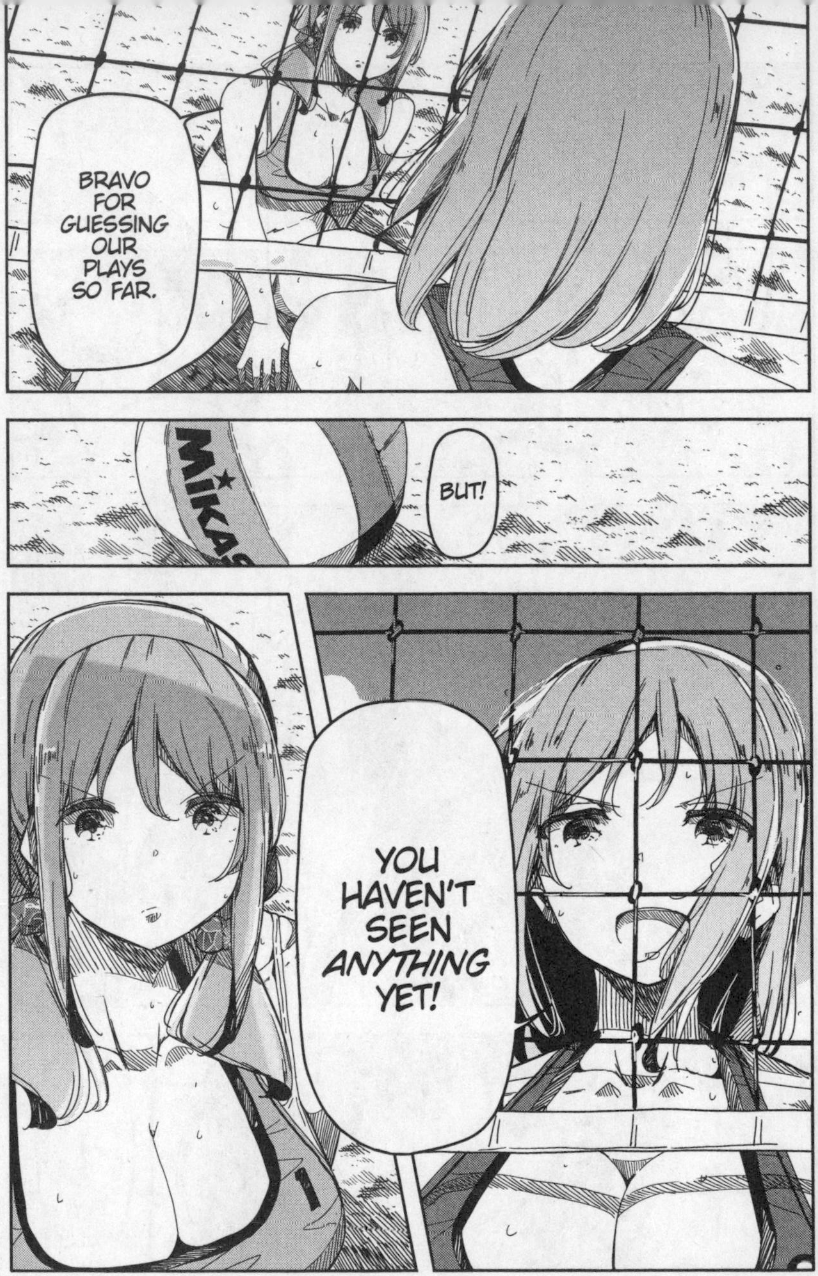
BRAVO FOR GUESSING OUR PLAYS SO FAR.
BUT!
YOU HAVEN'T SEEN *ANYTHING* YET!

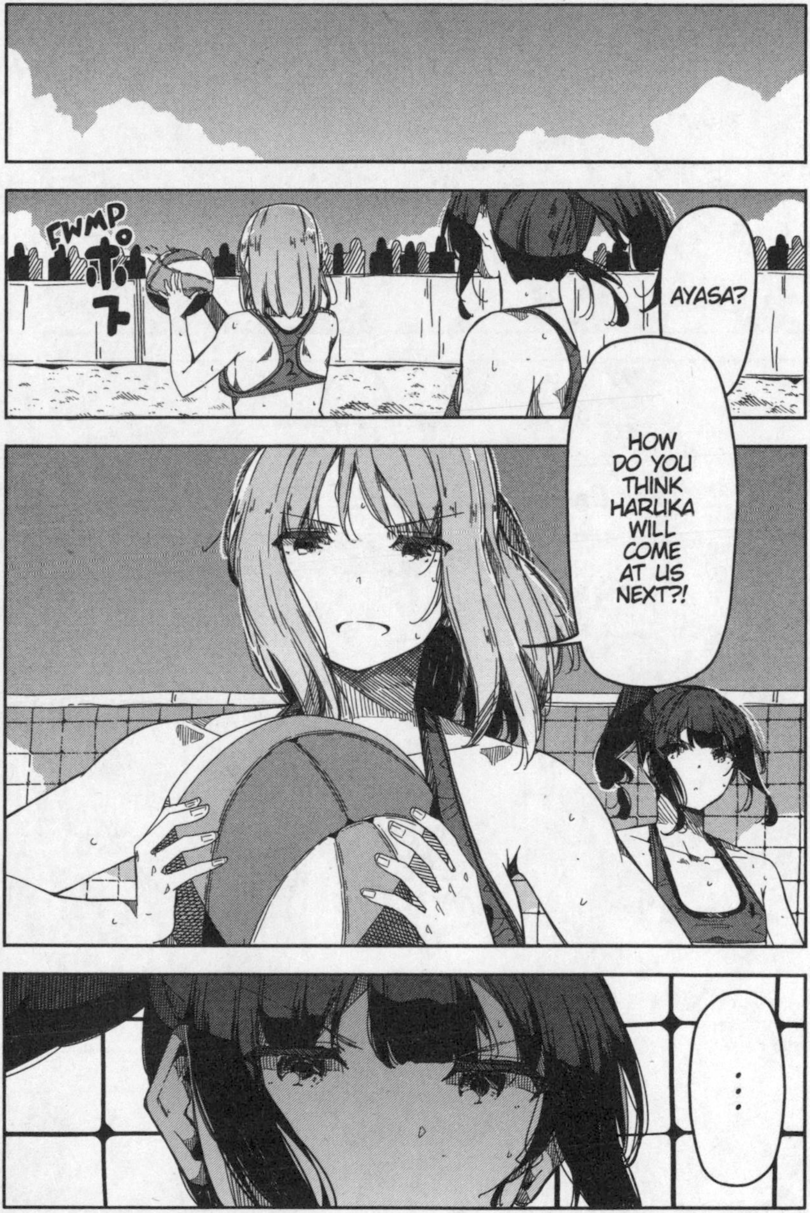
FWMP
ポフ
AYASA?
HOW DO YOU THINK HARUKA WILL COME AT US NEXT?!
...

Harukana★Receive

Presented by Nyoijizai

Harukana★Receive

Presented by Nyoijizai

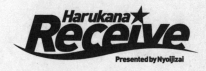

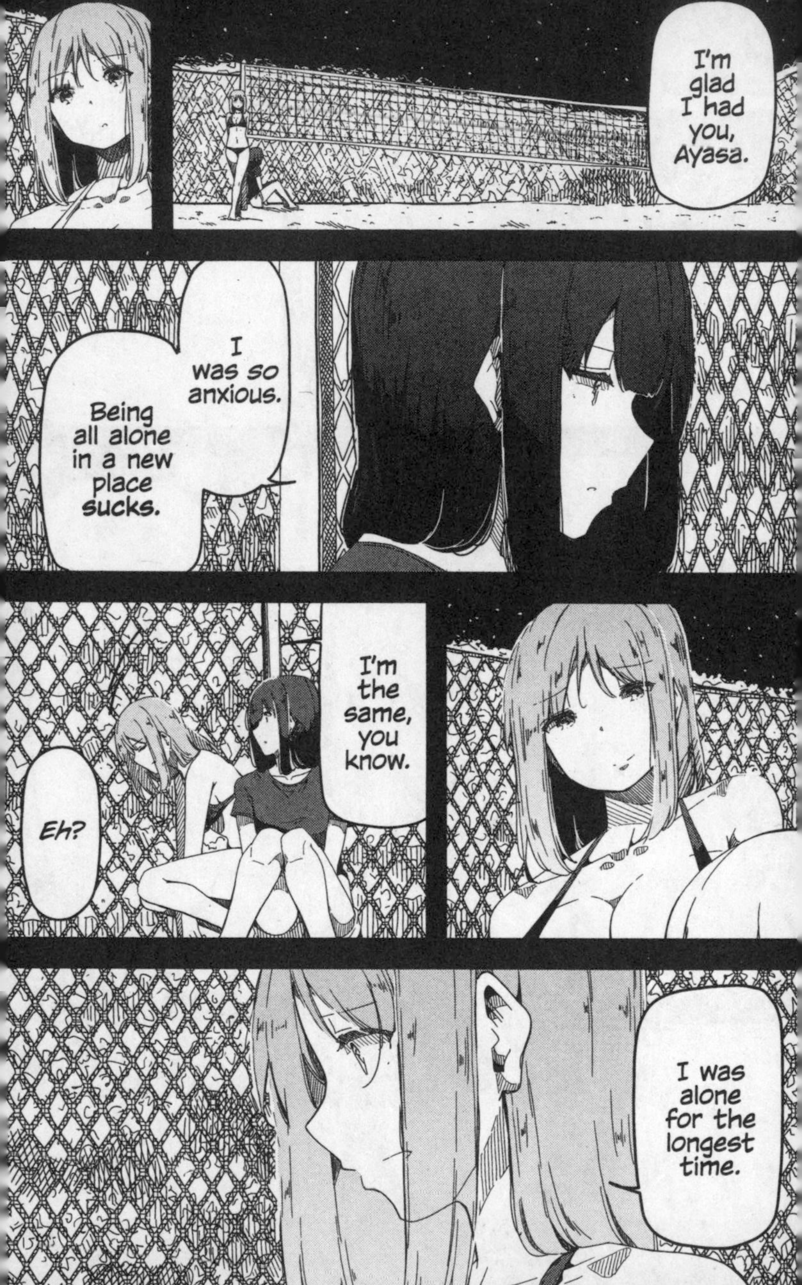
I'm glad I had you, Ayasa.
I was so anxious.
Being all alone in a new place sucks.
I'm the same, you know.
Eh?
I was alone for the longest time.

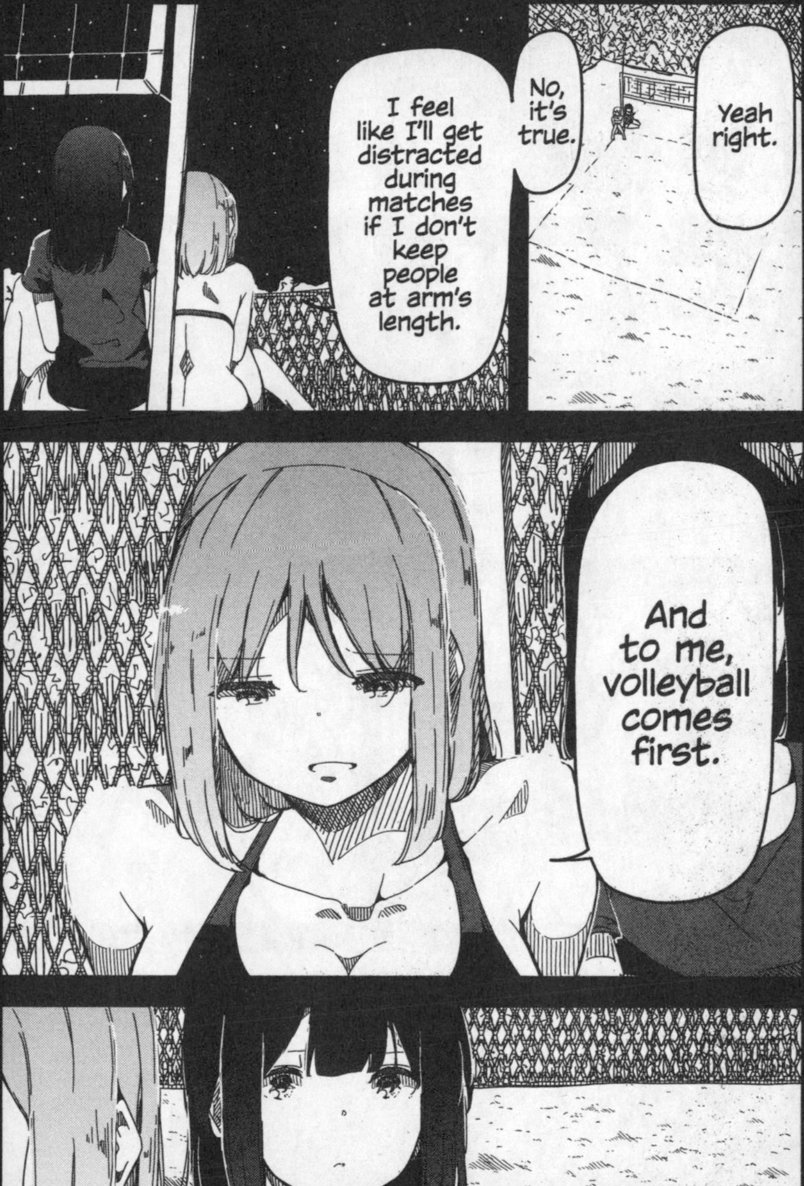
Yeah right.
No, it's true.
I feel like I'll get distracted during matches if I don't keep people at arm's length.
And to me, volleyball comes first.

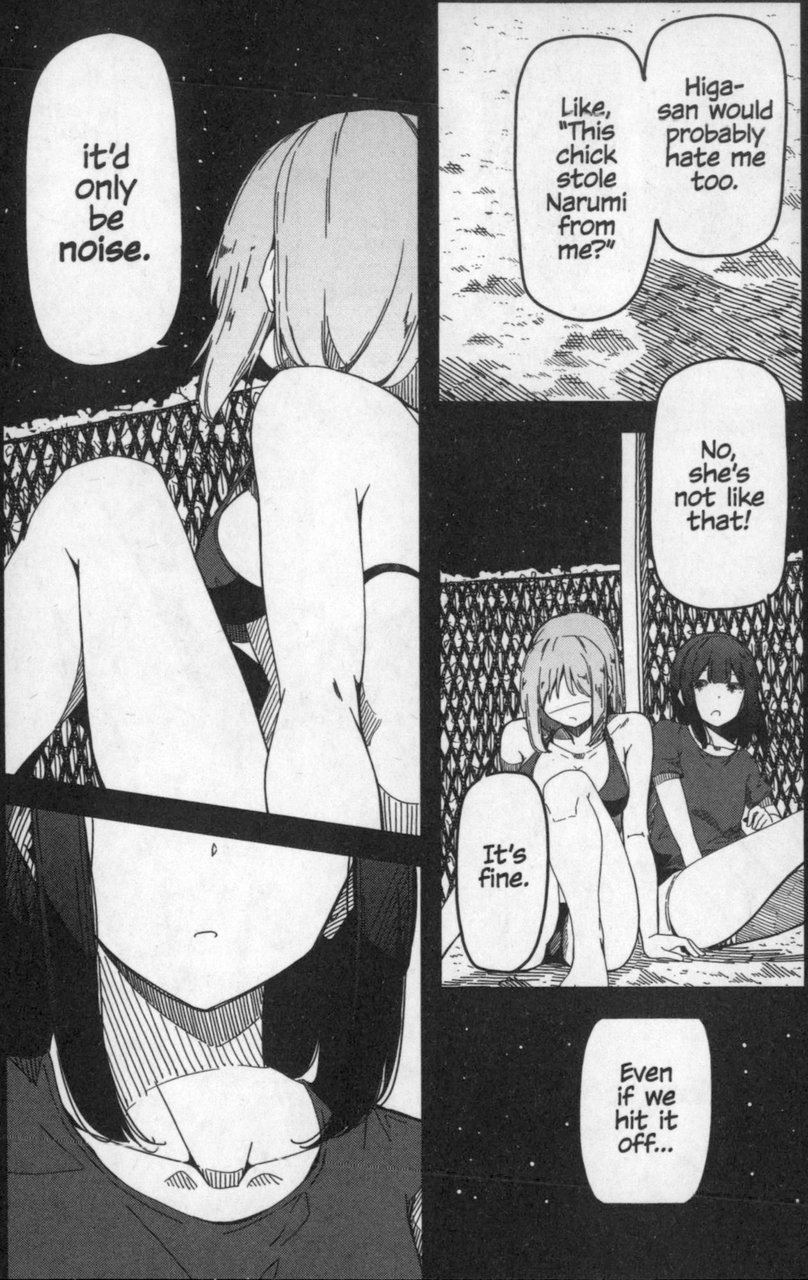
Higa-san would probably hate me too.
Like, "This chick stole Narumi from me?"
No, she's not like that!
It's fine.
Even if we hit it off...
it'd only be noise.

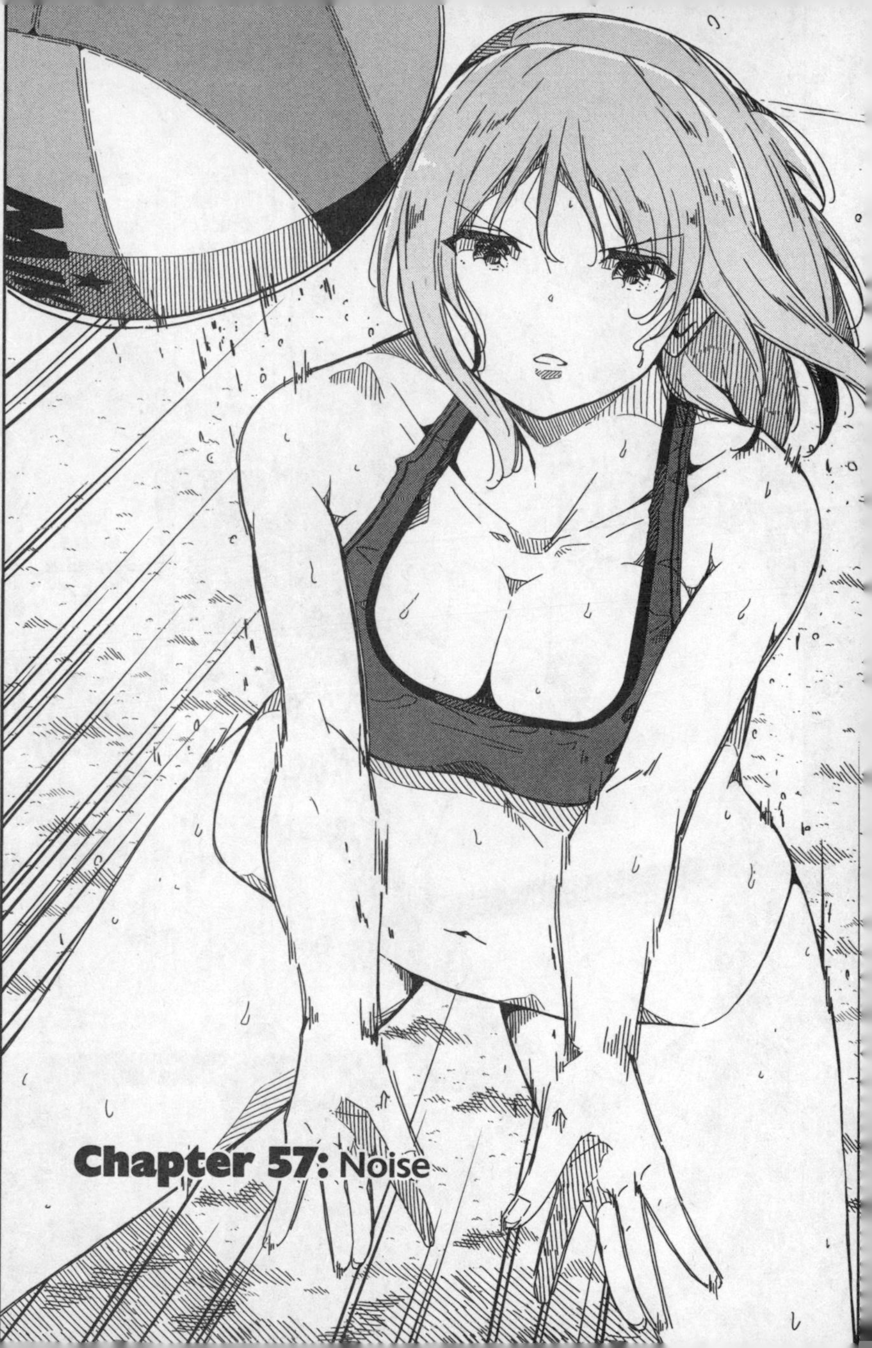
Chapter 57: Noise

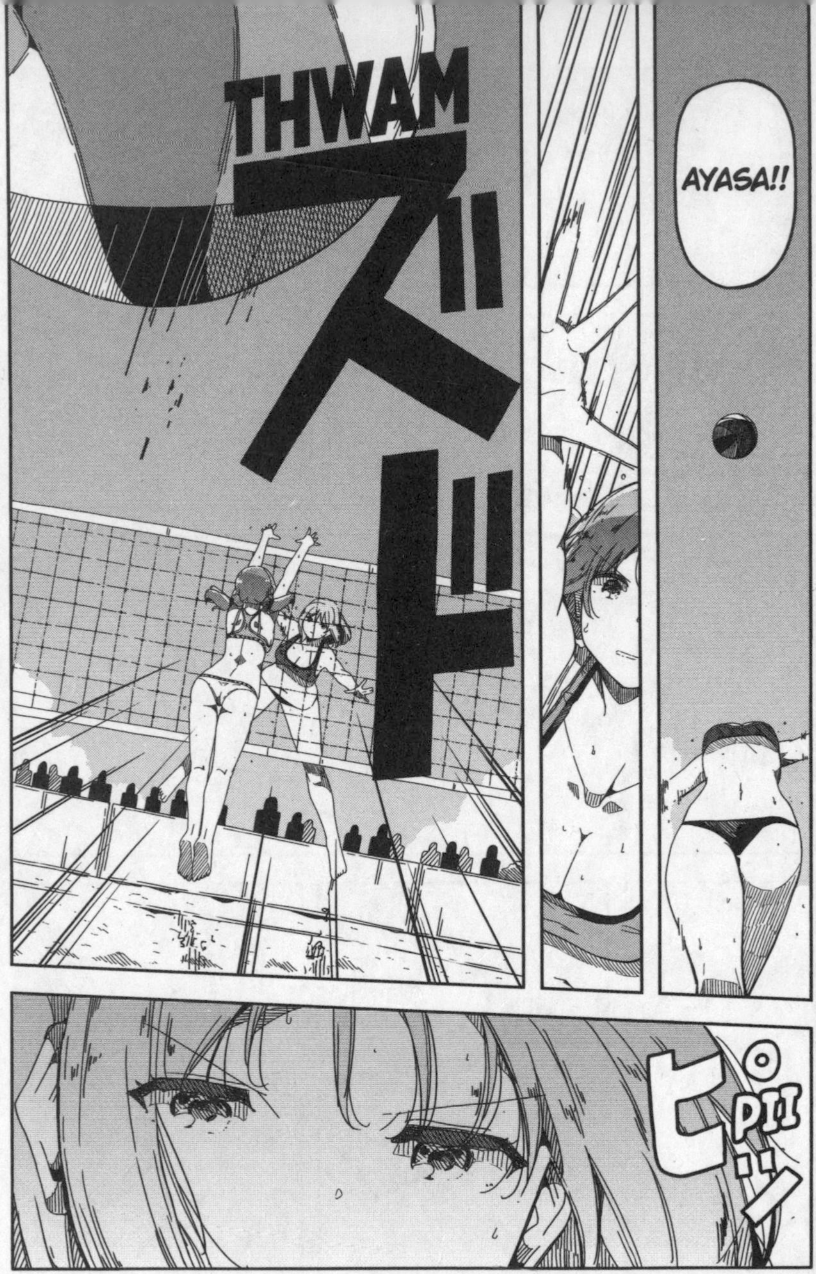
AYASA!!
THWAM
PII

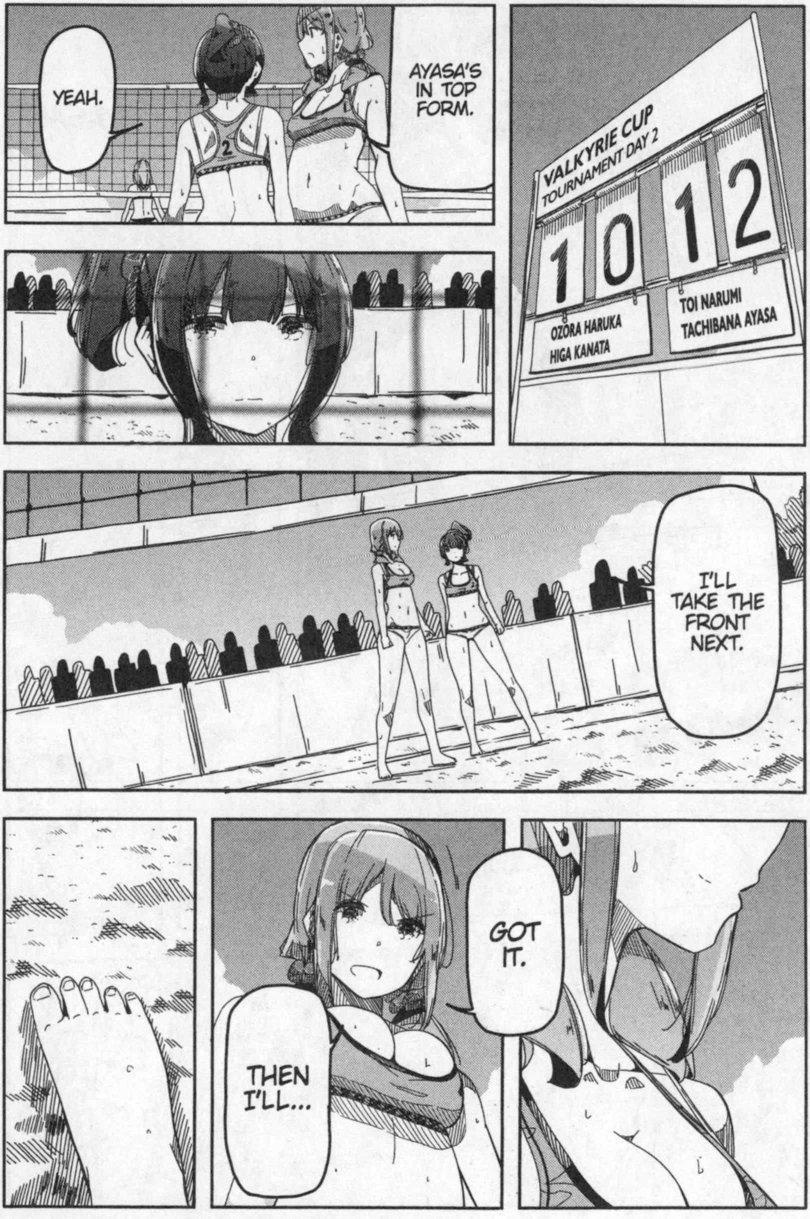
VALKYRIE CUP
TOURNAMENT DAY 2
10
12
OZORA HARUKA
HIGA KANATA
TOI NARUMI
TACHIBANA AYASA
AYASA'S IN TOP FORM.
YEAH.
I'LL TAKE THE FRONT NEXT.
GOT IT.
THEN I'LL...

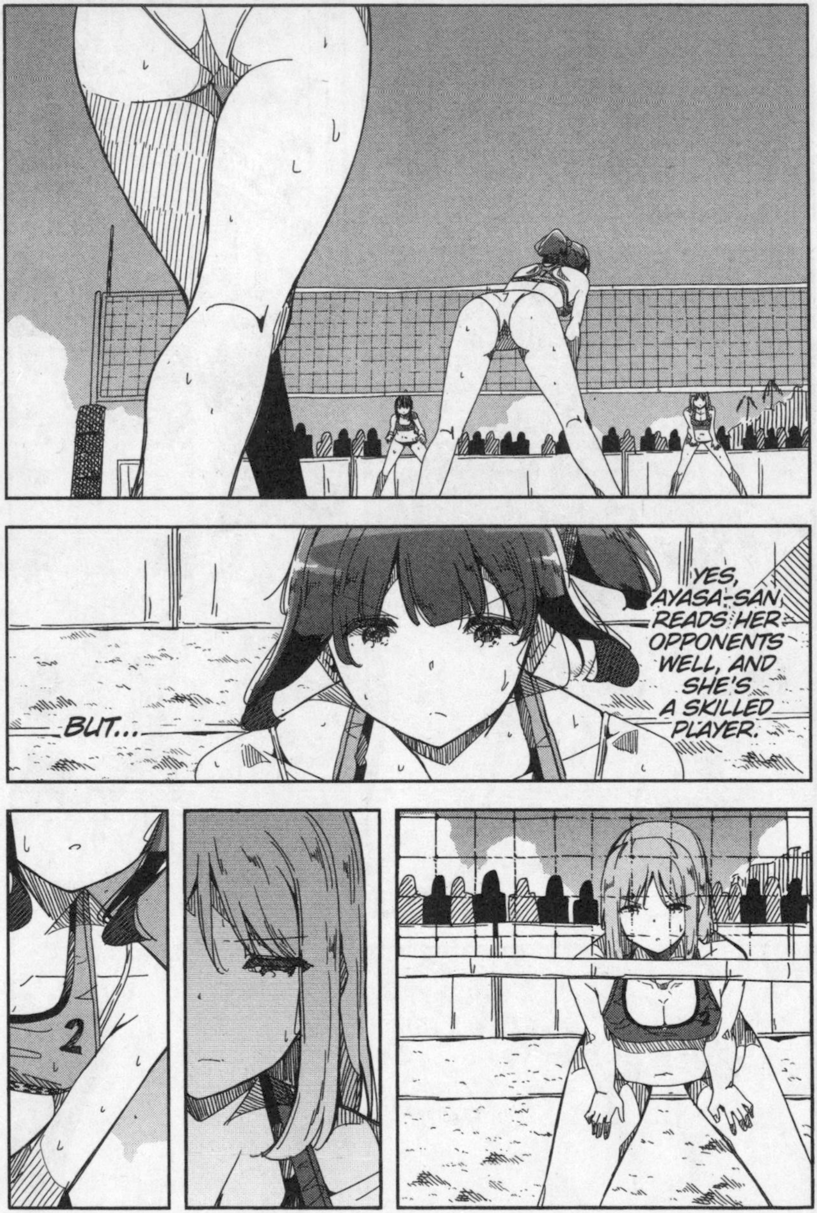
YES, AYASA-SAN READS HER OPPONENTS WELL, AND SHE'S A SKILLED PLAYER.
BUT...
2

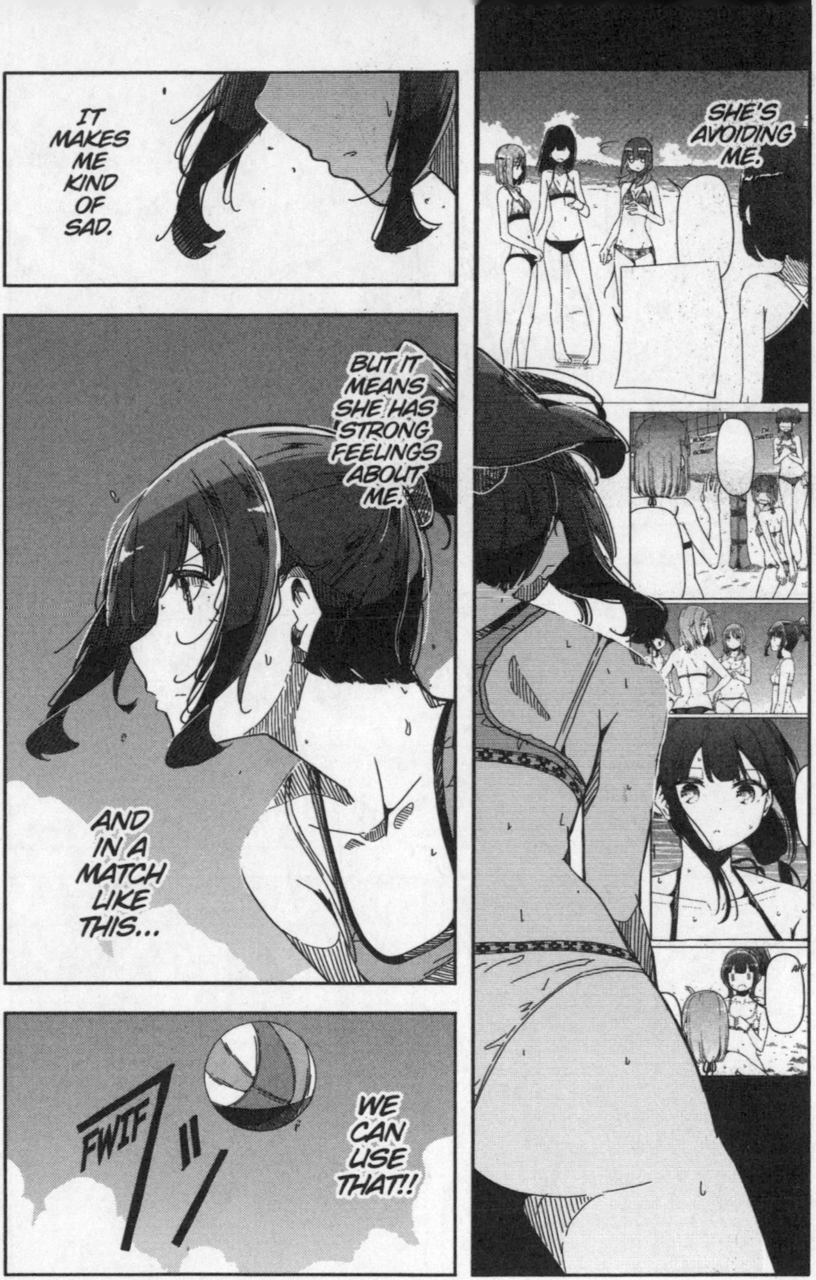
SHE'S AVOIDING ME.
I'M SAVED
HOW'S IT GOING?
AH!
IT MAKES ME KIND OF SAD.
BUT IT MEANS SHE HAS STRONG FEELINGS ABOUT ME.
AND IN A MATCH LIKE THIS...
WE CAN USE THAT!!
FWIP

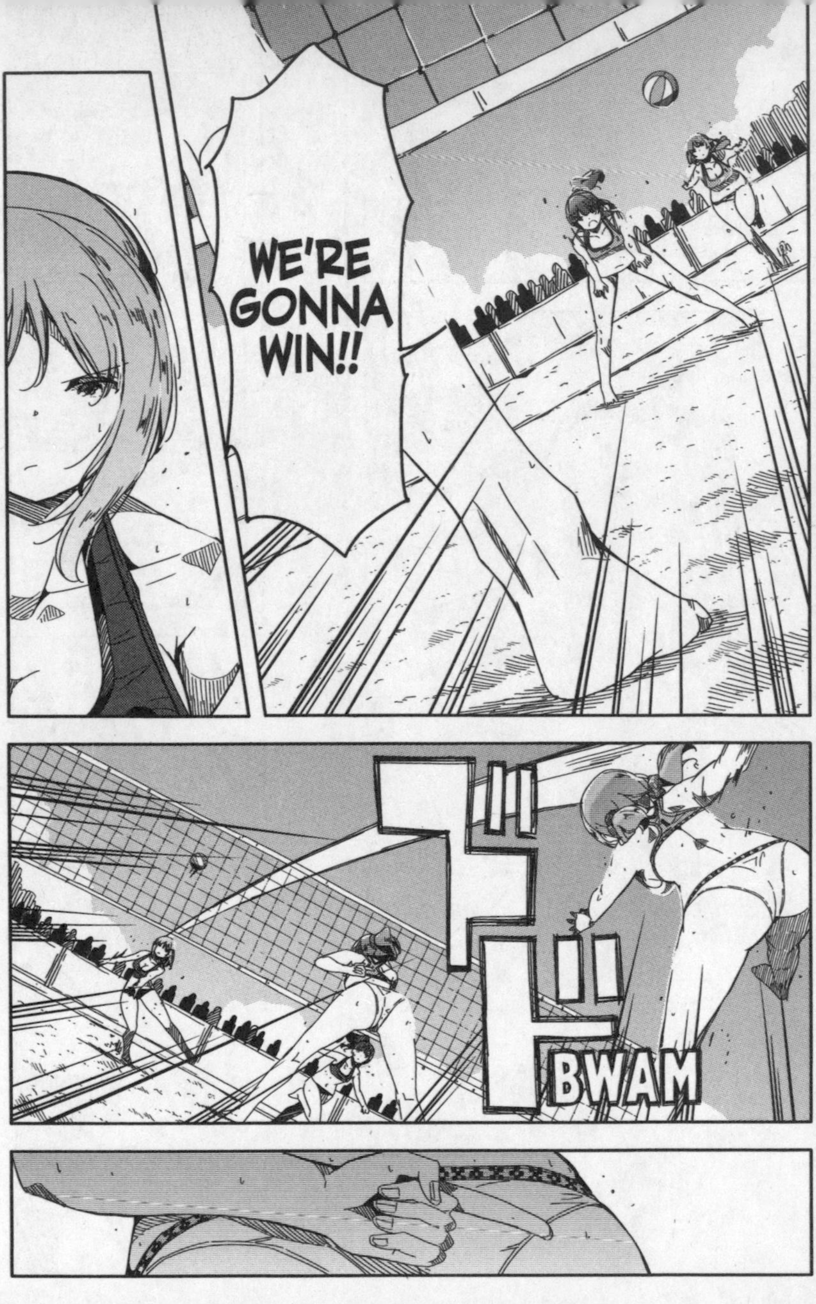
WE'RE GONNA WIN!!
BWAM

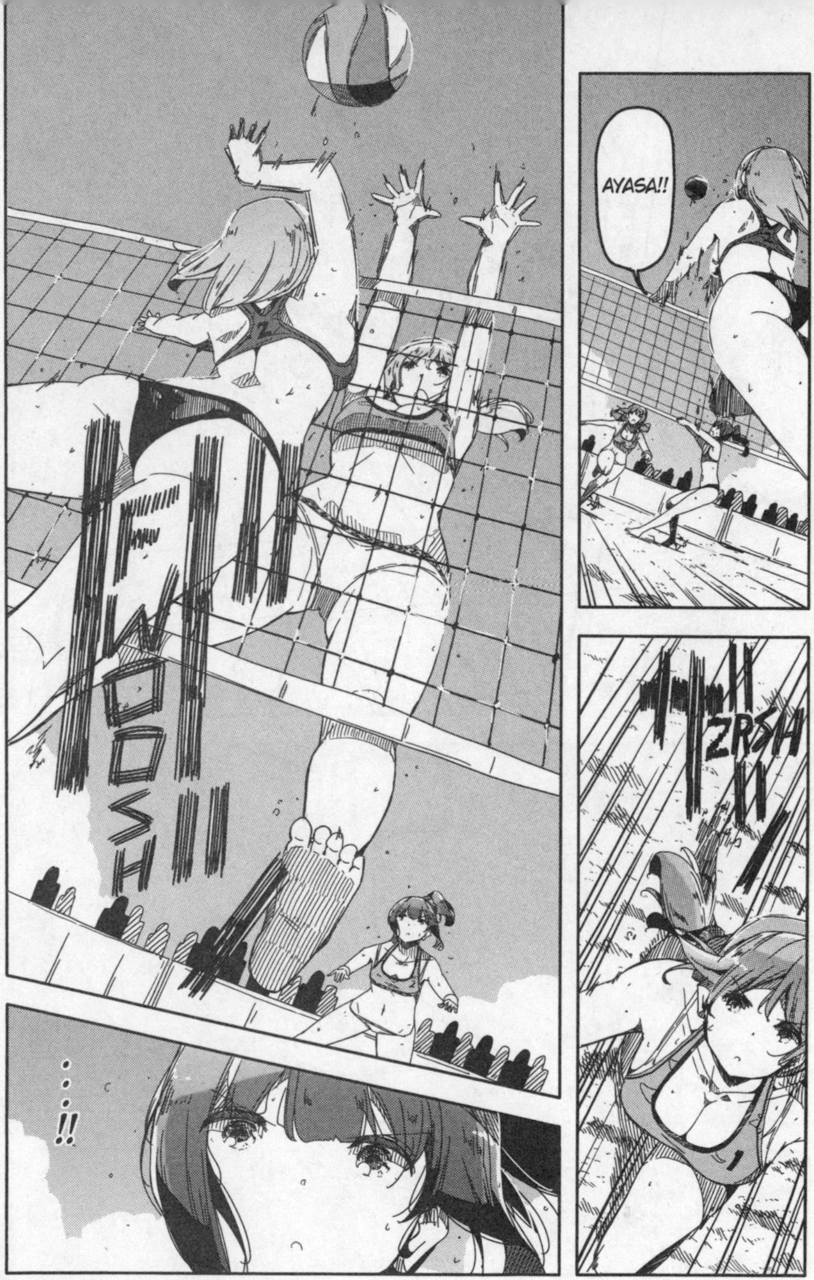
AYASA!!
ZRSH
FWOOSH
...!!

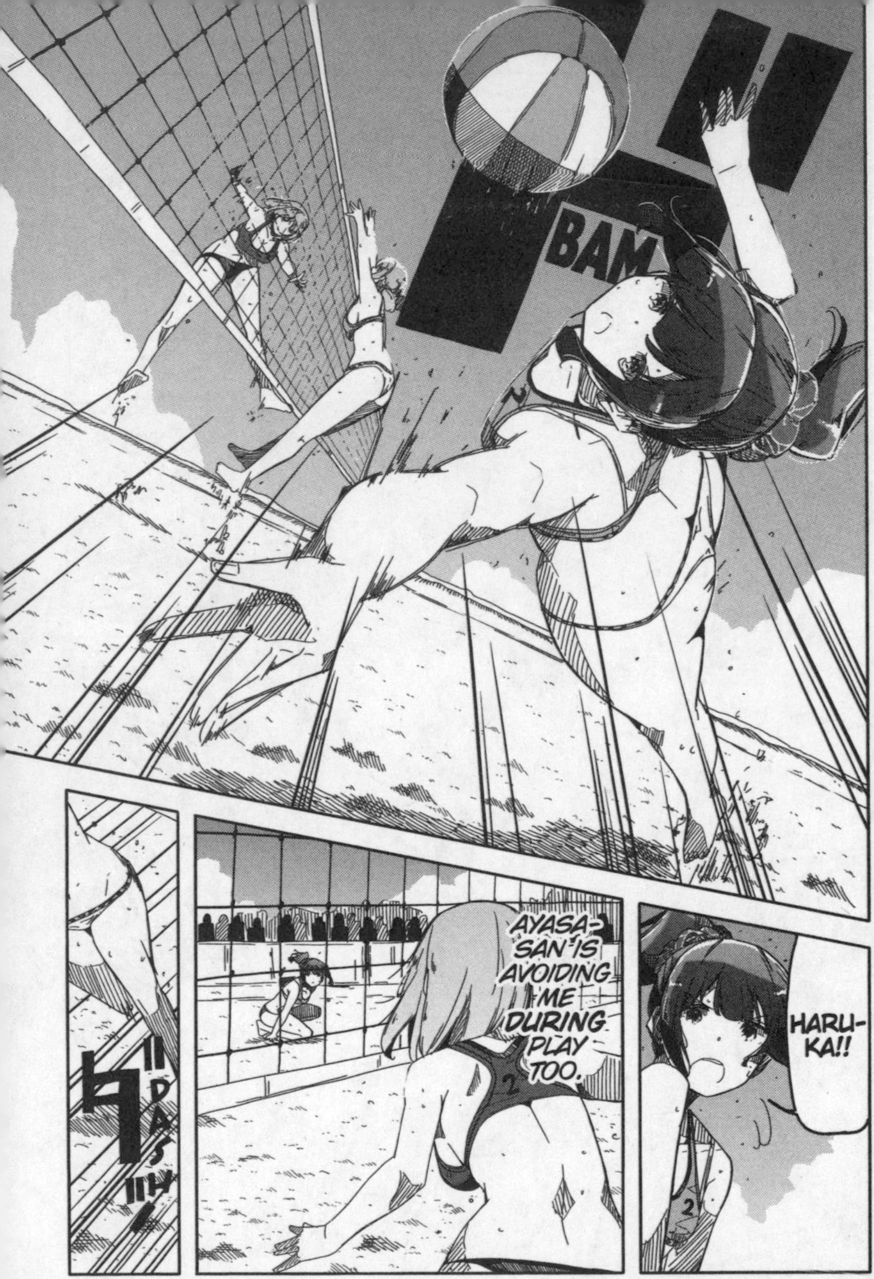
BAM
HARU-KA!!
AYASA-SAN IS AVOIDING ME DURING PLAY TOO.
DASH!!

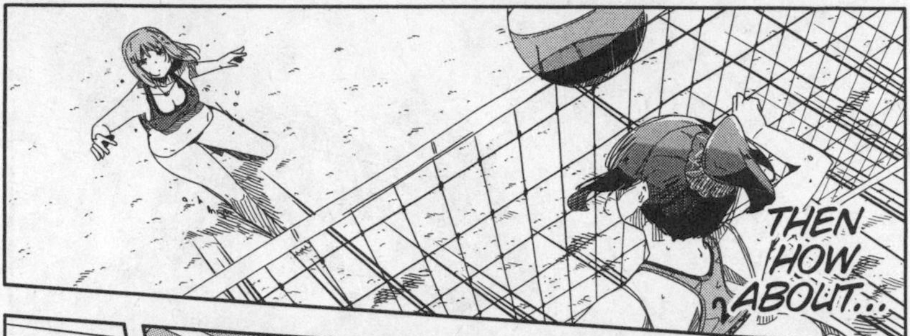
THEN HOW ABOUT...

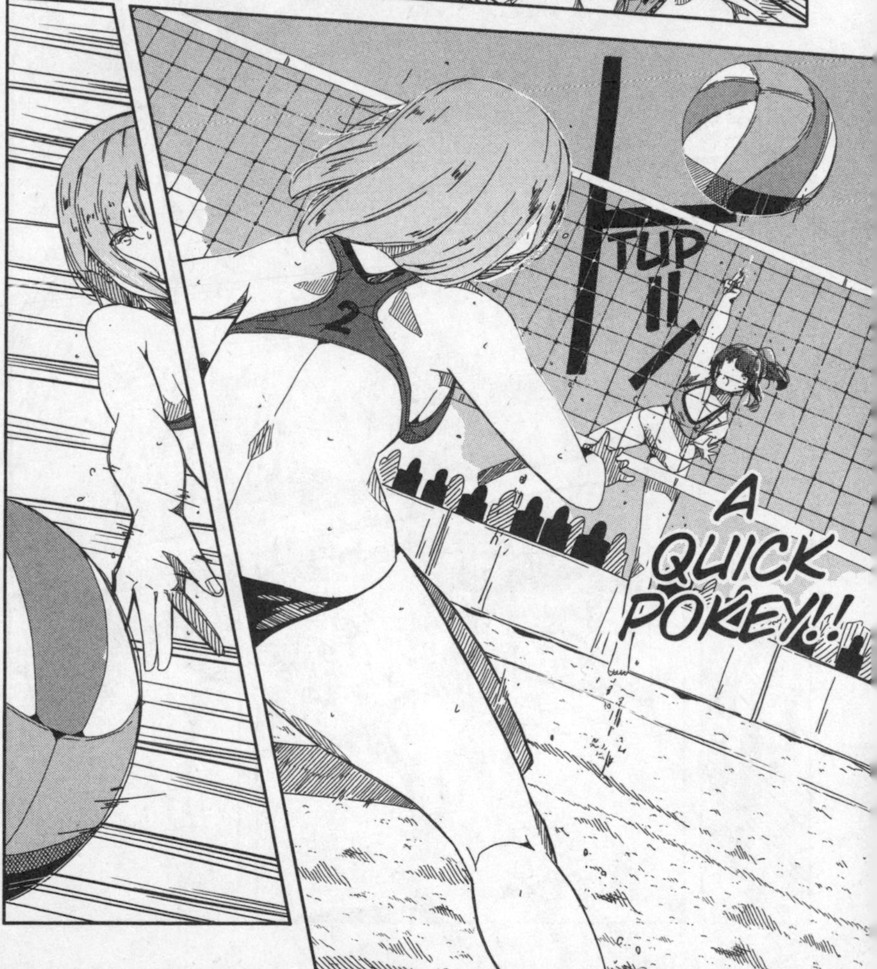
TUP
A QUICK POKEY!!

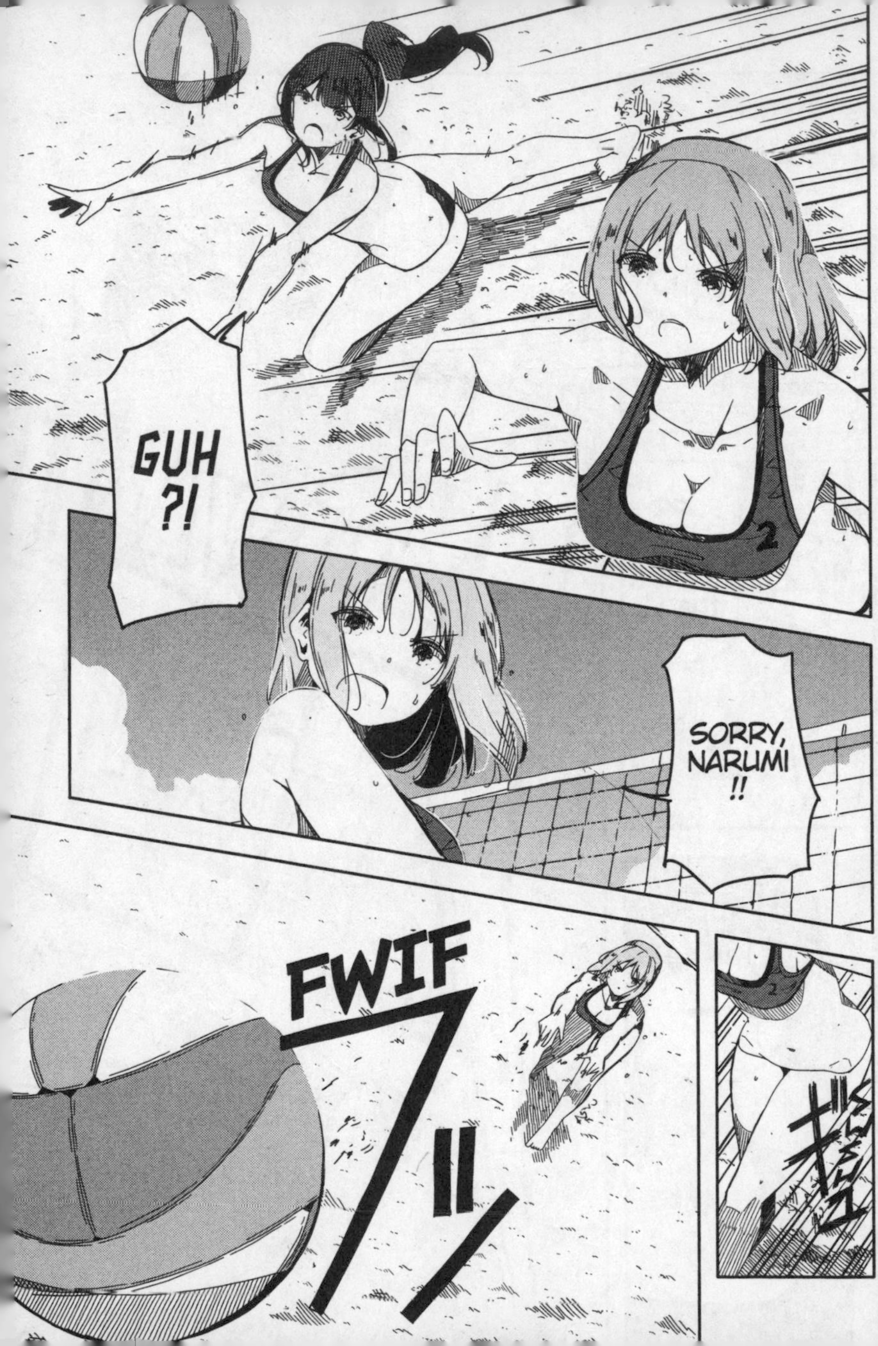
GUH ?!
SORRY, NARUMI !!
FWIF

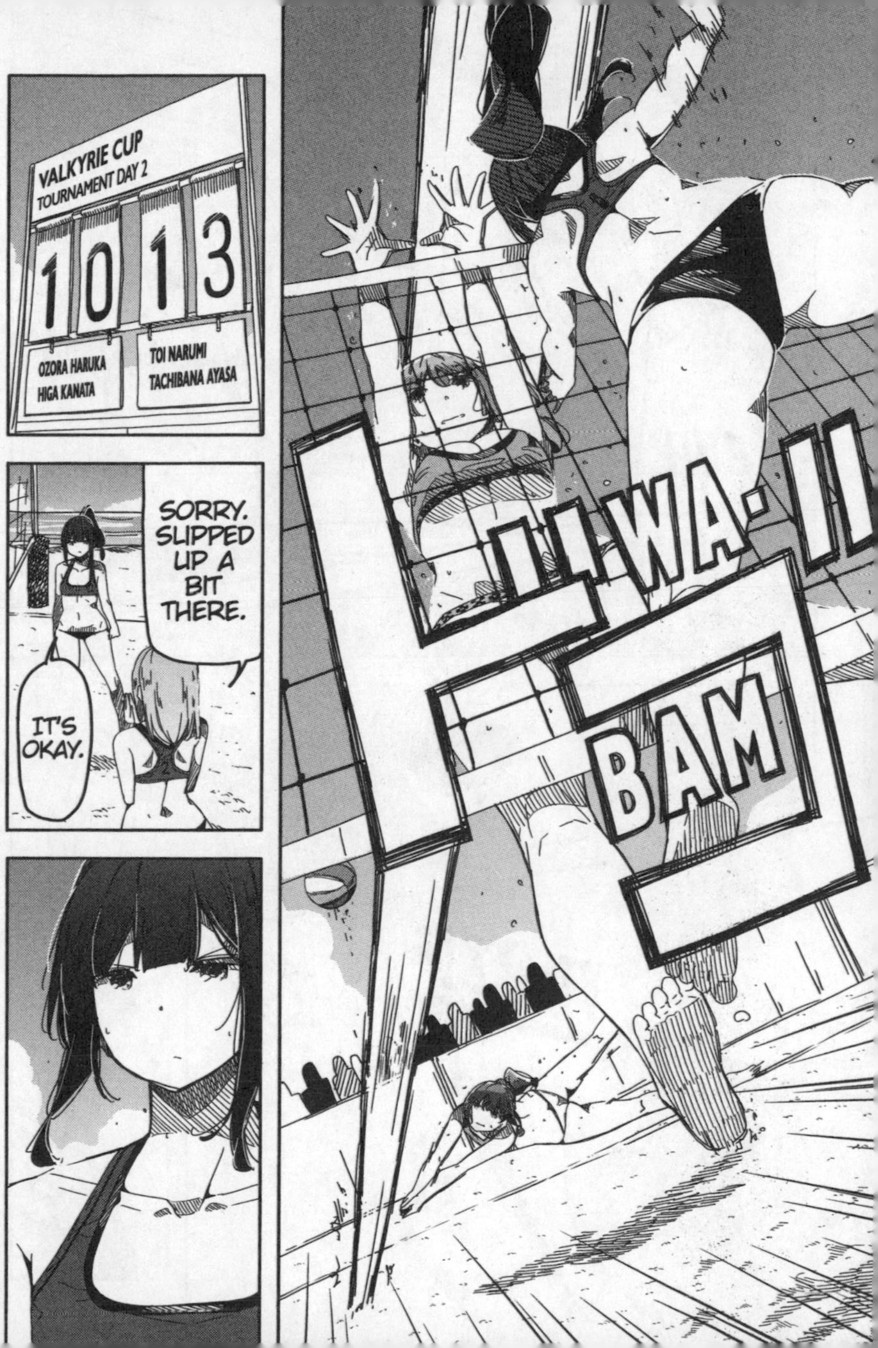
WA-!!
BAM
VALKYRIE CUP
TOURNAMENT DAY 2
10 13
OZORA HARUKA
HIGA KANATA
TOI NARUMI
TACHIBANA AYASA
SORRY. SLIPPED UP A BIT THERE.
IT'S OKAY.

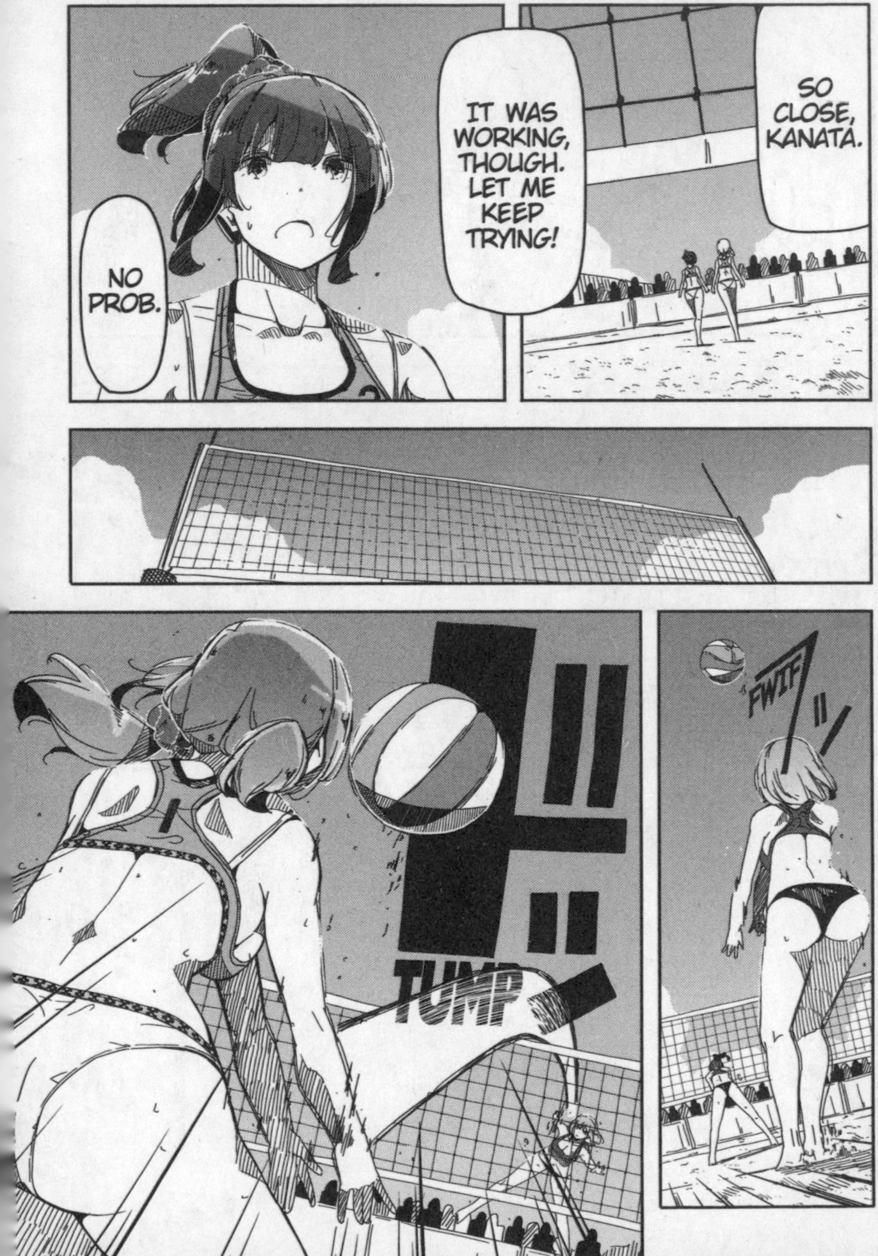
SO CLOSE, KANATA.
IT WAS WORKING, THOUGH. LET ME KEEP TRYING!
NO PROB.
FWIF
TUMP

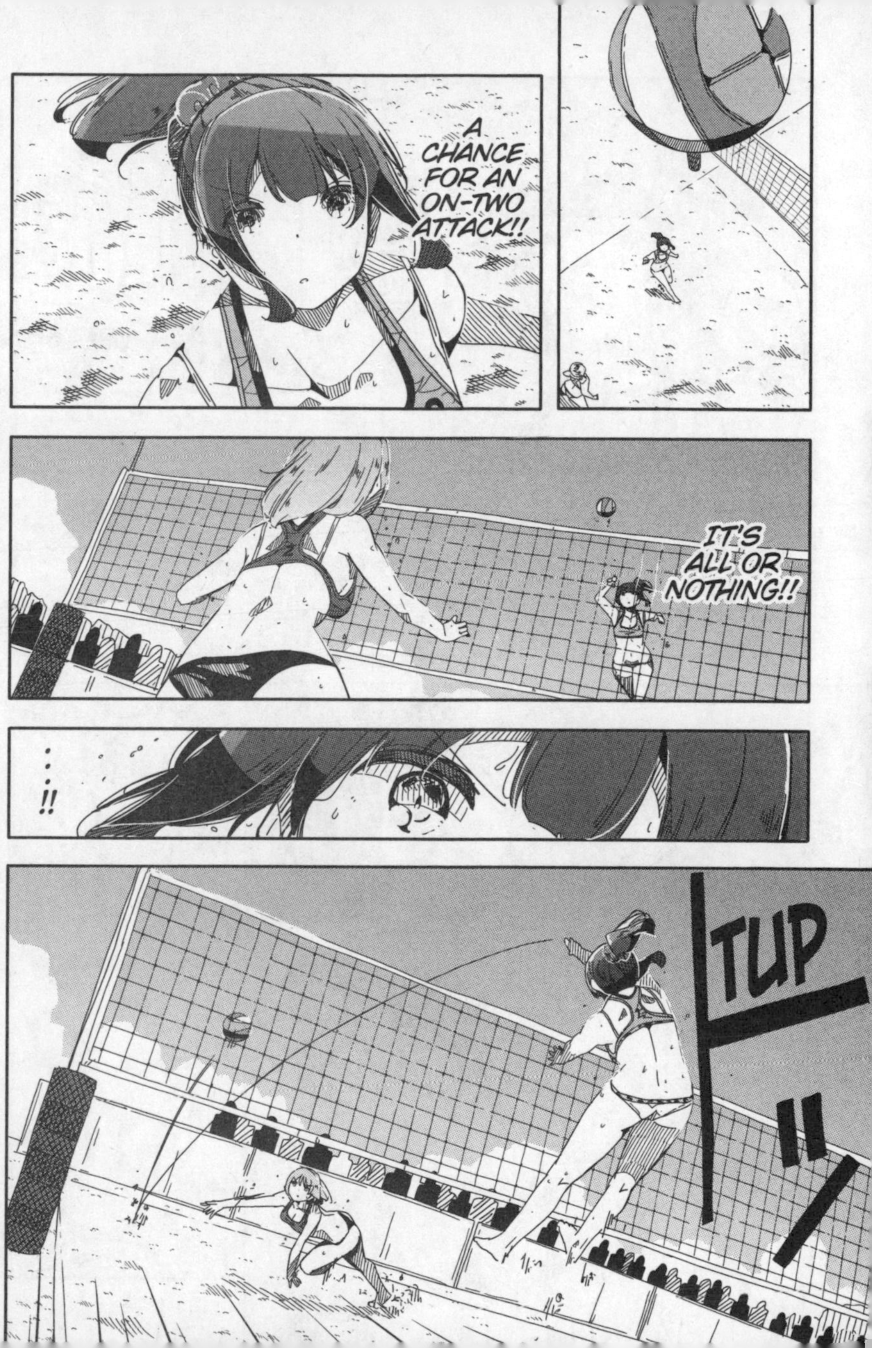
A CHANCE FOR AN ON-TWO ATTACK!!
IT'S ALL OR NOTHING!!
...!!
TUP

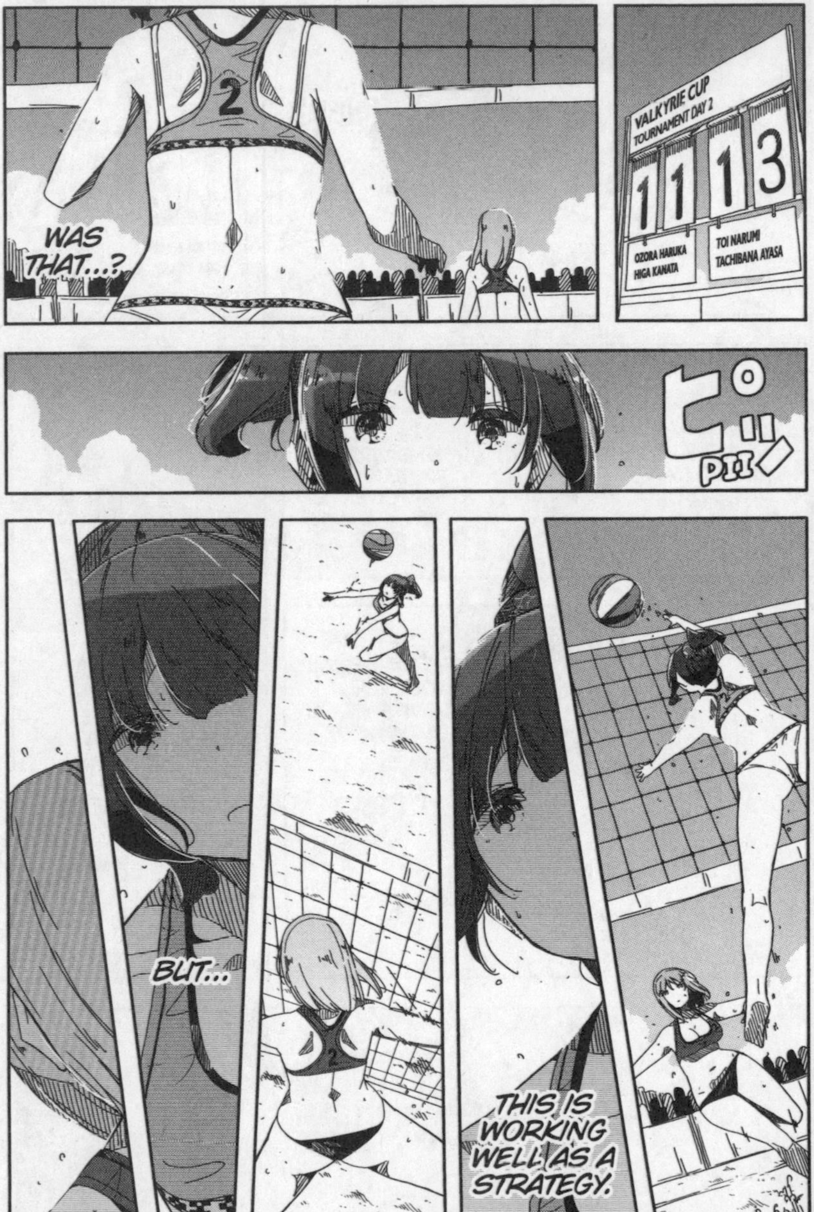
VALKYRIE CUP
TOURNAMENT DAY 2
1 1 1 3
OZORA HARUKA
HIGA KANATA
TOI NARUMI
TACHIBANA AYASA
WAS THAT...?
ピッ
PII
BUT...
THIS IS WORKING WELL AS A STRATEGY.

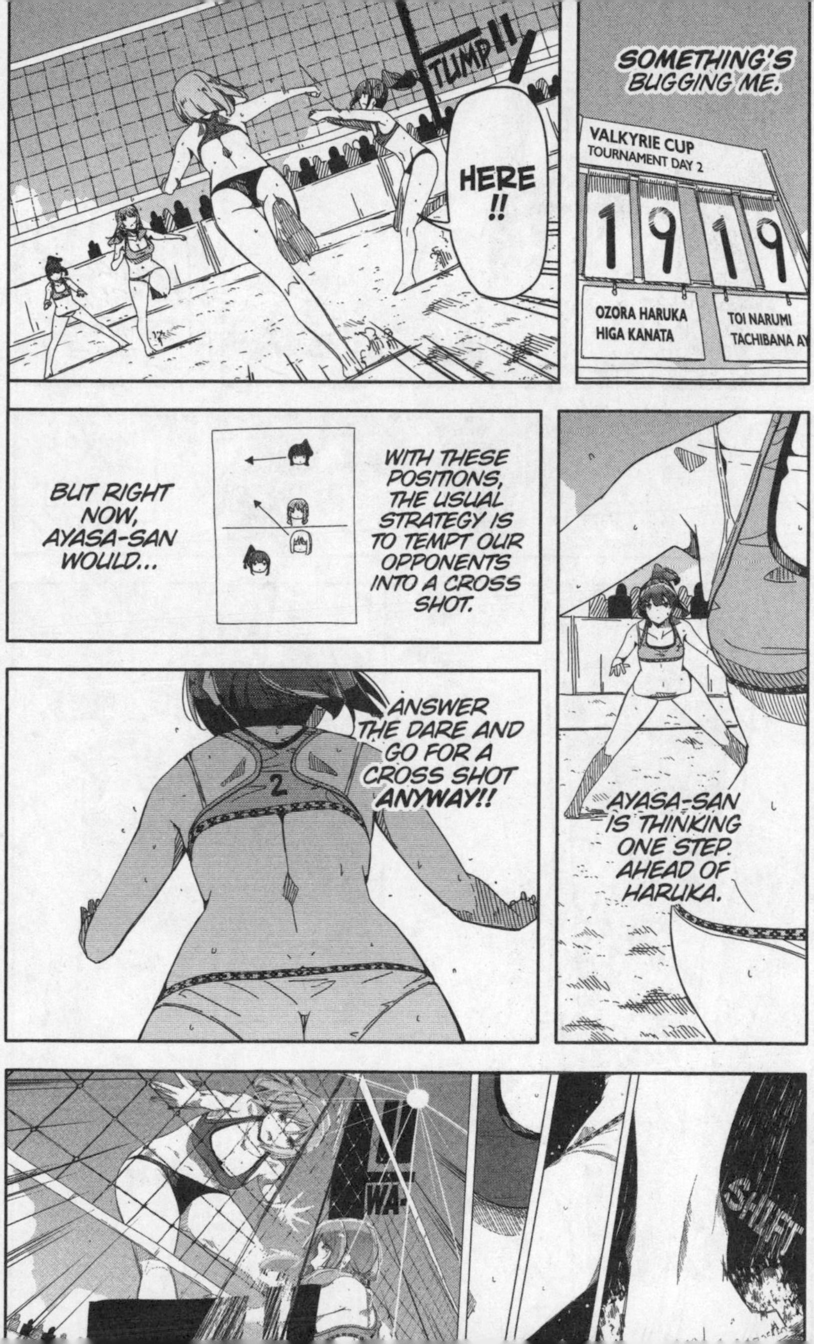
SOMETHING'S BUGGING ME.
VALKYRIE CUP
TOURNAMENT DAY 2
19 19
OZORA HARUKA
HIGA KANATA
TOI NARUMI
TACHIBANA AY
TUMP!!
HERE!!
AYASA-SAN IS THINKING ONE STEP AHEAD OF HARUKA.
WITH THESE POSITIONS, THE USUAL STRATEGY IS TO TEMPT OUR OPPONENTS INTO A CROSS SHOT.
BUT RIGHT NOW, AYASA-SAN WOULD...
ANSWER THE DARE AND GO FOR A CROSS SHOT ANYWAY!!
SHIFT
WA-

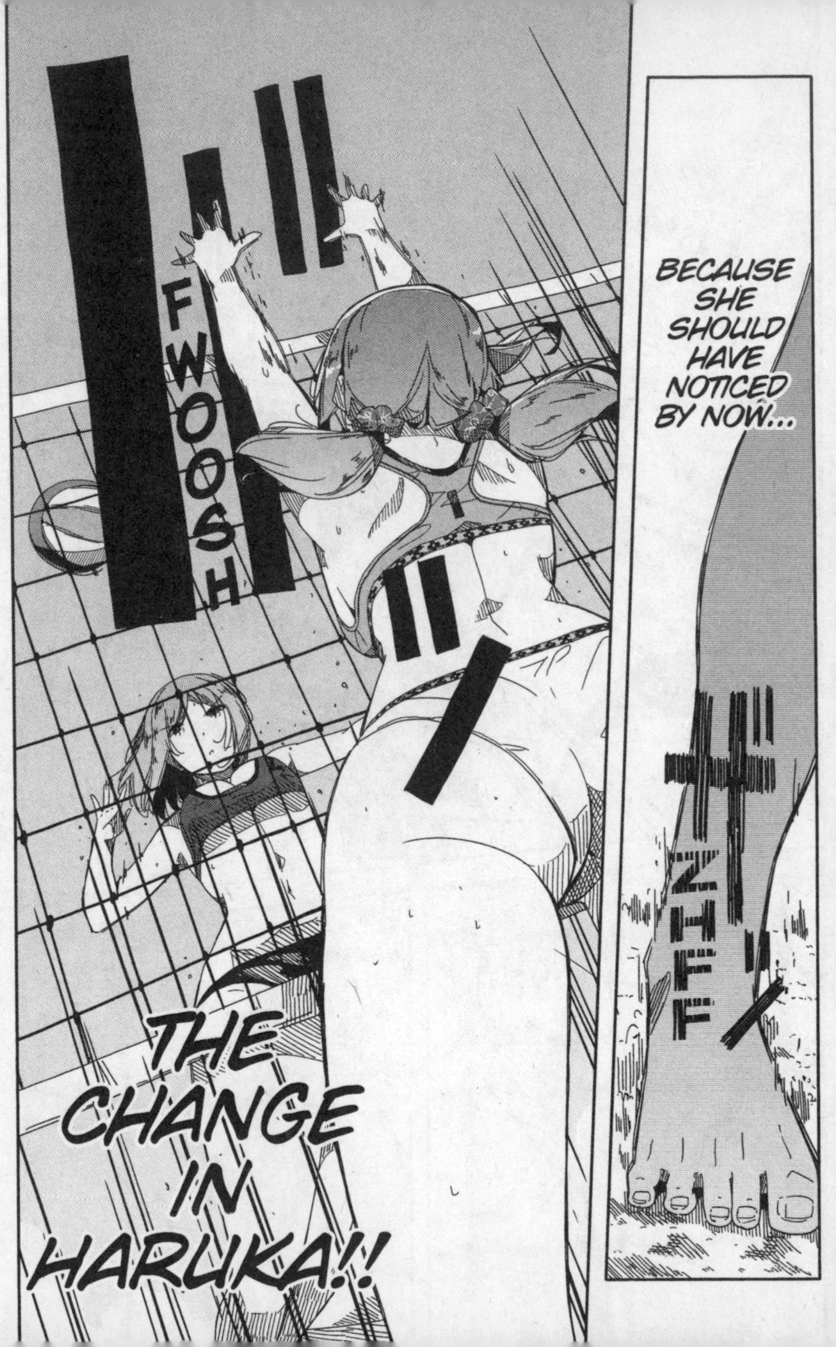
BECAUSE SHE SHOULD HAVE NOTICED BY NOW...
ZHFF
FWOOSH
THE CHANGE IN HARUKA!!

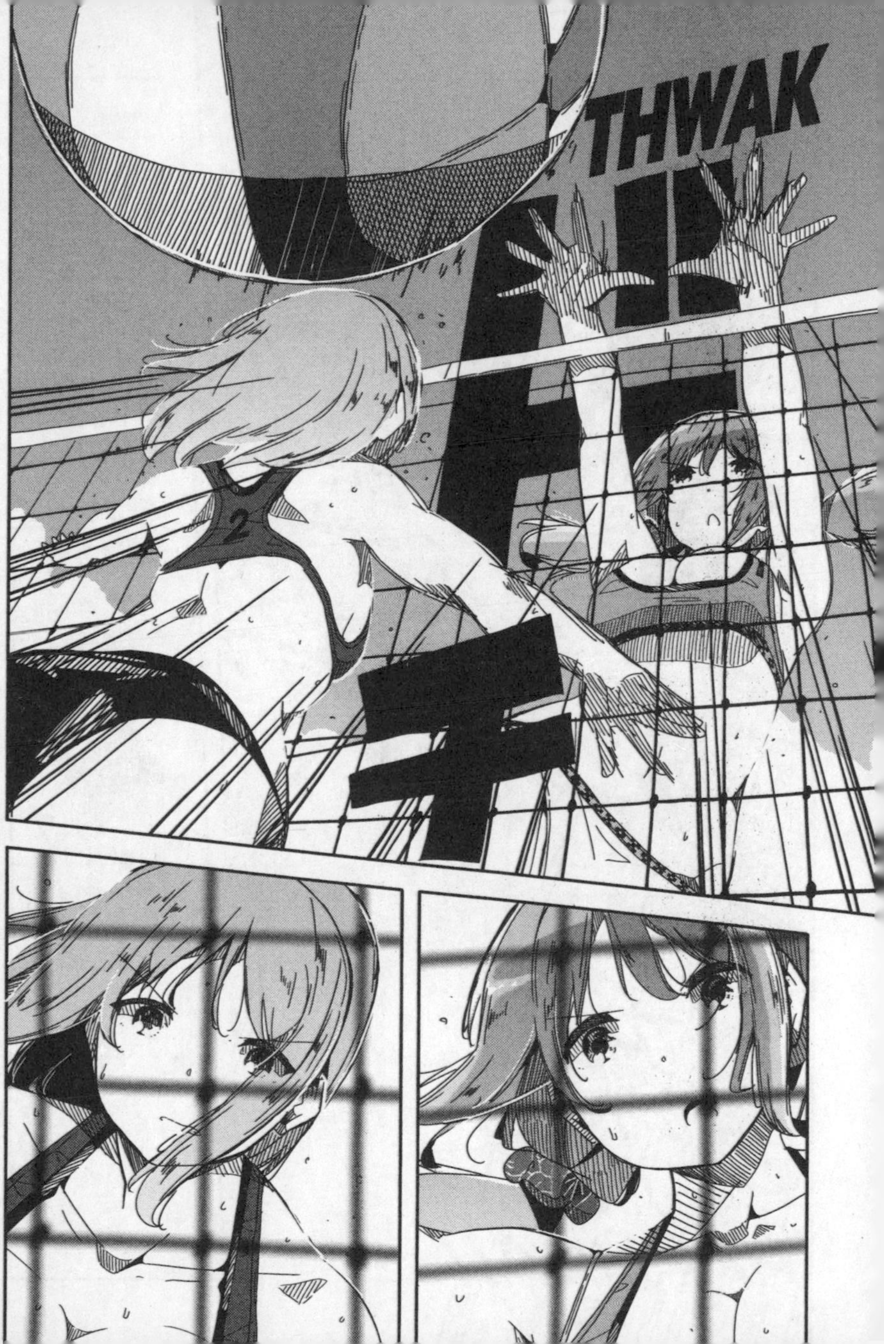
THWAK

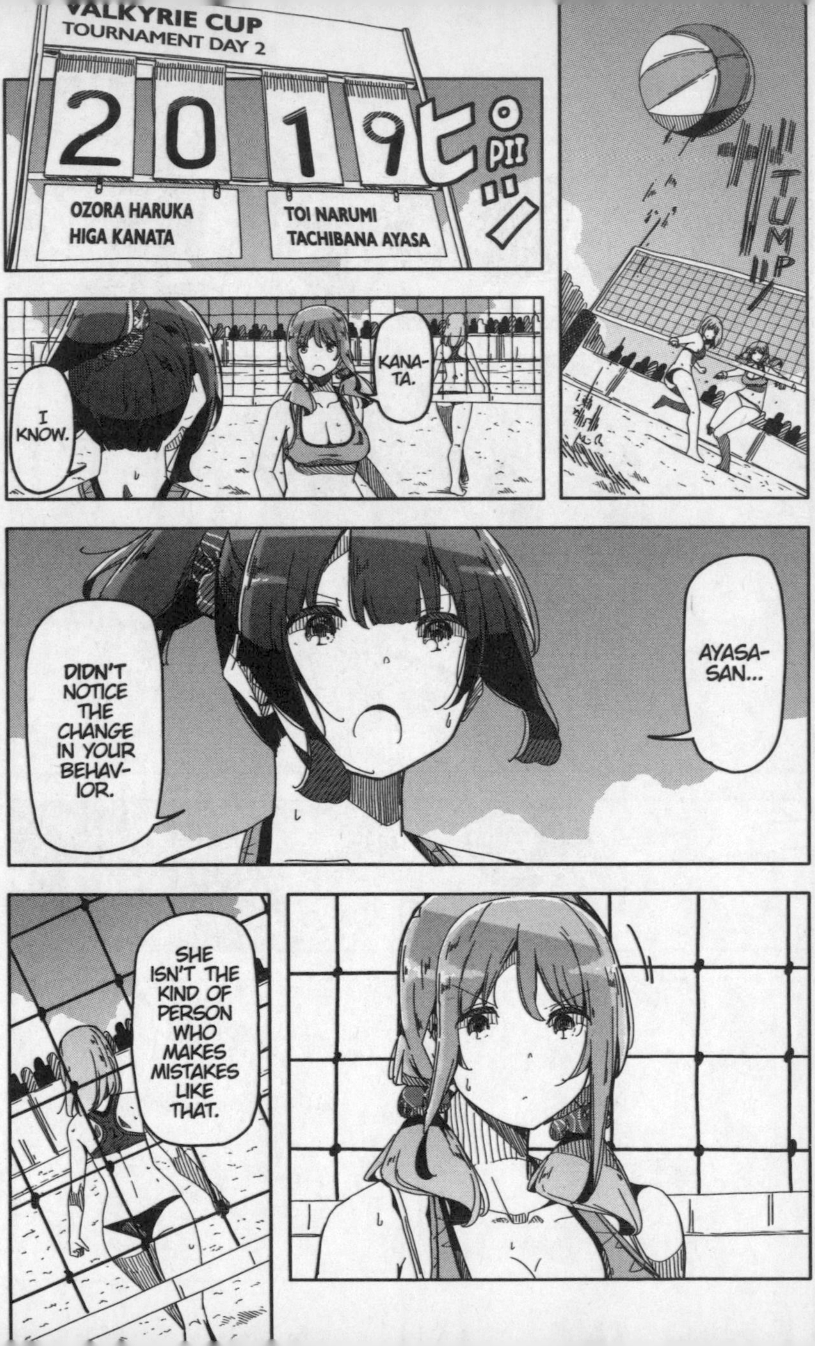
TUMP
VALKYRIE CUP
TOURNAMENT DAY 2
20 19
PII
OZORA HARUKA
HIGA KANATA
TOI NARUMI
TACHIBANA AYASA
KANA-TA.
I KNOW.
AYASA-SAN...
DIDN'T NOTICE THE CHANGE IN YOUR BEHAV-IOR.
SHE ISN'T THE KIND OF PERSON WHO MAKES MISTAKES LIKE THAT.

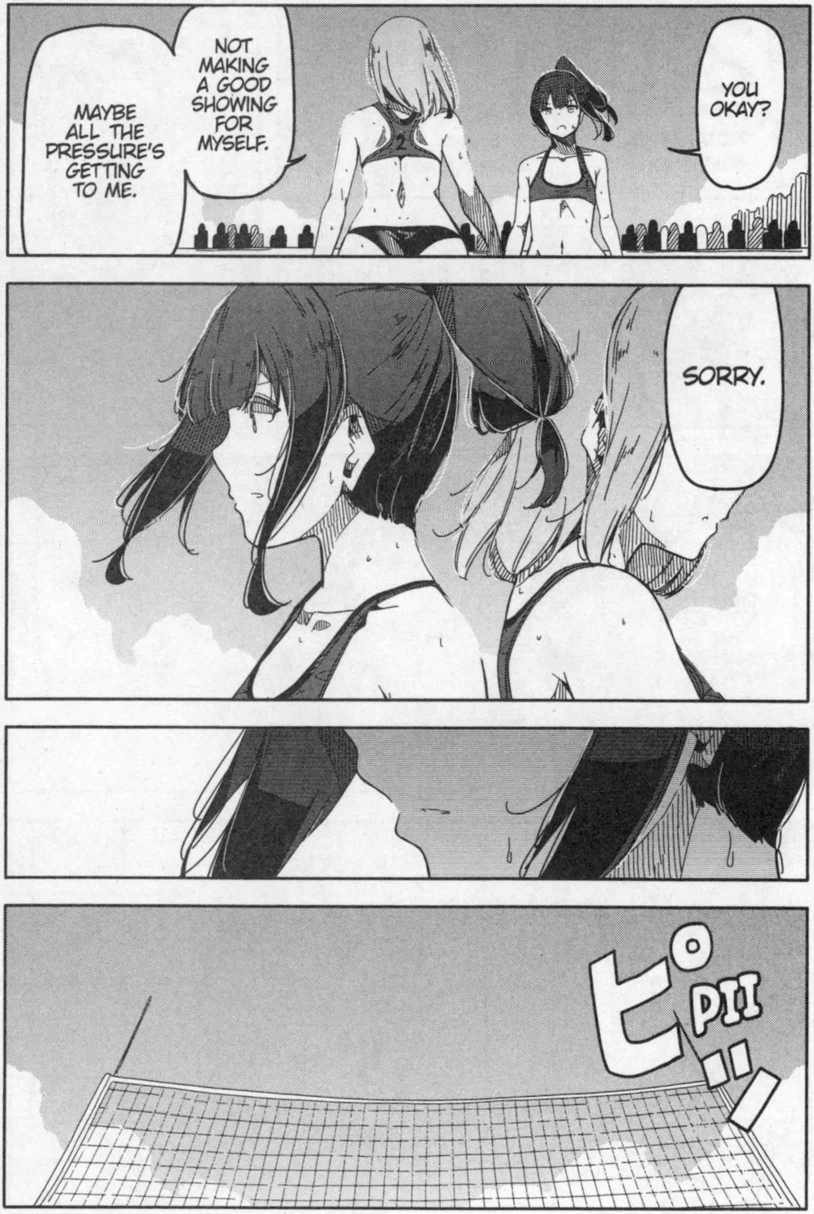
YOU OKAY?
NOT MAKING A GOOD SHOWING FOR MYSELF.
MAYBE ALL THE PRESSURE'S GETTING TO ME.
SORRY.
ピ PII

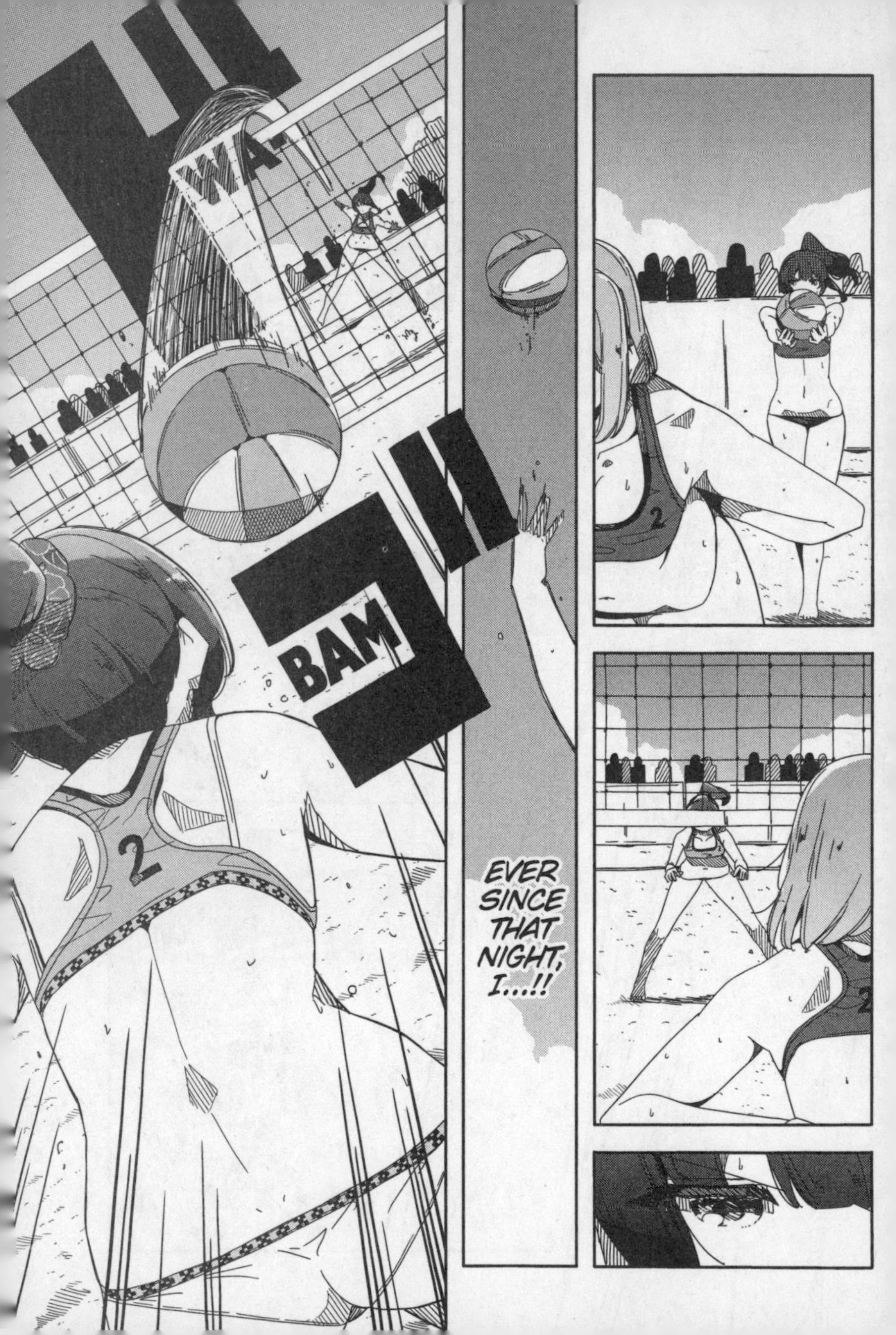
EVER SINCE THAT NIGHT, I...!!
WA-
BAM

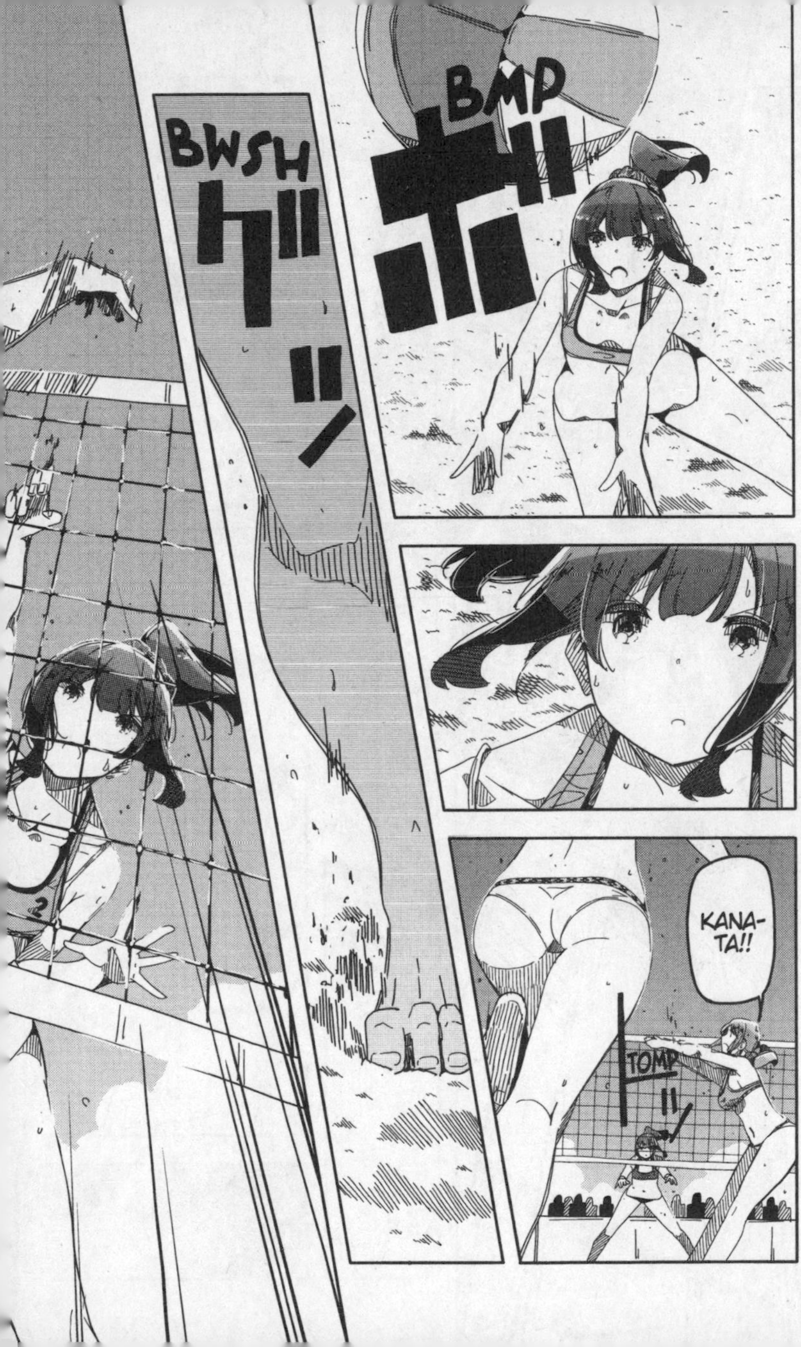
BMP
KANA-TA!!
TOMP
BWSH

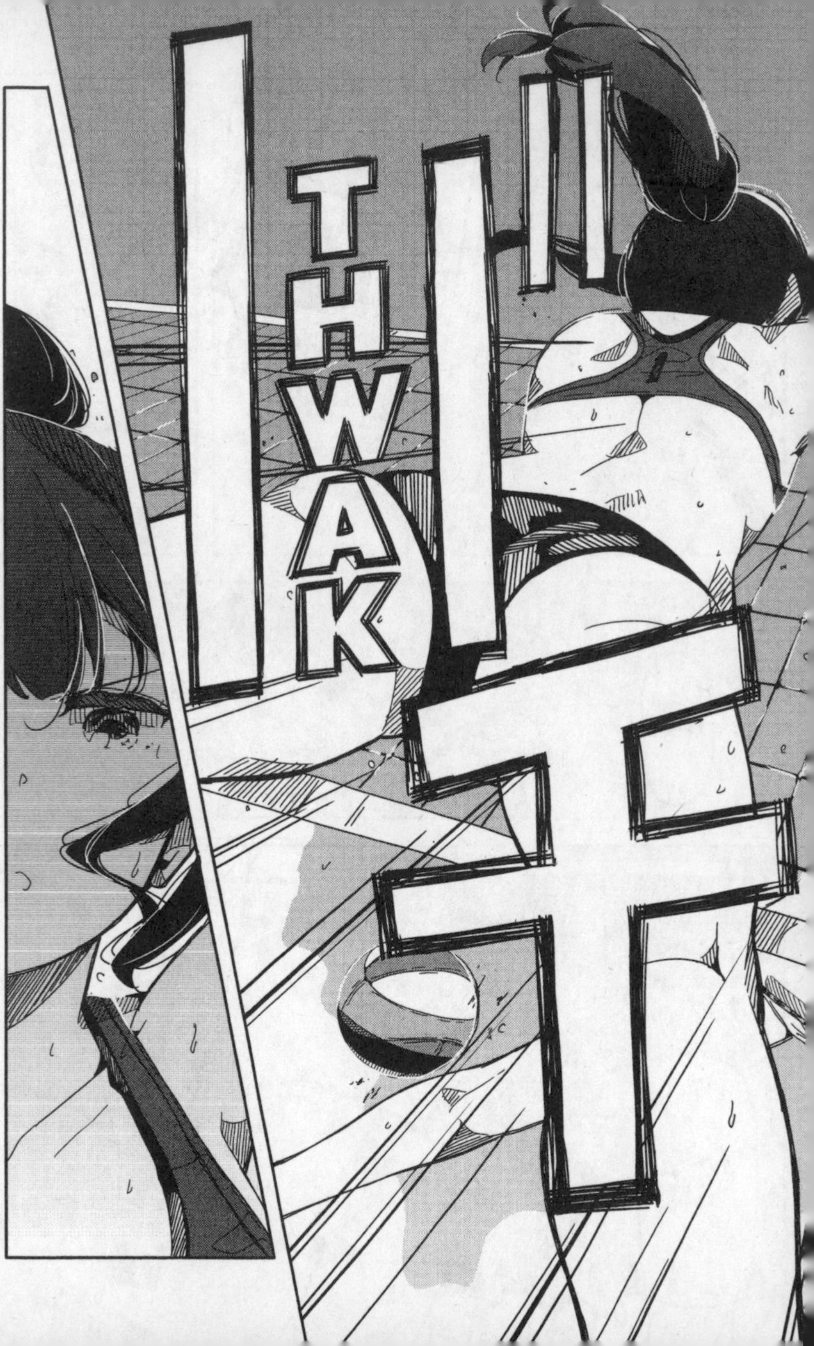
THWAK

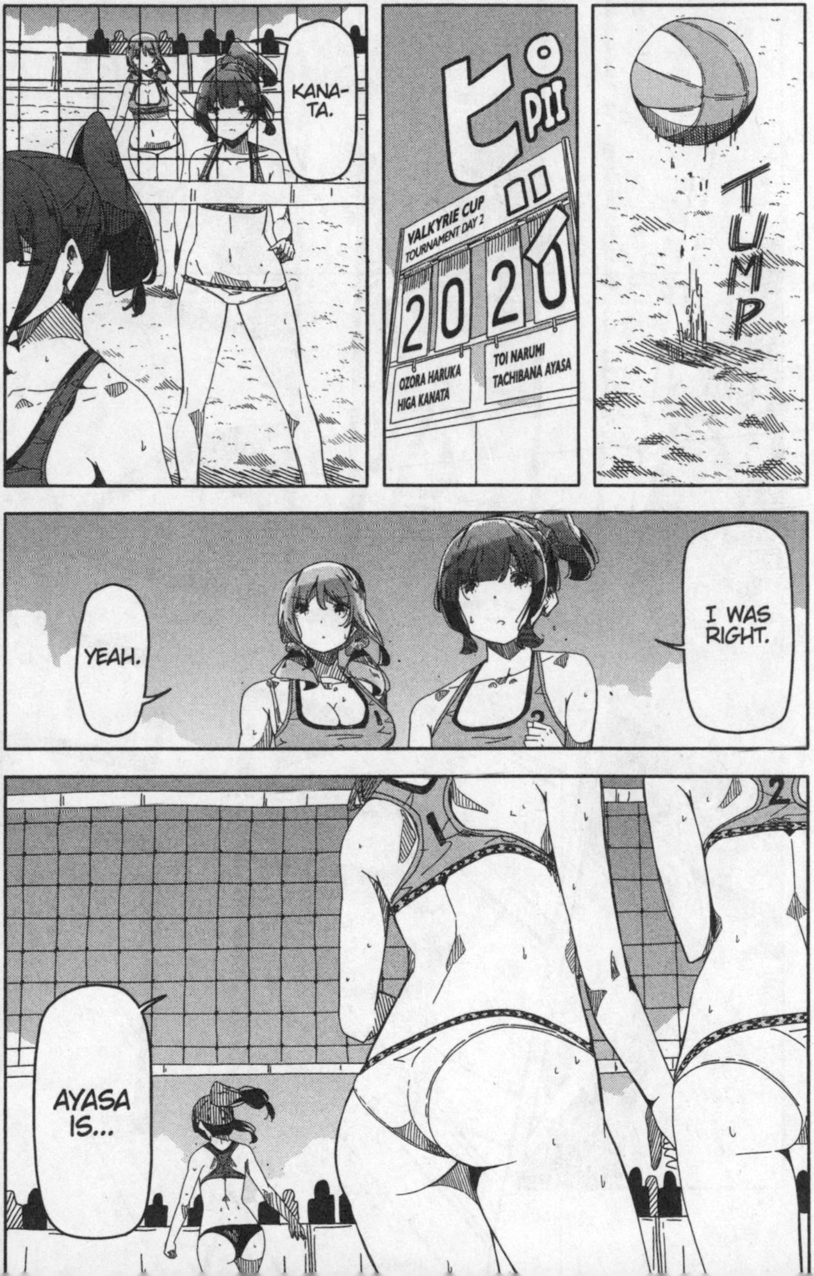
TUMP
ピ PII
VALKYRIE CUP
TOURNAMENT DAY 2
20 20
OZORA HARUKA
HIGA KANATA
TOI NARUMI
TACHIBANA AYASA
KANA-TA.
I WAS RIGHT.
YEAH.
AYASA IS...

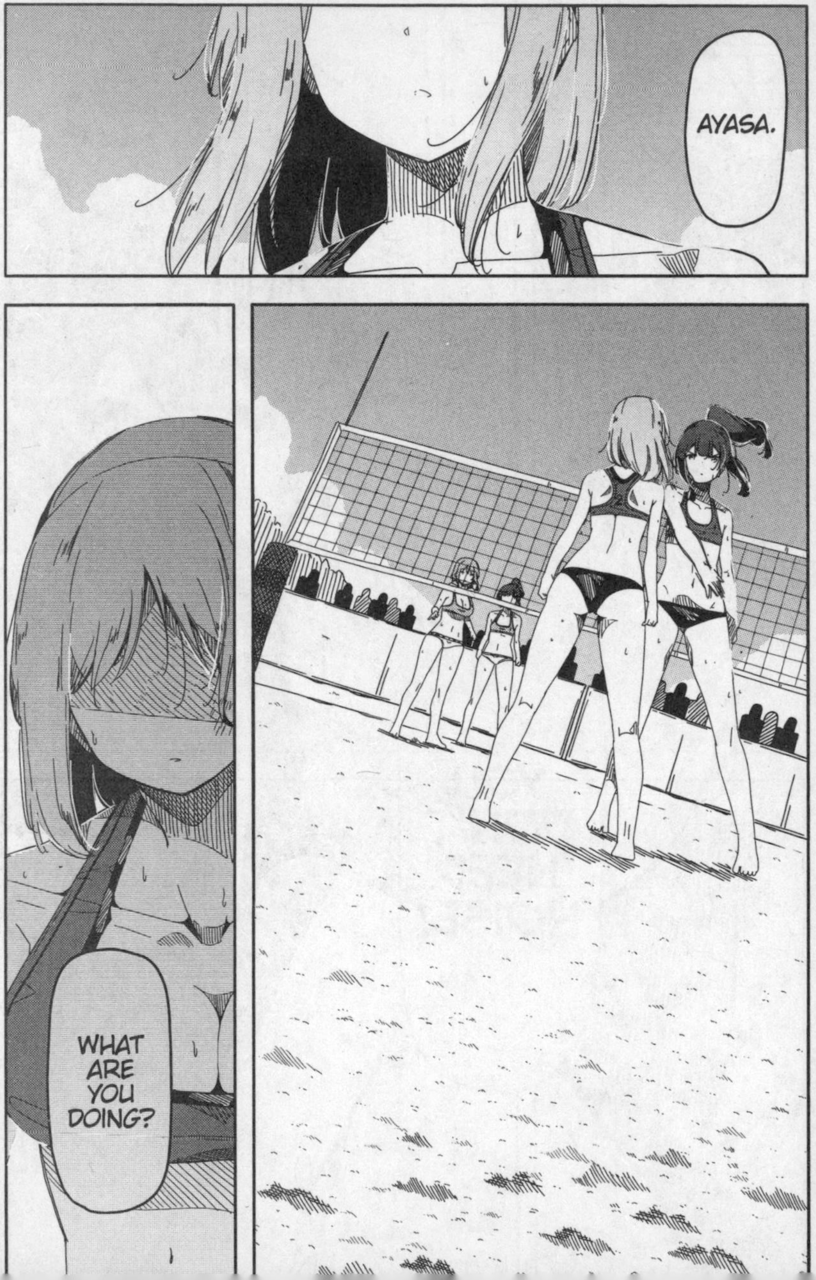
AYASA.
WHAT ARE YOU DOING?

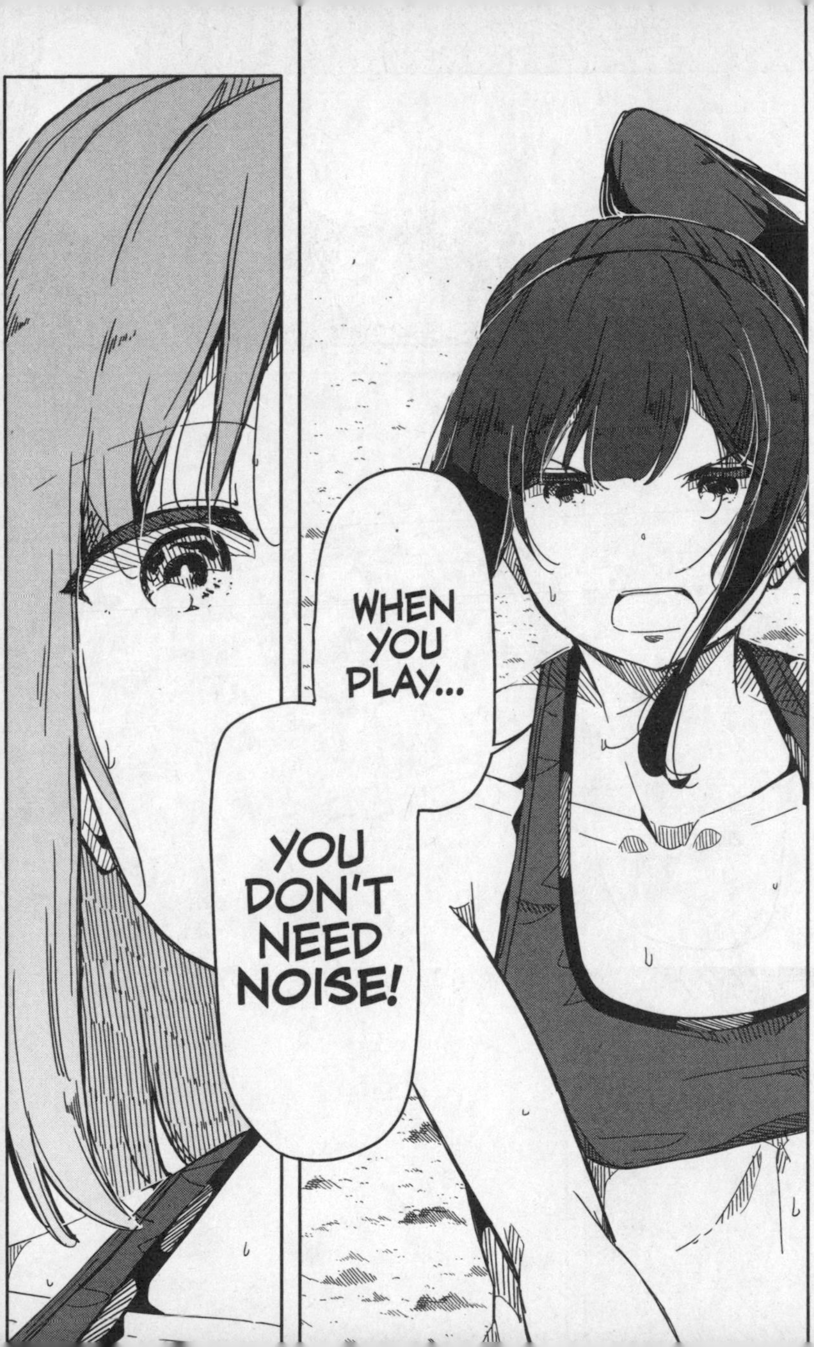
WHEN YOU PLAY...
YOU DON'T NEED NOISE!

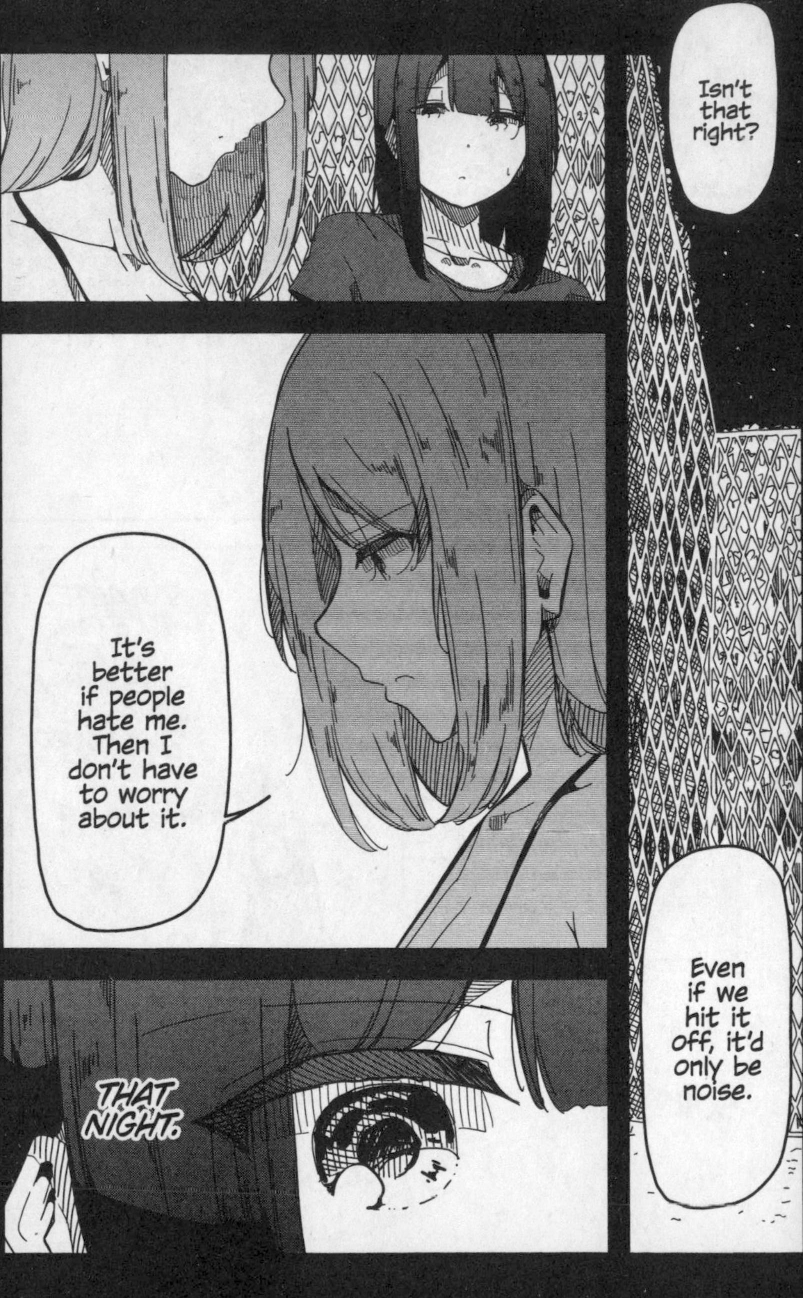
Isn't that right?
Even if we hit it off, it'd only be noise.
It's better if people hate me. Then I don't have to worry about it.
THAT NIGHT.

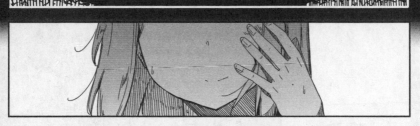

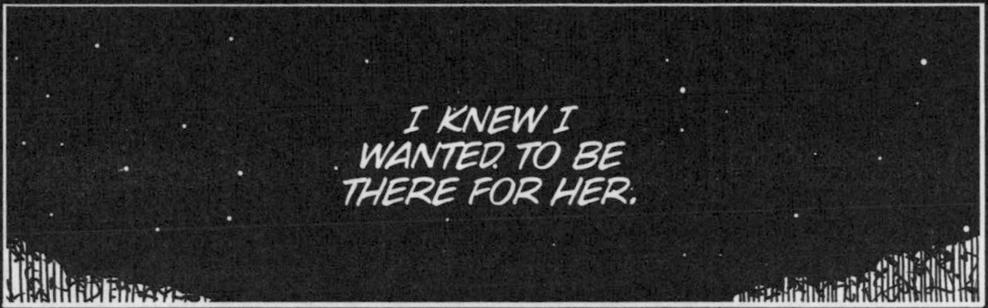
I KNEW I WANTED TO BE THERE FOR HER.
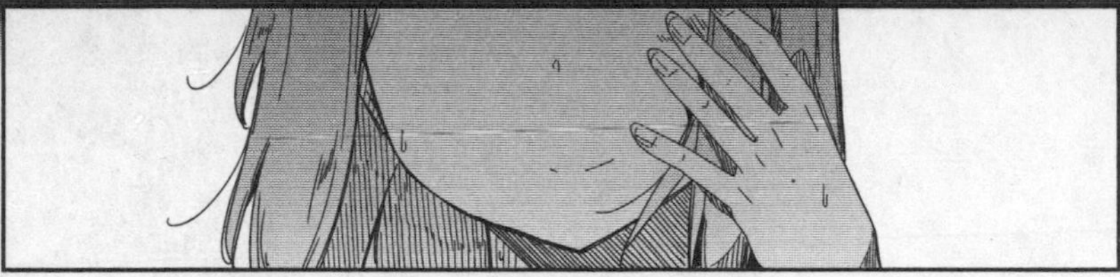
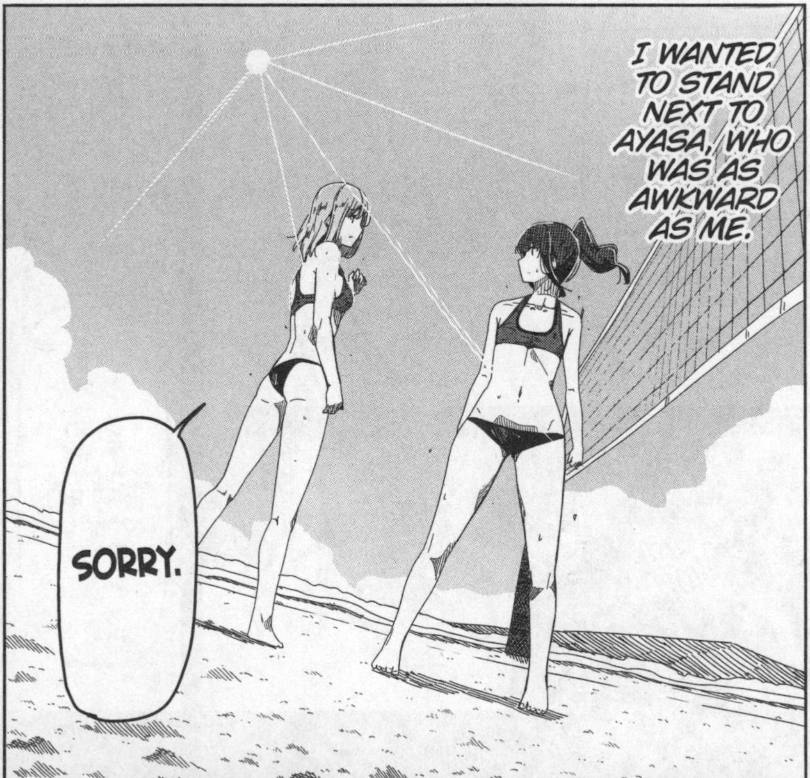
I WANTED TO STAND NEXT TO AYASA, WHO WAS AS AWKWARD AS ME.
SORRY.

Harukana★Receive

Presented by Nyoijizai

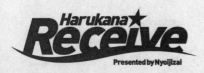

Harukana★Receive

Presented by Nyoijizai

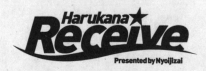

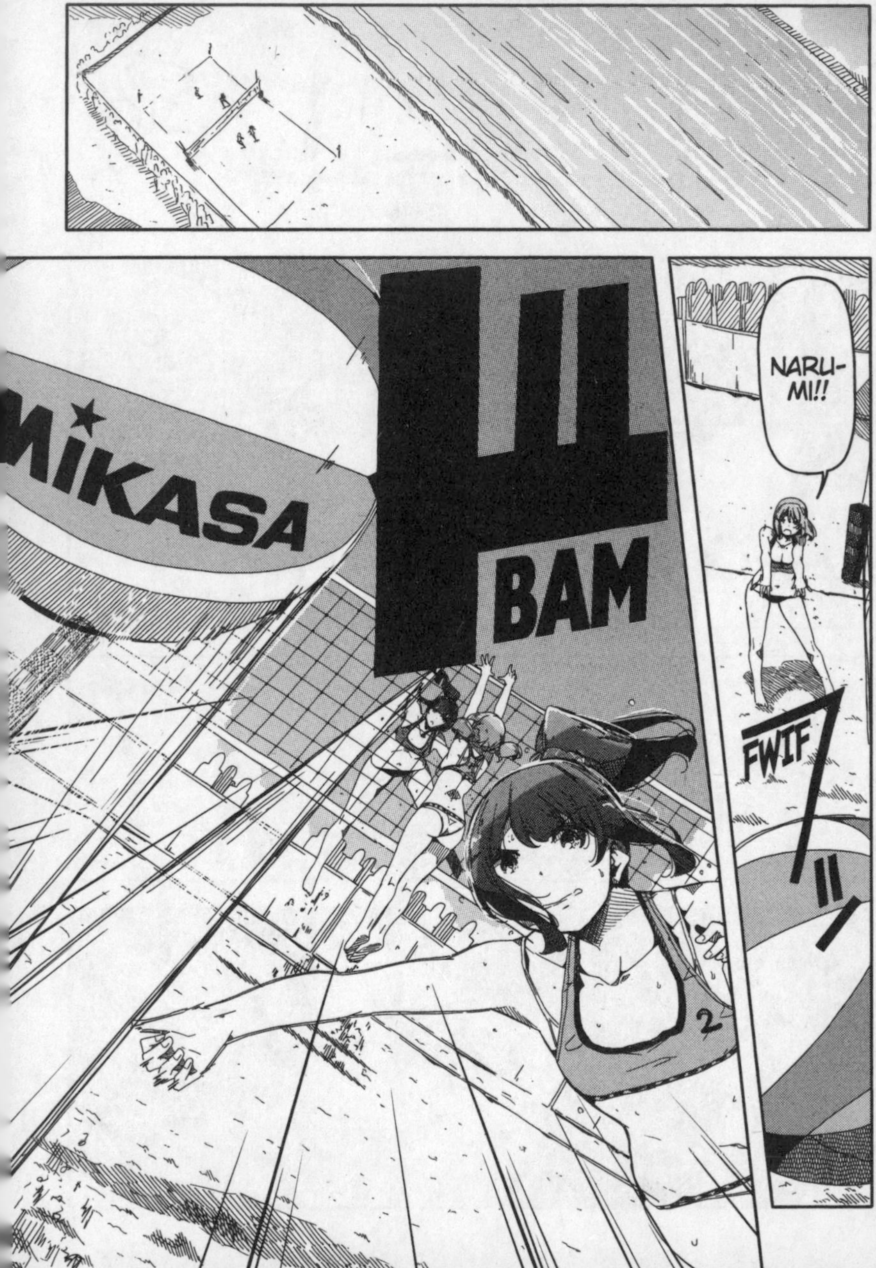
NARU-MI!!
FWIF
MIKASA
BAM

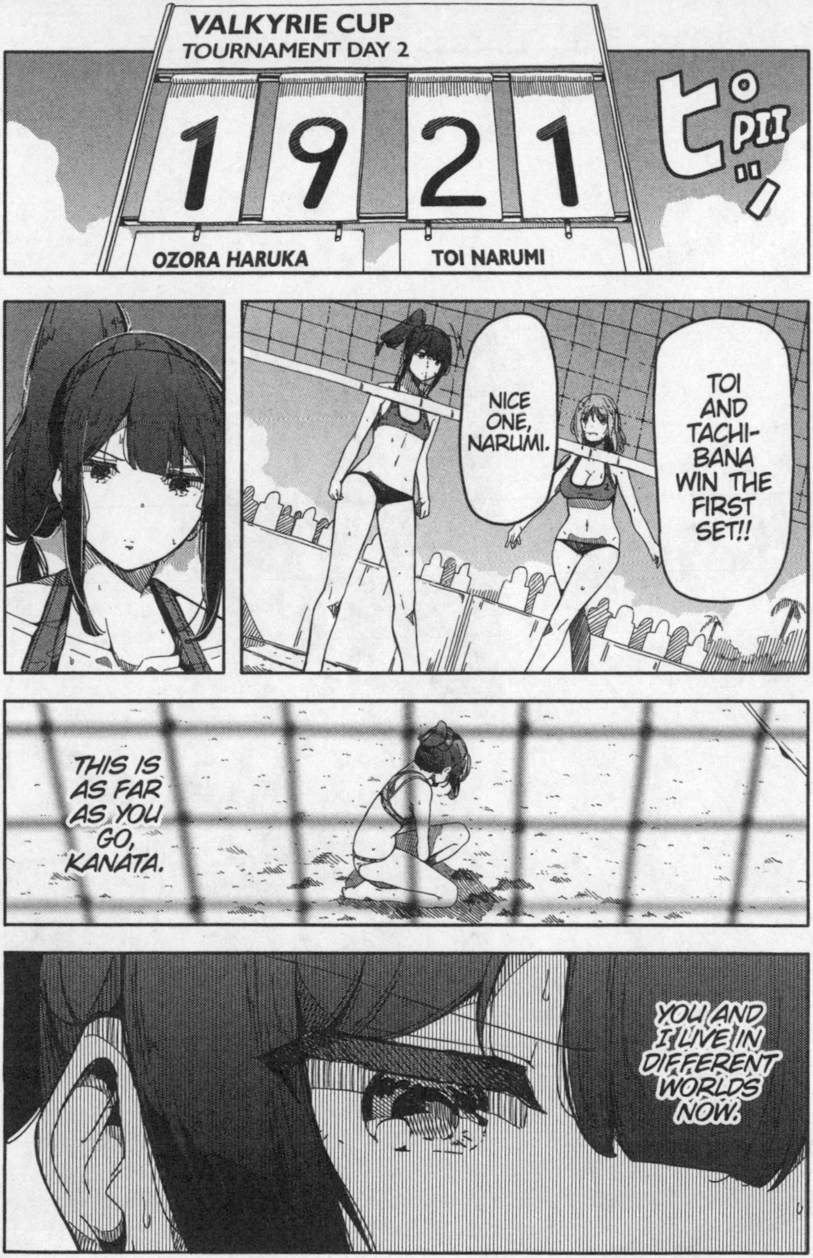
VALKYRIE CUP
TOURNAMENT DAY 2
19 21
OZORA HARUKA
TOI NARUMI
PII
TOI AND TACHIBANA WIN THE FIRST SET!!
NICE ONE, NARUMI.
THIS IS AS FAR AS YOU GO, KANATA.
YOU AND I LIVE IN DIFFERENT WORLDS NOW.

Chapter 58: Princess of Whales

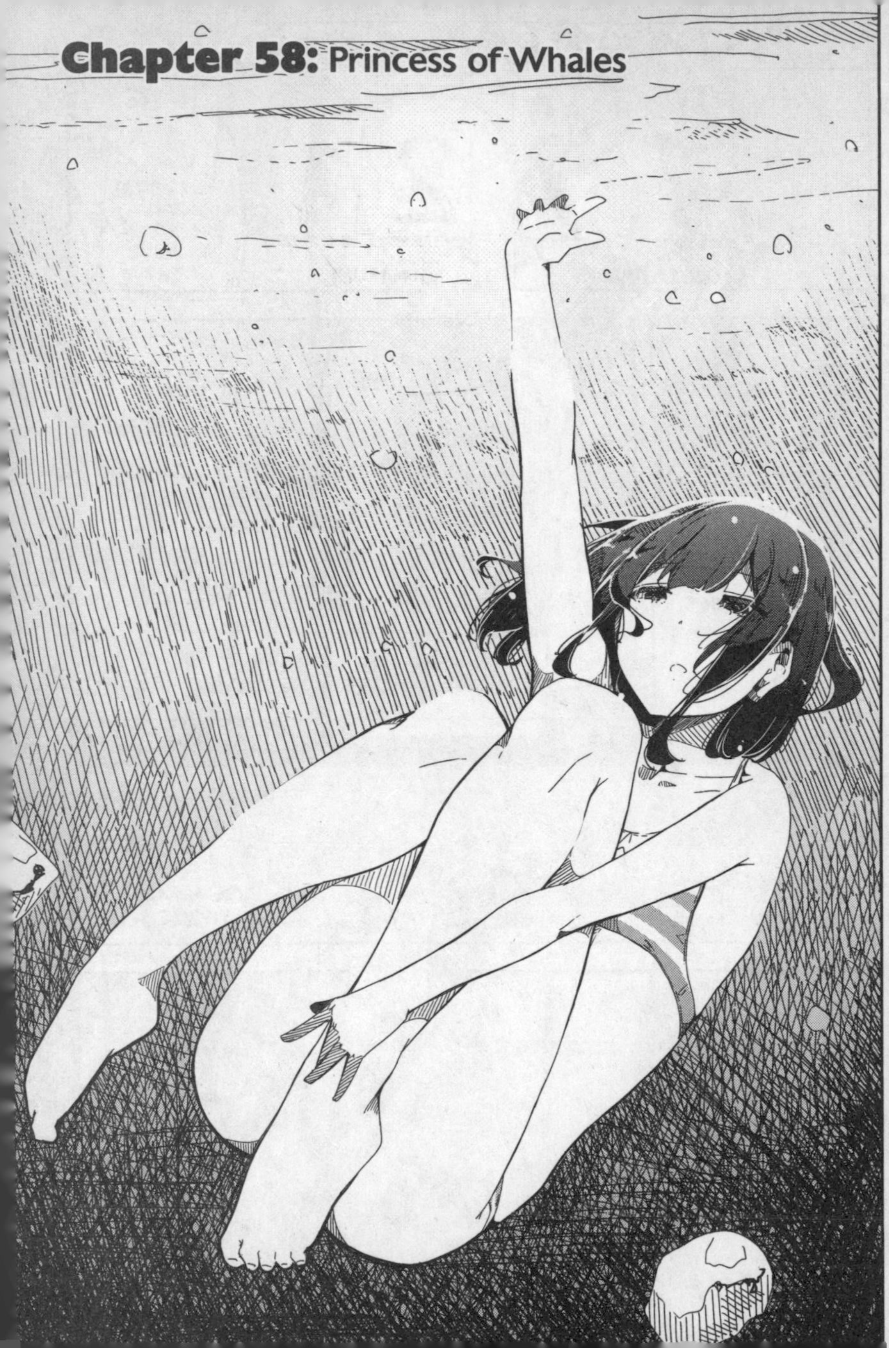

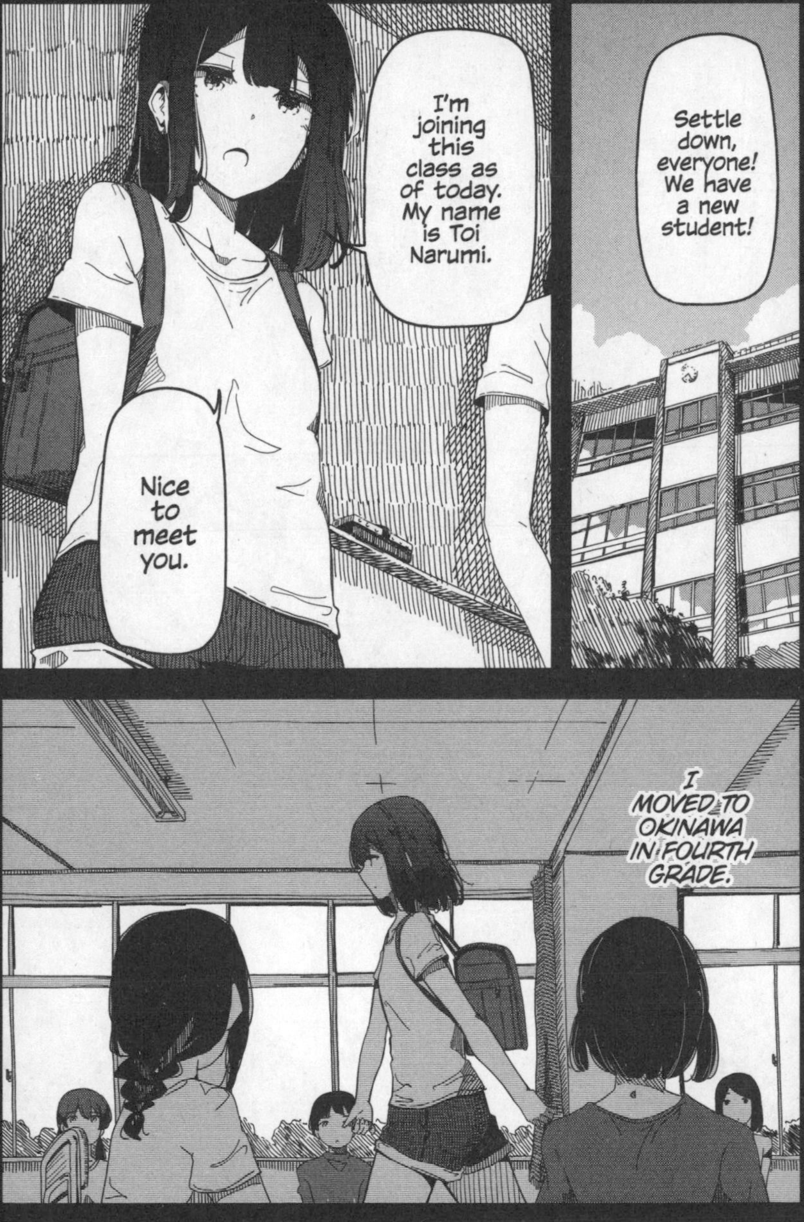
Settle down, everyone! We have a new student!
I'm joining this class as of today. My name is Toi Narumi.
Nice to meet you.
I MOVED TO OKINAWA IN FOURTH GRADE.

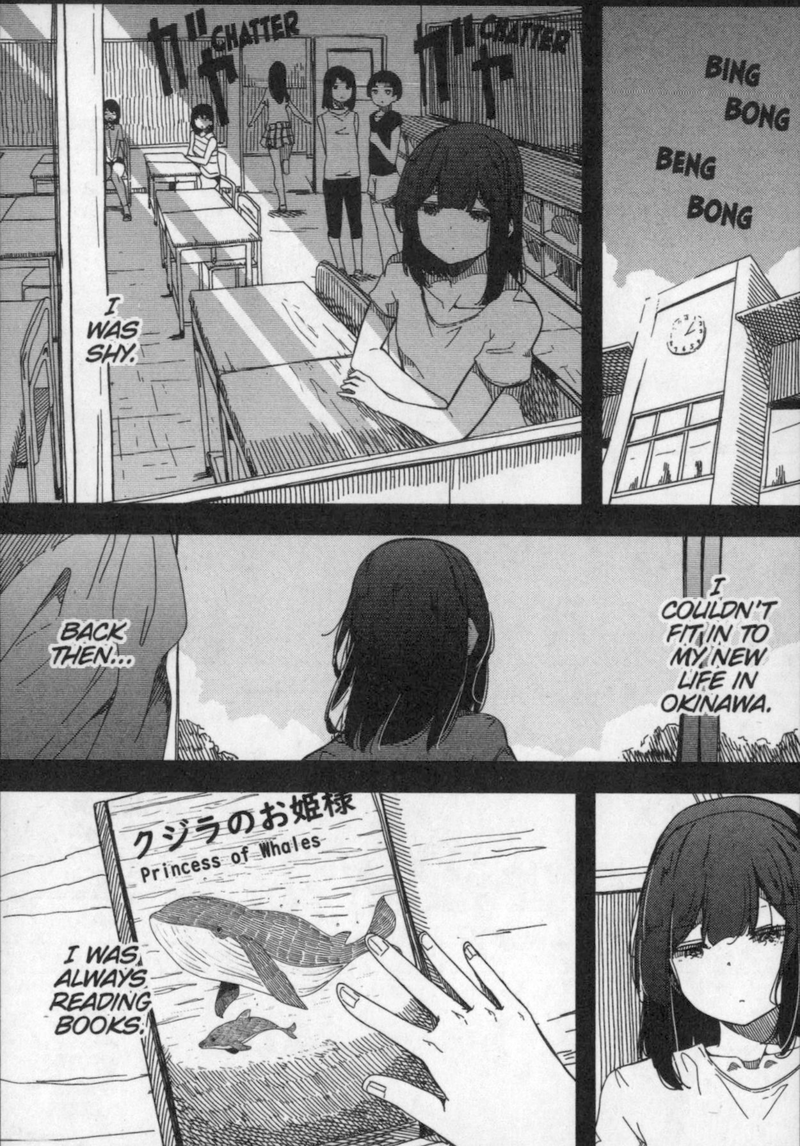
BING BONG
BENG BONG
ガヤ
CHATTER
ガヤ
CHATTER
I WAS SHY.
I COULDN'T FIT IN TO MY NEW LIFE IN OKINAWA.
BACK THEN...
クジラのお姫様
Princess of Whales
I WAS ALWAYS READING BOOKS.

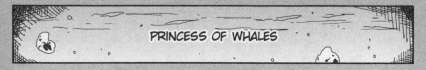

PRINCESS OF WHALES
THIS IS A LOST WHALE.
SEPARATED FROM HER POD, SHE WANDERED THROUGH THE OCEAN ALONE.
AS THE WHALE WANDERED...
SHE CAME ACROSS A SCHOOL OF FISH.
BUT THE FISH...
WERE AFRAID OF THE WHALE'S SIZE.
THAT WAS WHEN...

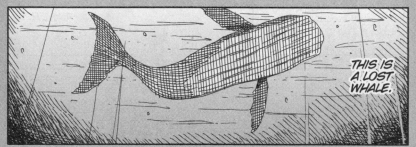

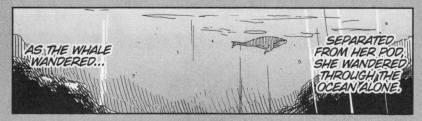

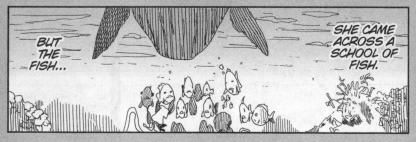

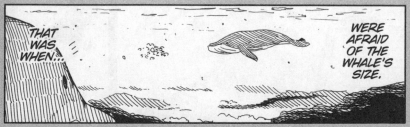

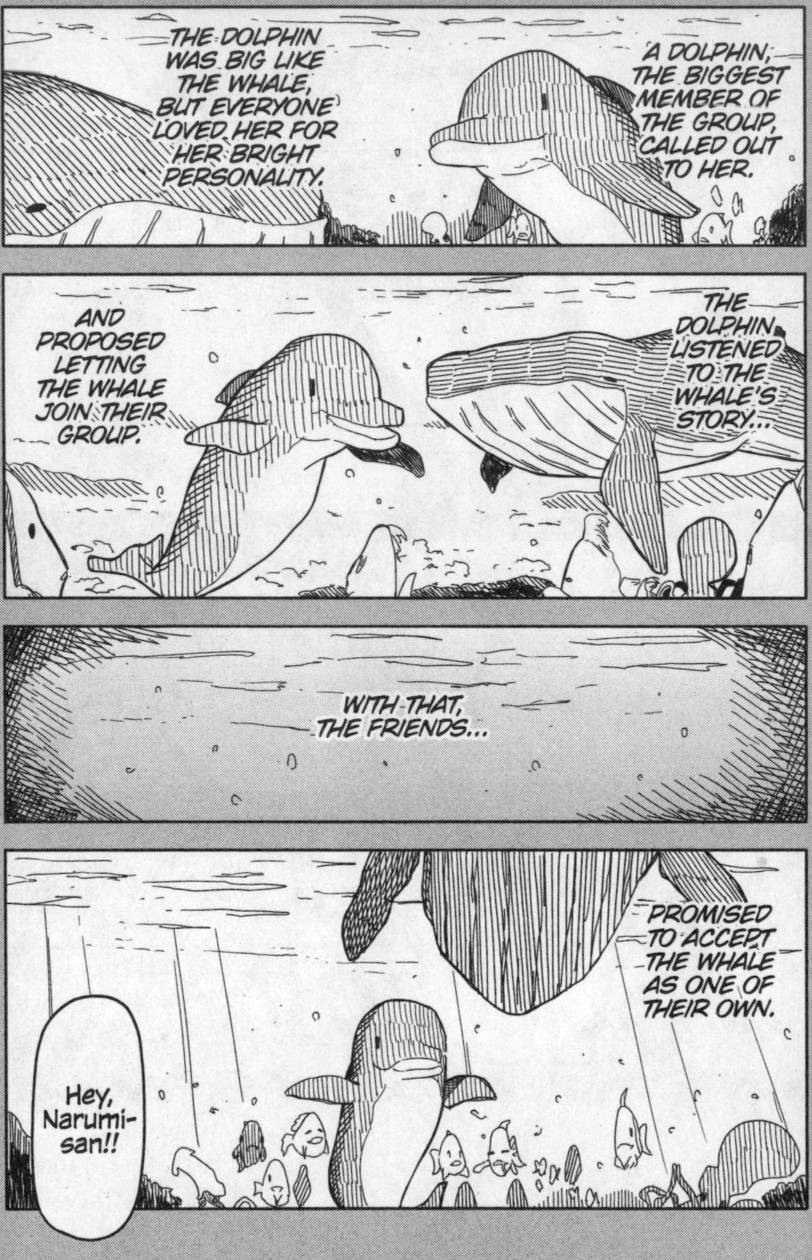
A DOLPHIN, THE BIGGEST MEMBER OF THE GROUP, CALLED OUT TO HER.
THE DOLPHIN WAS BIG LIKE THE WHALE, BUT EVERYONE LOVED HER FOR HER BRIGHT PERSONALITY.
THE DOLPHIN LISTENED TO THE WHALE'S STORY...
AND PROPOSED LETTING THE WHALE JOIN THEIR GROUP.
WITH THAT, THE FRIENDS...
PROMISED TO ACCEPT THE WHALE AS ONE OF THEIR OWN.
Hey, Narumi-san!!

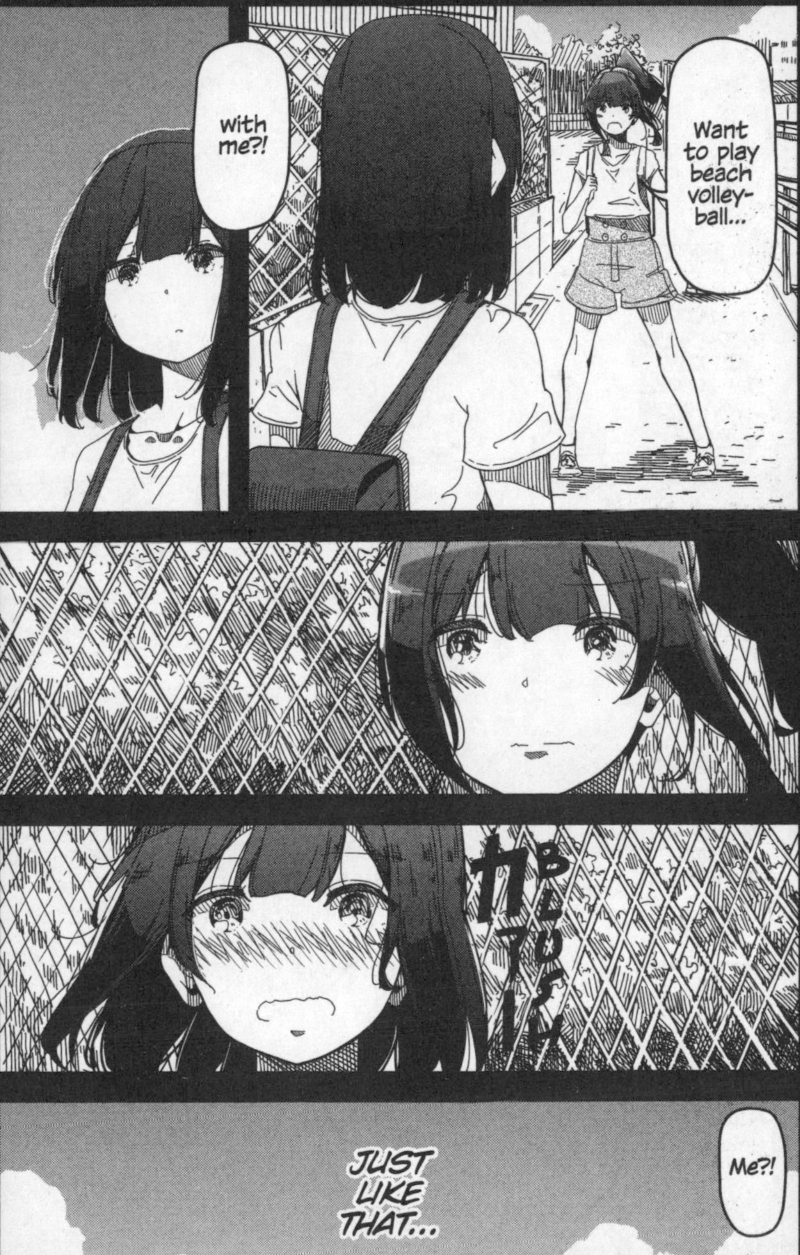
Want to play beach volley-ball...
with me?!
BLUSH
Me?!
JUST LIKE THAT...

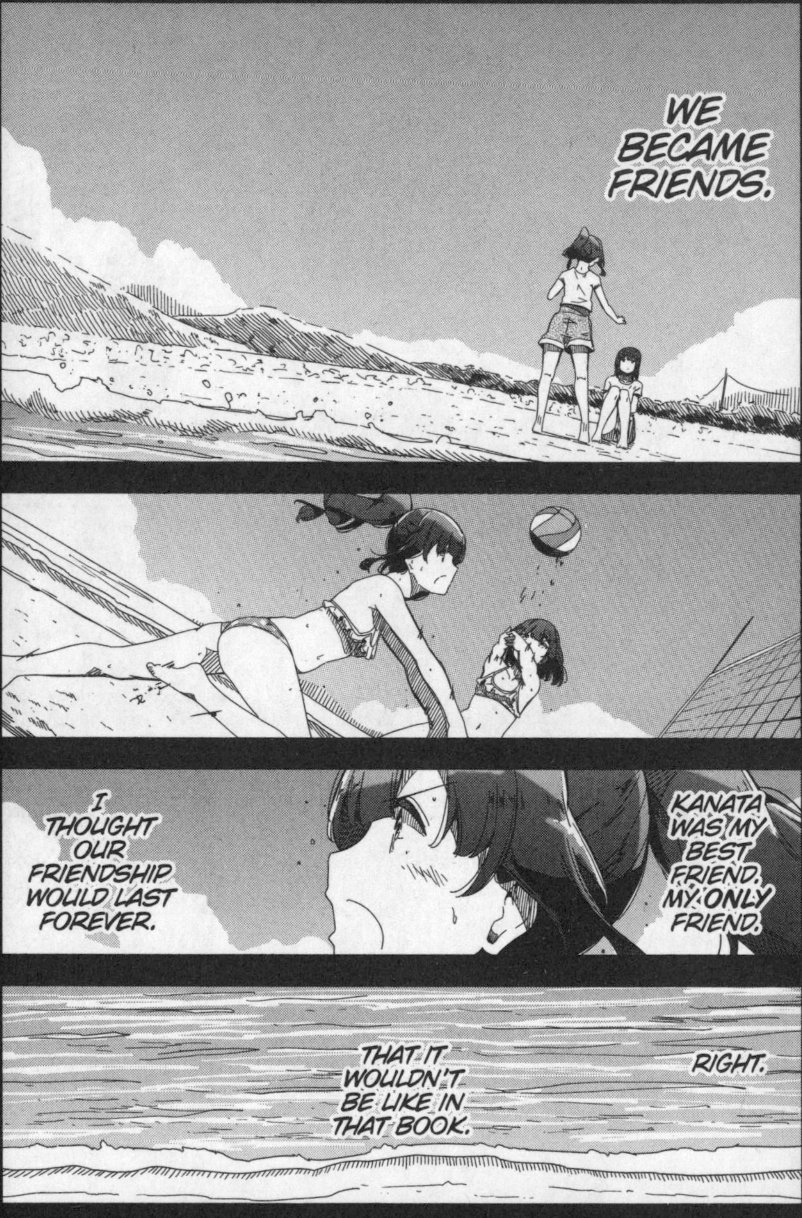
WE BECAME FRIENDS.
KANATA WAS MY BEST FRIEND. MY ONLY FRIEND.
I THOUGHT OUR FRIENDSHIP WOULD LAST FOREVER.
RIGHT.
THAT IT WOULDN'T BE LIKE IN THAT BOOK.

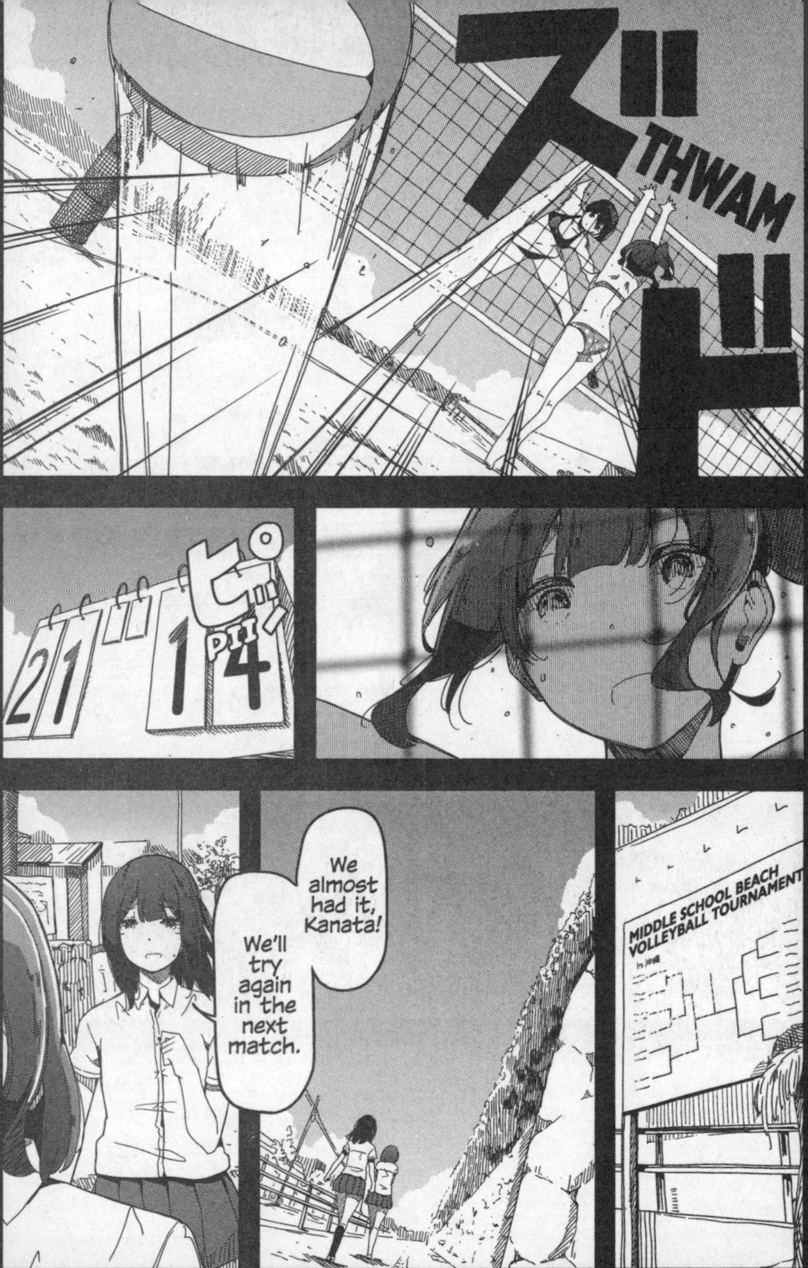
THWAM
PII
21 14
MIDDLE SCHOOL BEACH VOLLEYBALL TOURNAMENT
In 沖縄
We almost had it, Kanata! We'll try again in the next match.

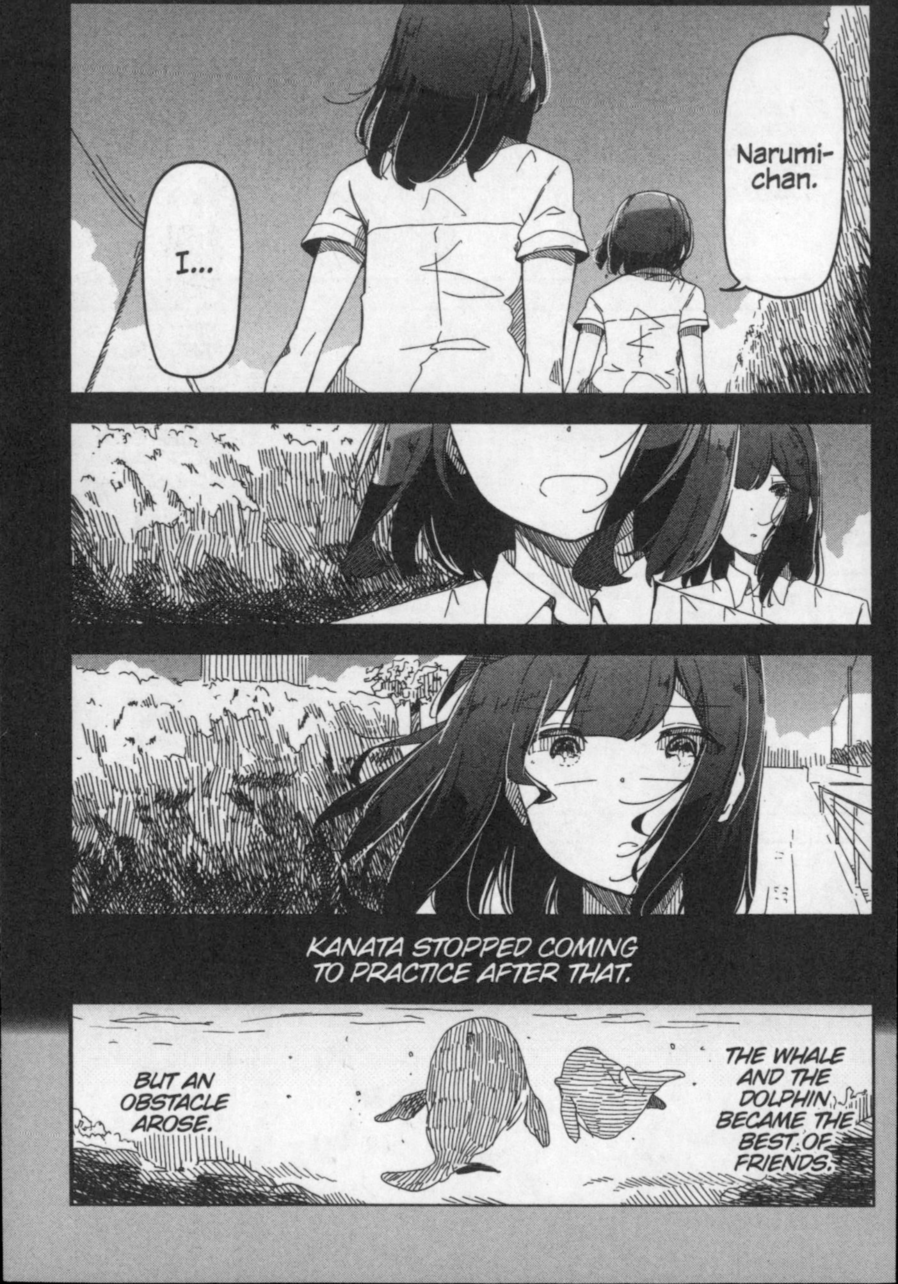
Narumi-chan.
I...
KANATA STOPPED COMING TO PRACTICE AFTER THAT.
THE WHALE AND THE DOLPHIN BECAME THE BEST OF FRIENDS.
BUT AN OBSTACLE AROSE.

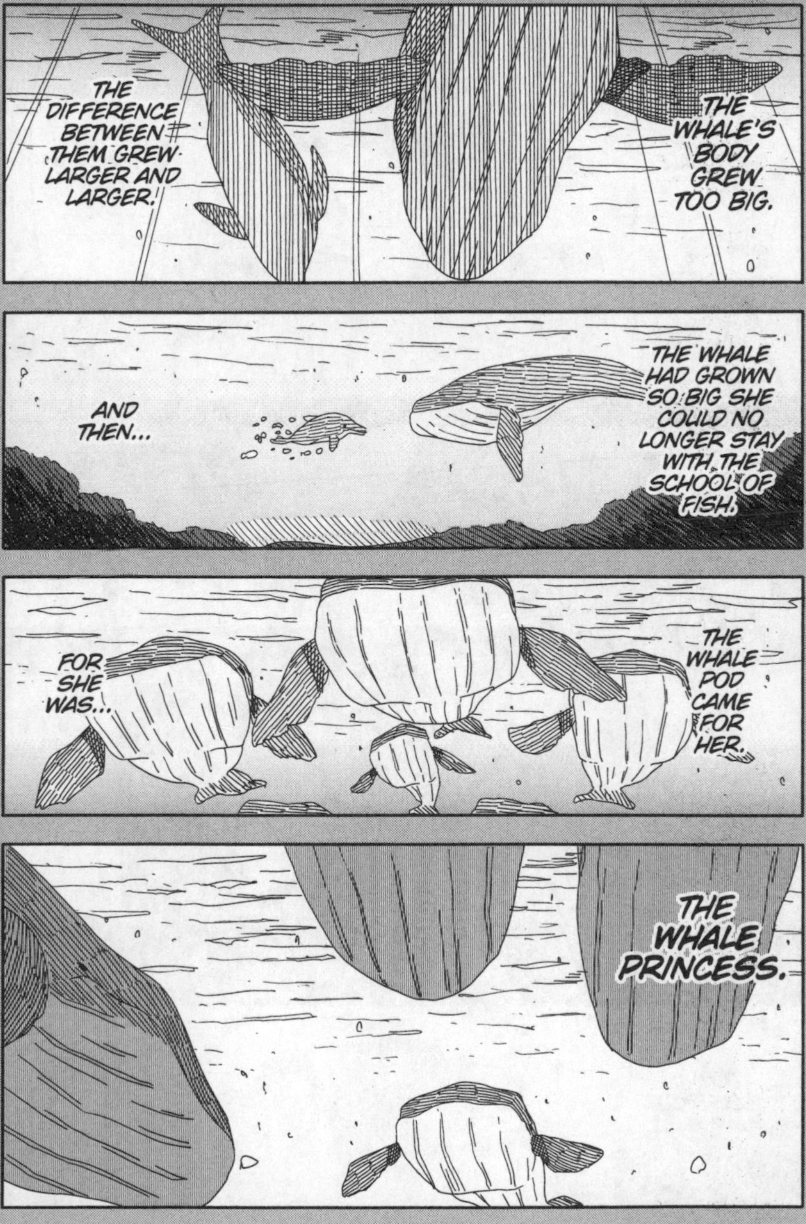
THE WHALE'S BODY GREW TOO BIG.
THE DIFFERENCE BETWEEN THEM GREW LARGER AND LARGER.
THE WHALE HAD GROWN SO BIG SHE COULD NO LONGER STAY WITH THE SCHOOL OF FISH.
AND THEN...
THE WHALE POD CAME FOR HER.
FOR SHE WAS...
THE WHALE PRINCESS.

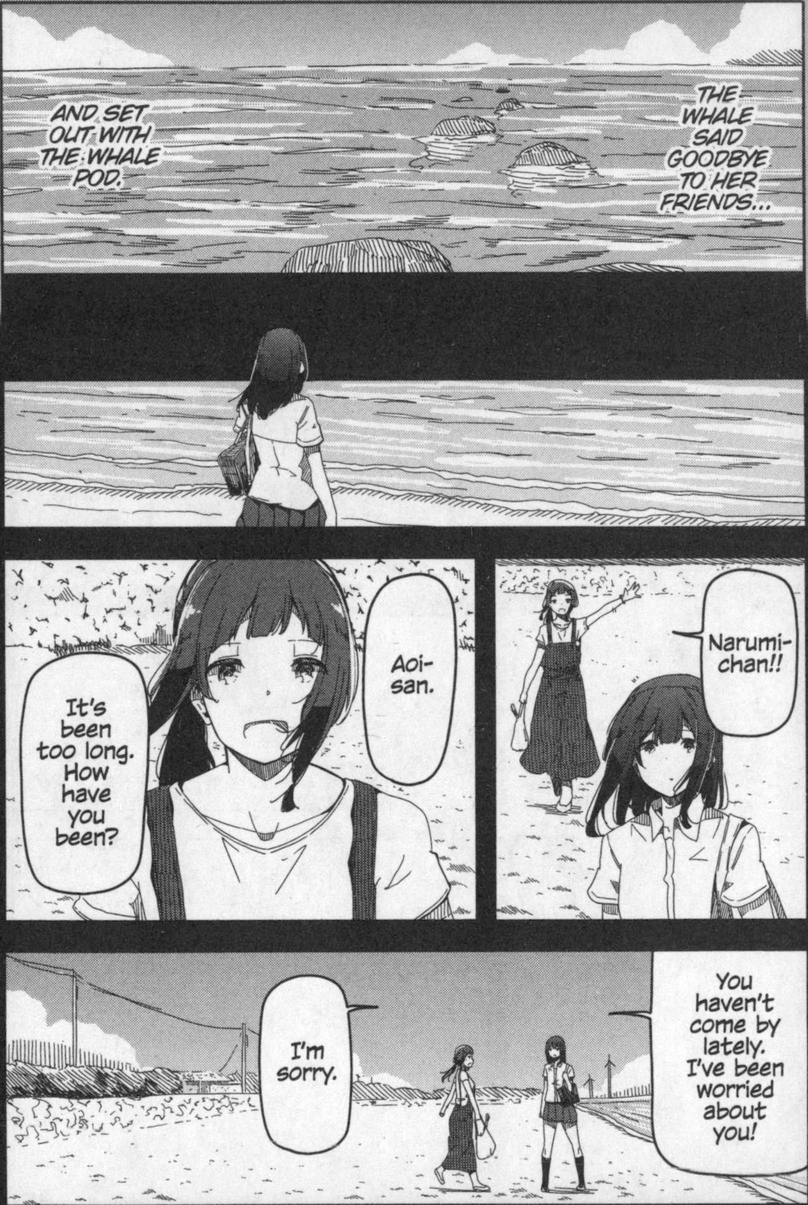
THE WHALE SAID GOODBYE TO HER FRIENDS...
AND SET OUT WITH THE WHALE POD.
Narumi-chan!!
Aoi-san.
It's been too long. How have you been?
You haven't come by lately. I've been worried about you!
I'm sorry.

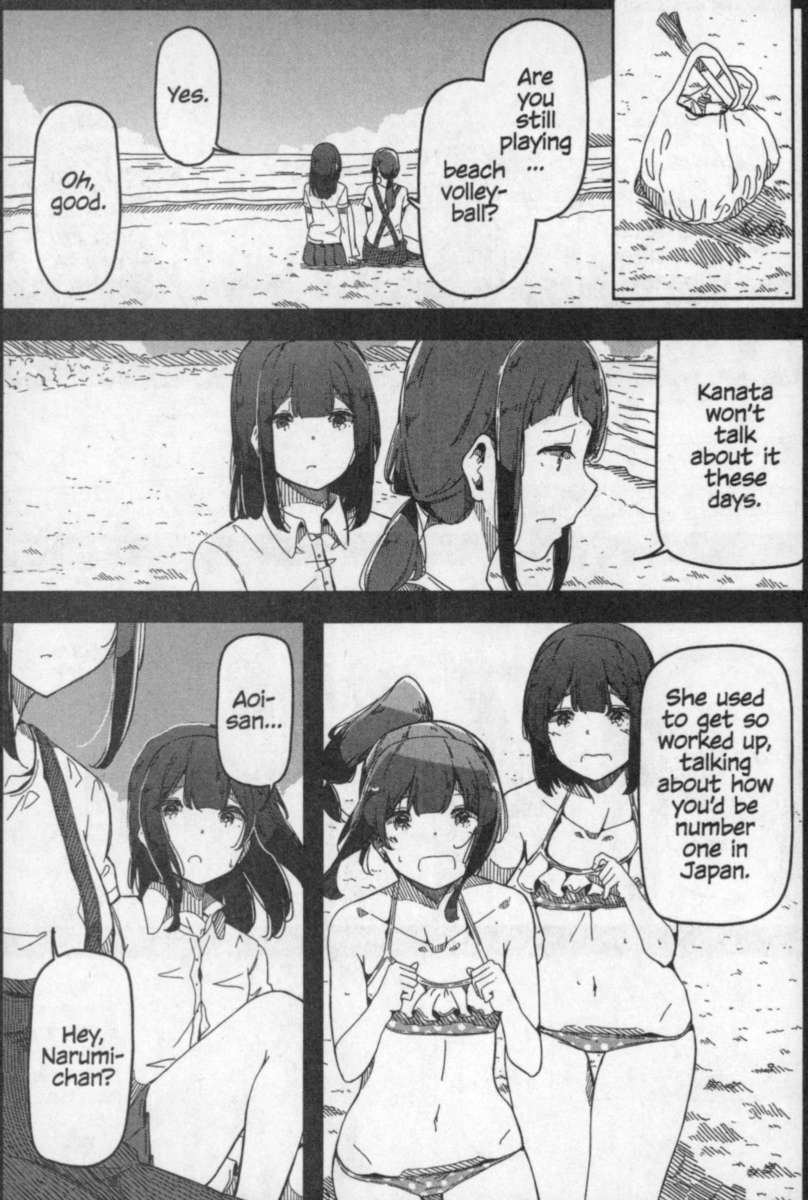
Are you still playing... beach volley-ball?
Yes.
Oh, good.
Kanata won't talk about it these days.
She used to get so worked up, talking about how you'd be number one in Japan.
Aoi-san...
Hey, Narumi-chan?

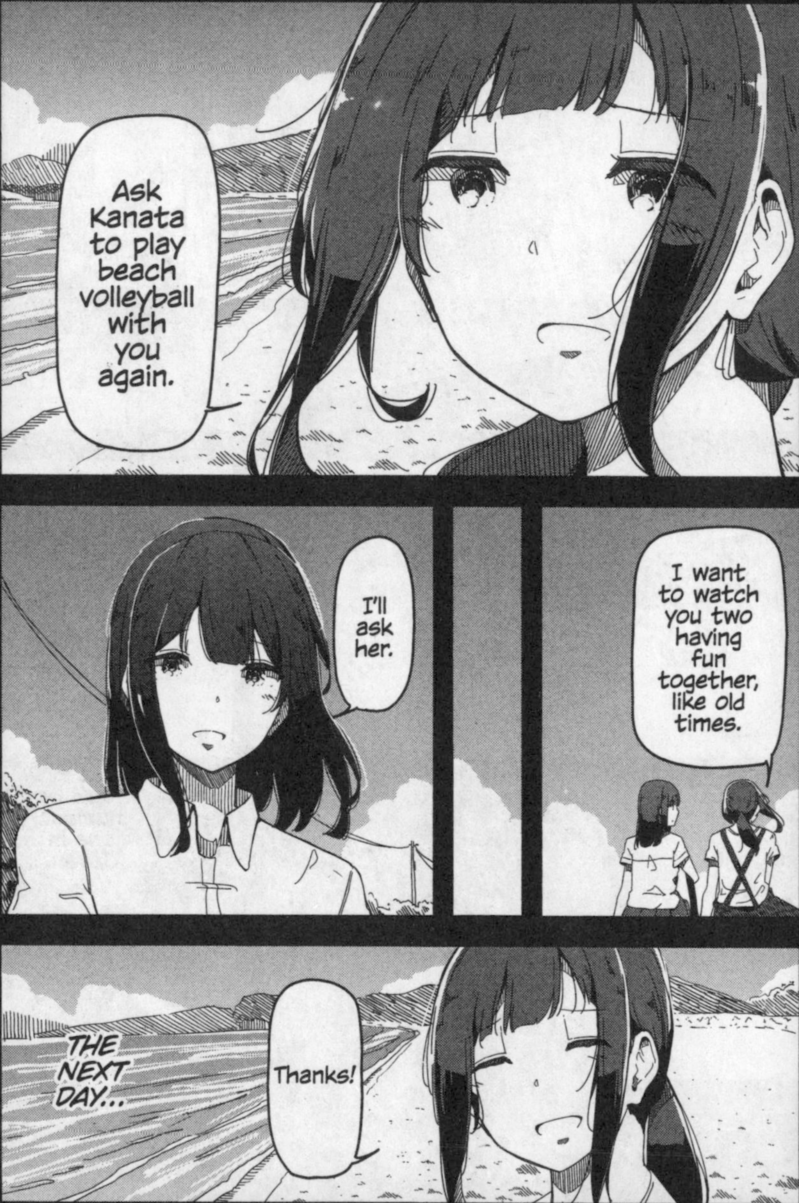
Ask Kanata to play beach volleyball with you again.
I want to watch you two having fun together, like old times.
I'll ask her.
Thanks!
THE NEXT DAY...

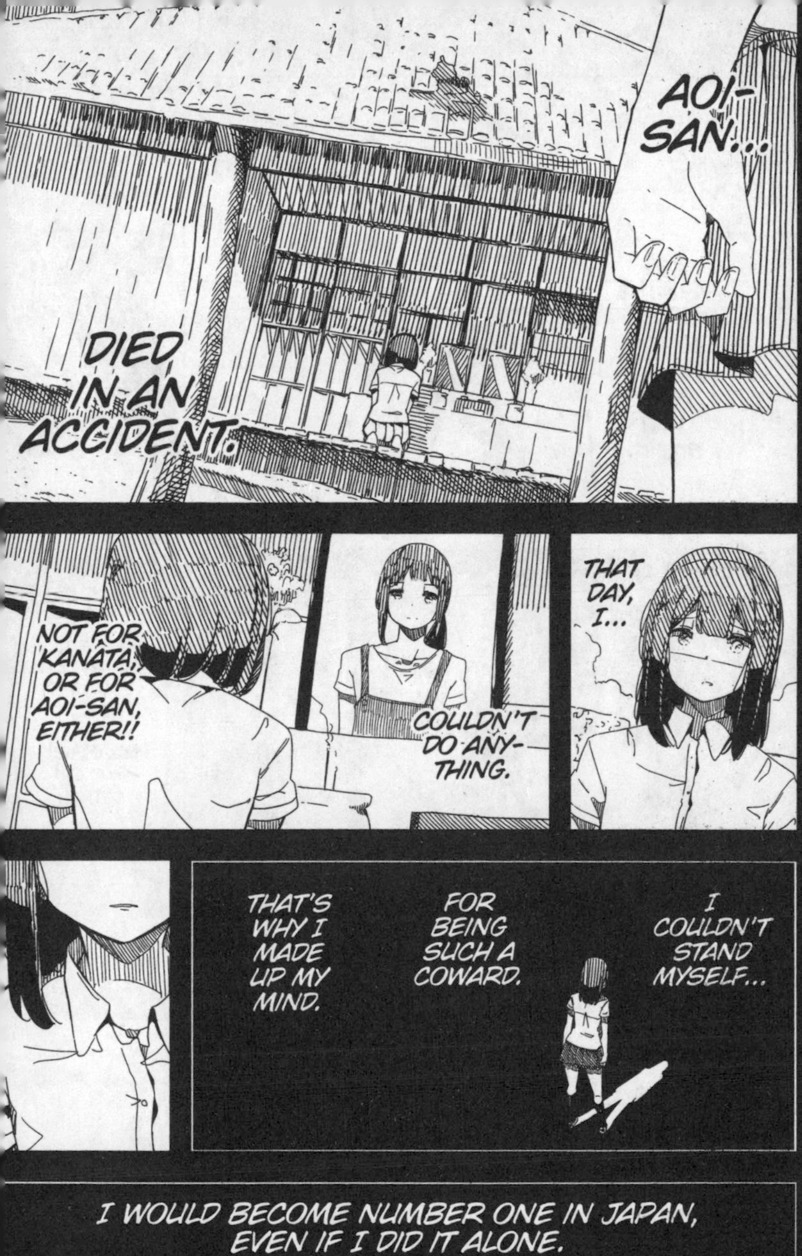
AOI-SAN...
DIED IN AN ACCIDENT.
THAT DAY, I...
COULDN'T DO ANYTHING.
NOT FOR KANATA, OR FOR AOI-SAN, EITHER!!
I COULDN'T STAND MYSELF...
FOR BEING SUCH A COWARD.
THAT'S WHY I MADE UP MY MIND.
I WOULD BECOME NUMBER ONE IN JAPAN, EVEN IF I DID IT ALONE.

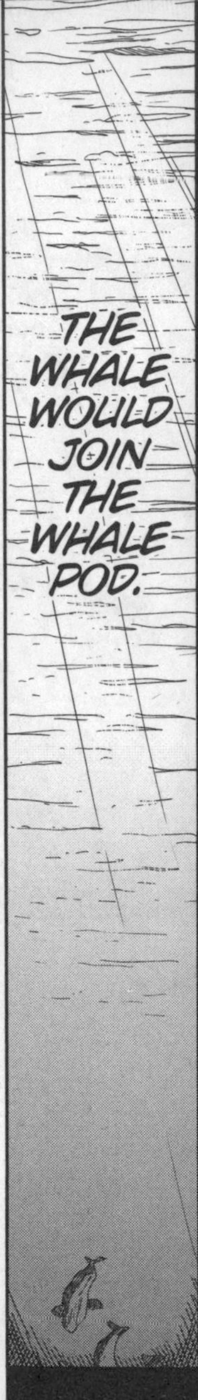
THE WHALE WOULD JOIN THE WHALE POD.
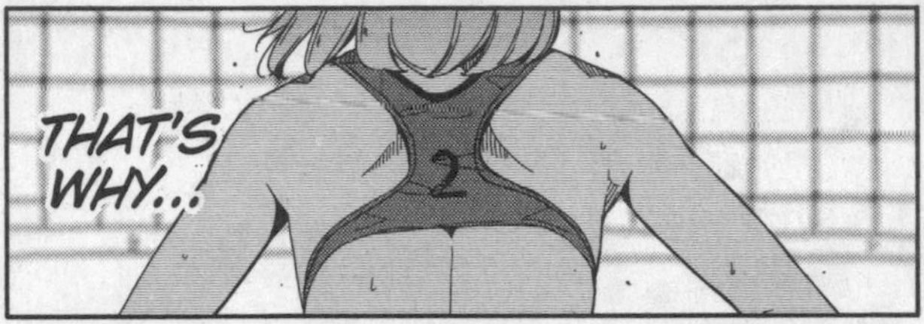
THAT'S WHY...
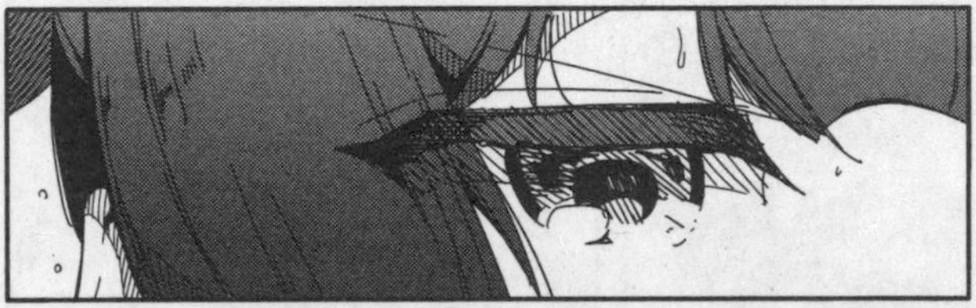
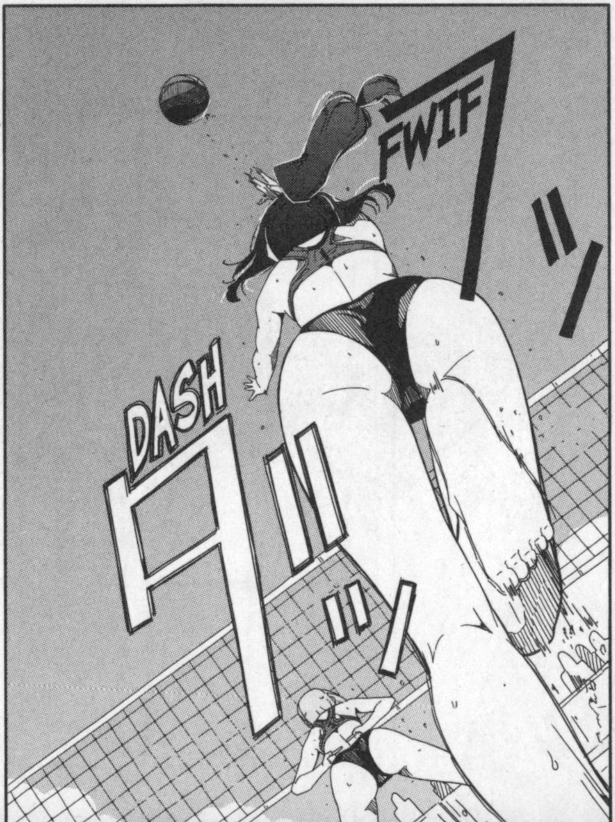
FWIF
DASH

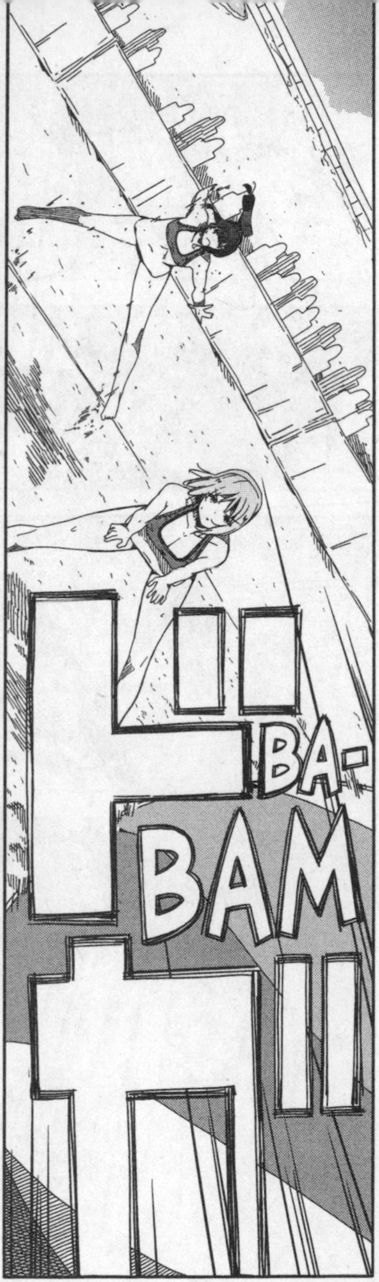
BA-BAM!!
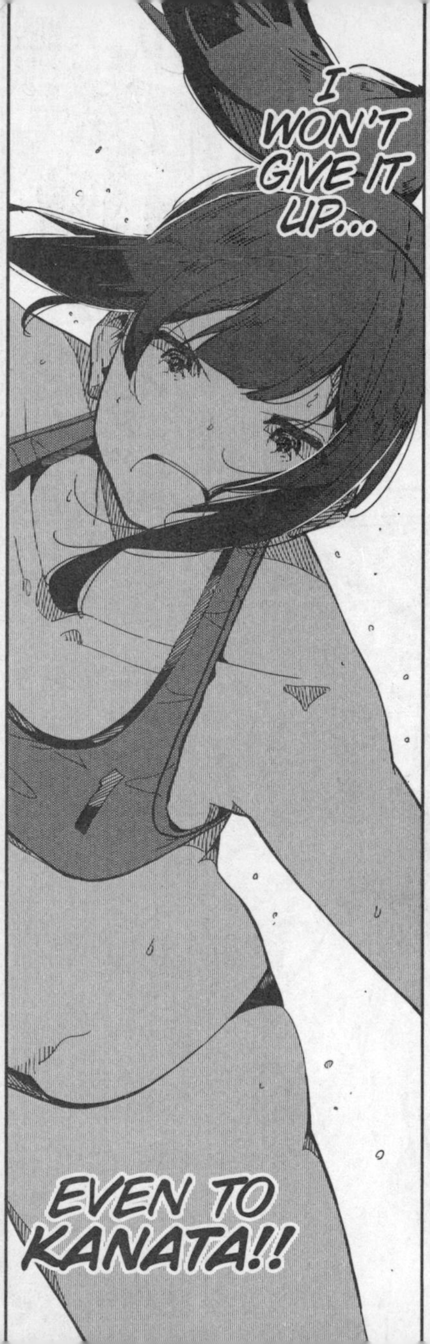
I WON'T GIVE IT UP...
EVEN TO KANATA!!

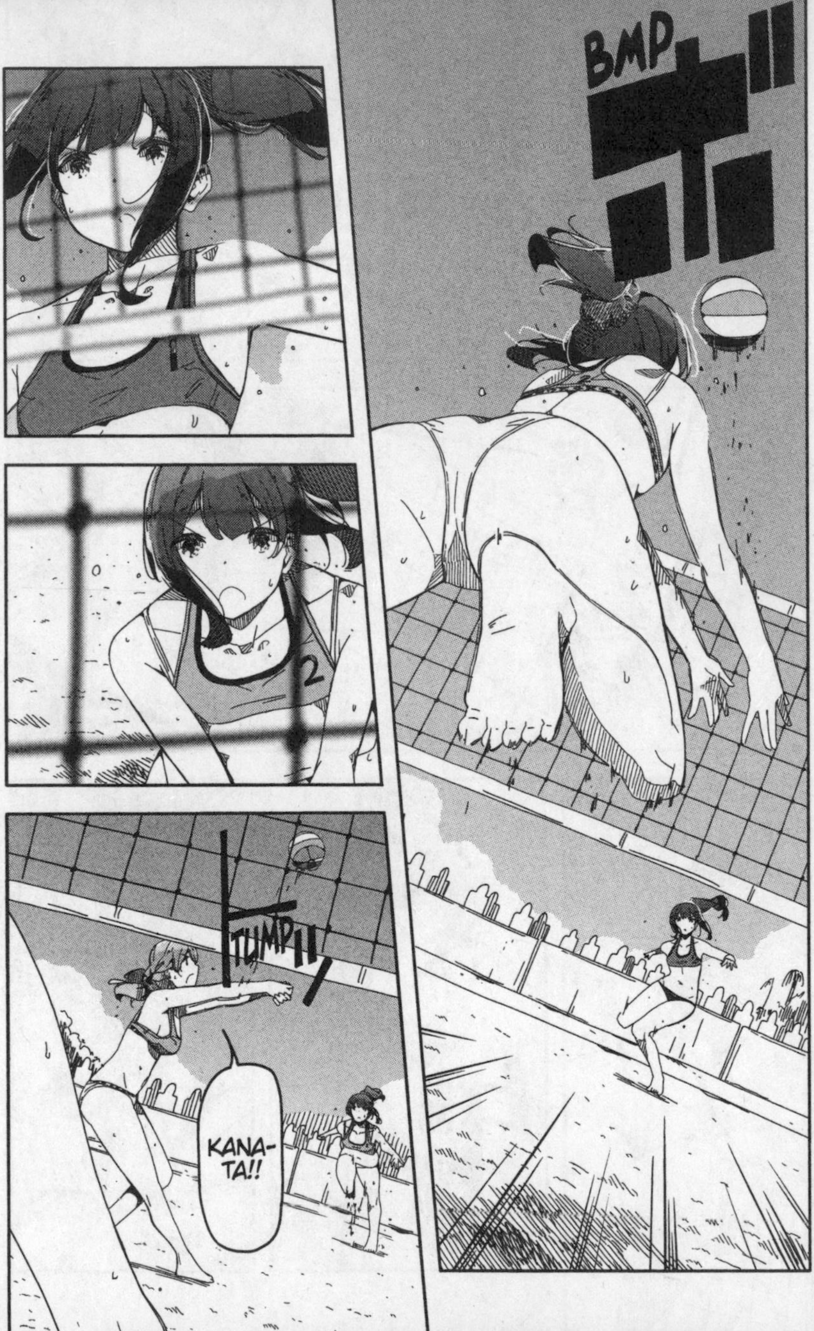
BMP
TUMP!!
KANA-
TA!!

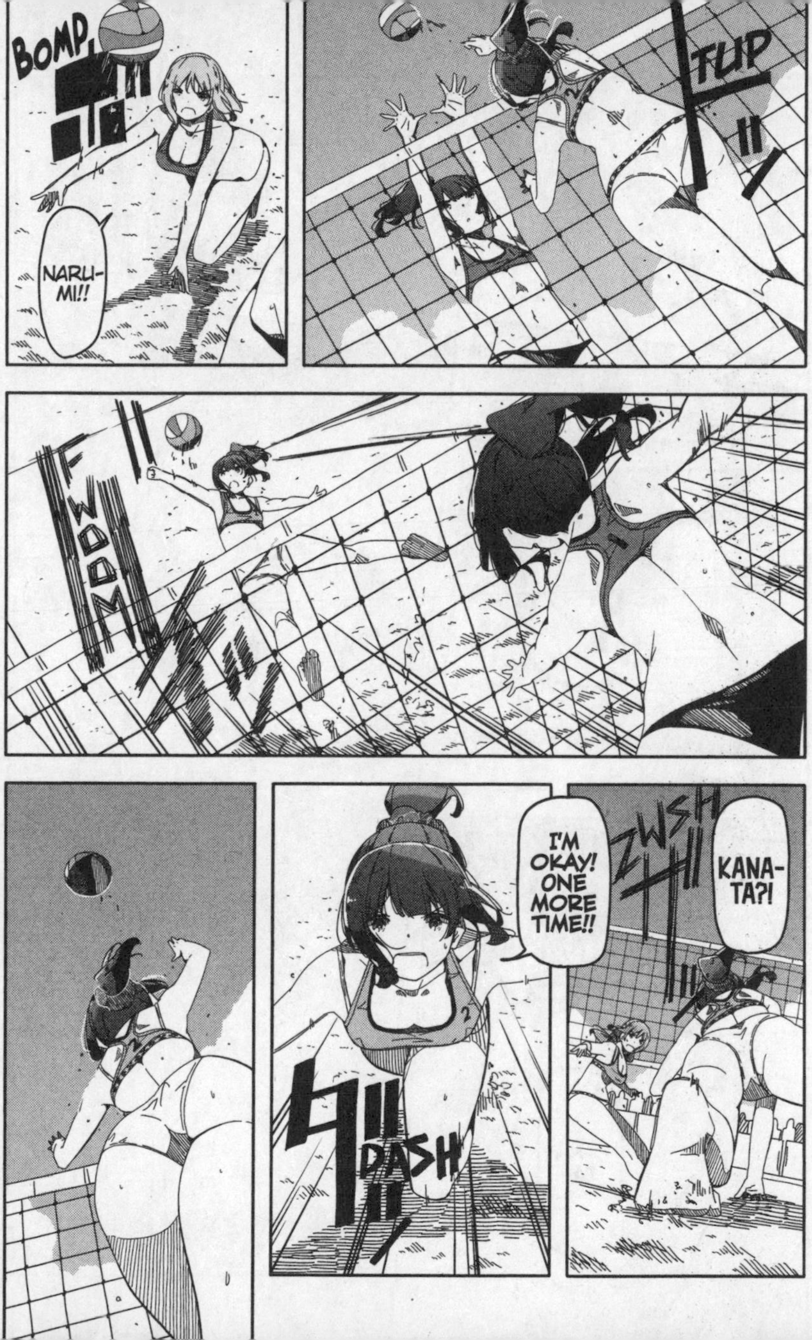
TUP
BOMP
NARU-MI!!
FWOOM
ZWSH
KANA-TA?!
I'M OKAY! ONE MORE TIME!!
DASH

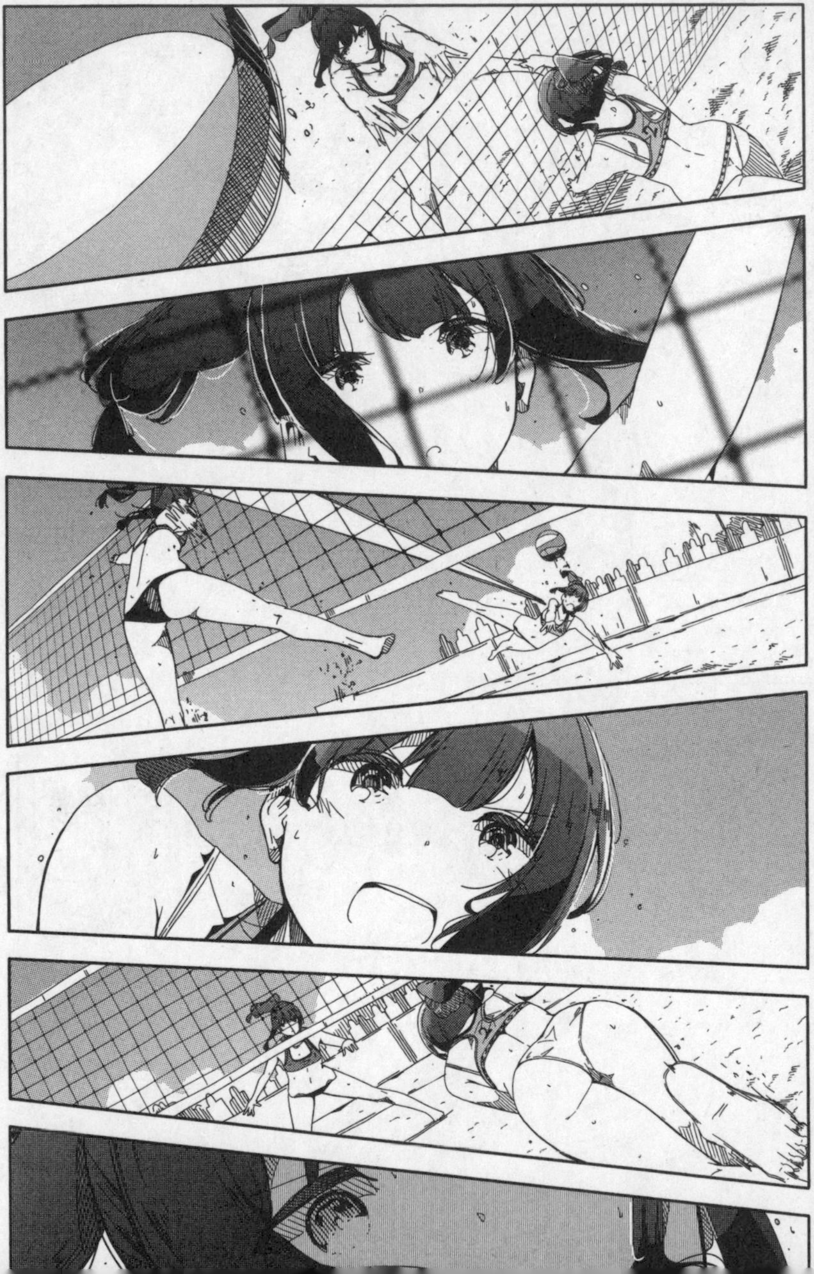

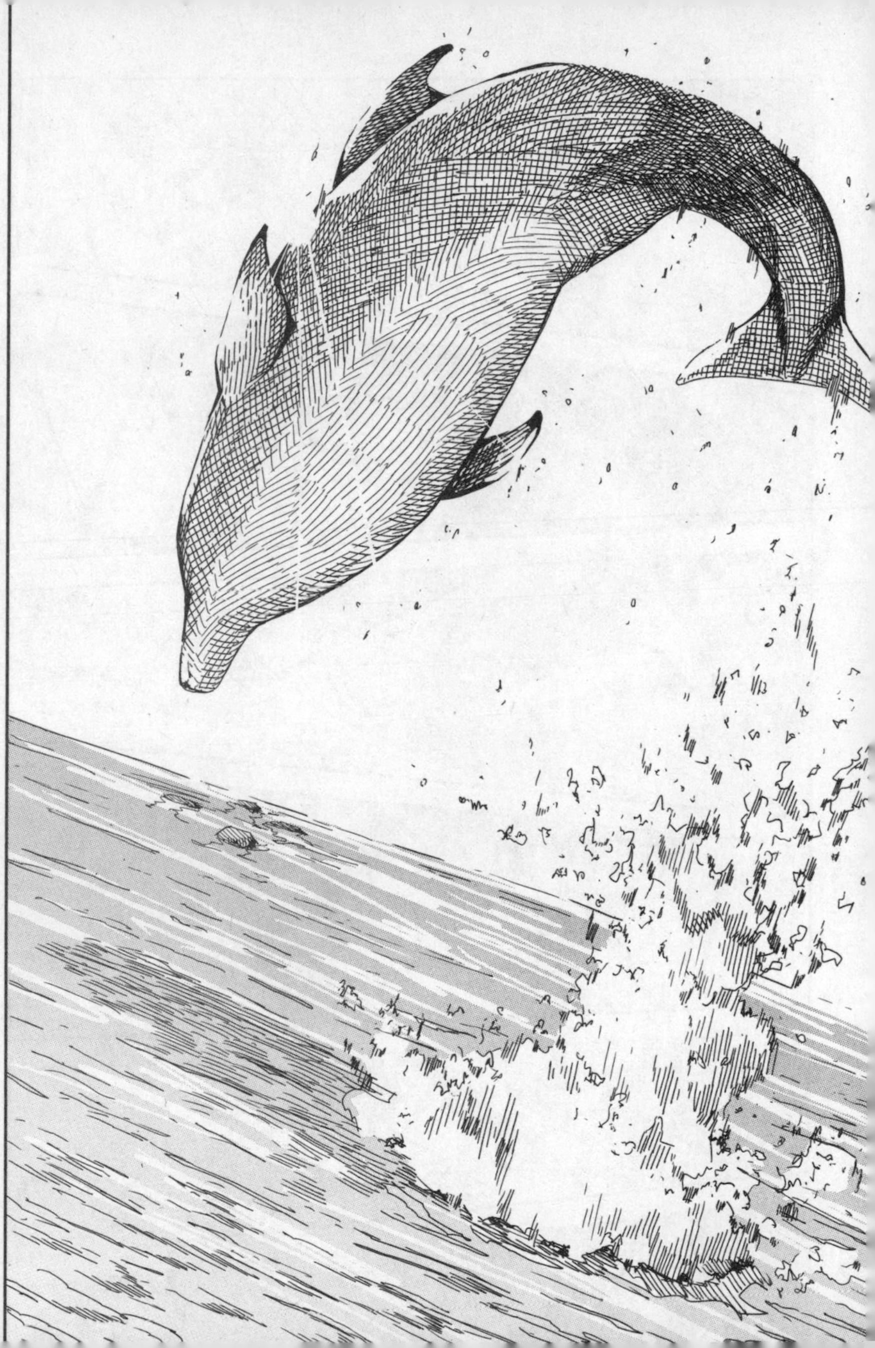

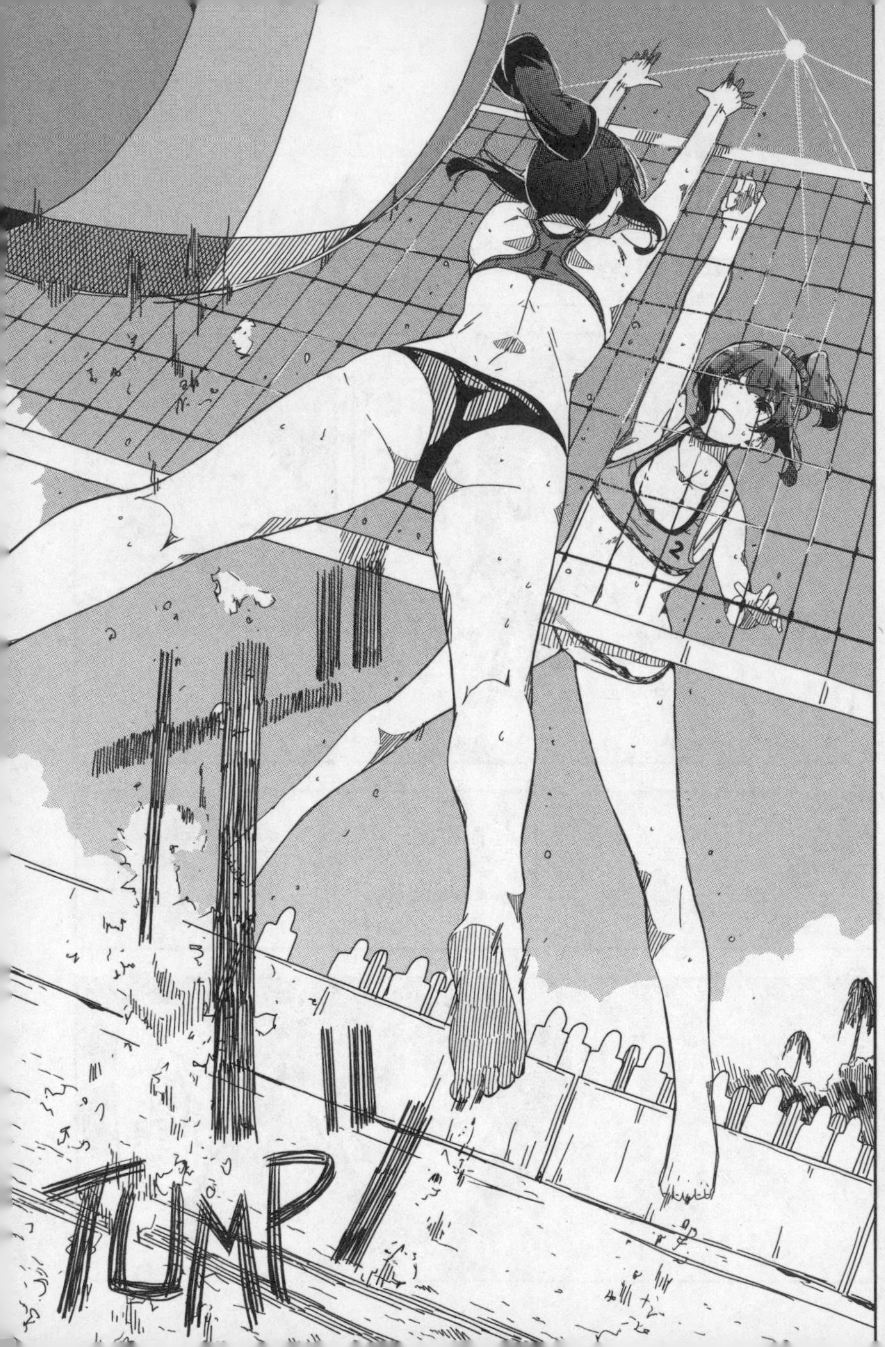
TUMP!!

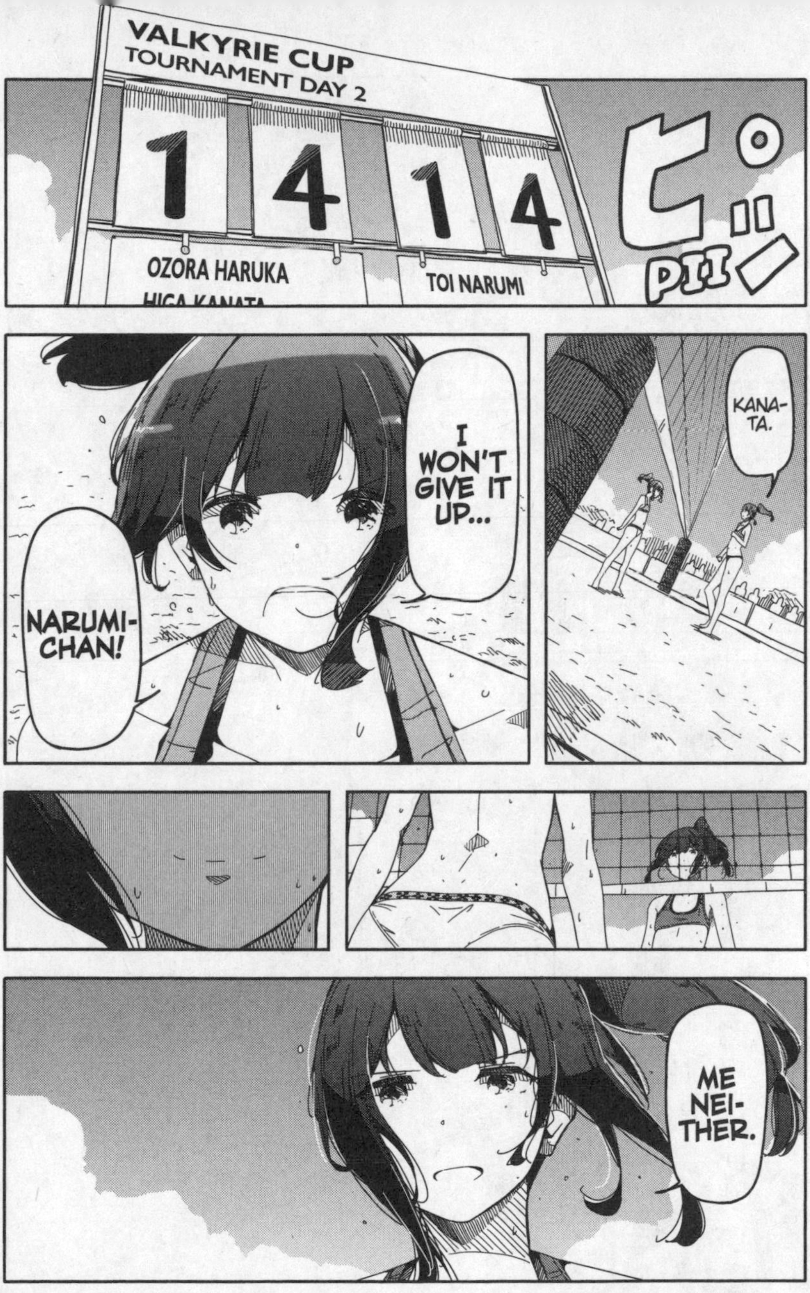
VALKYRIE CUP
TOURNAMENT DAY 2
14
14
OZORA HARUKA
HIGA KANATA
TOI NARUMI
ピー
PII
KANA-TA.
I WON'T GIVE IT UP...
NARUMI-CHAN!
ME NEI-THER.

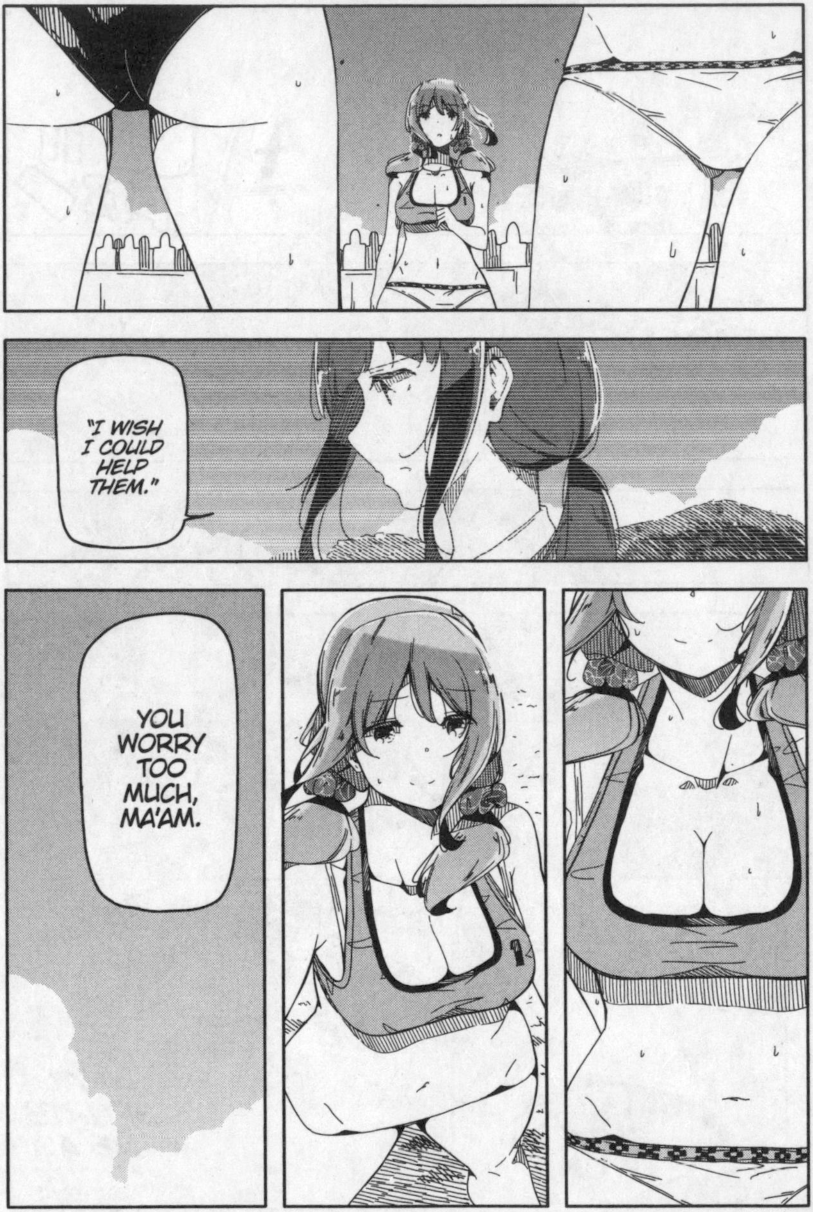
"I WISH I COULD HELP THEM."
YOU WORRY TOO MUCH, MA'AM.

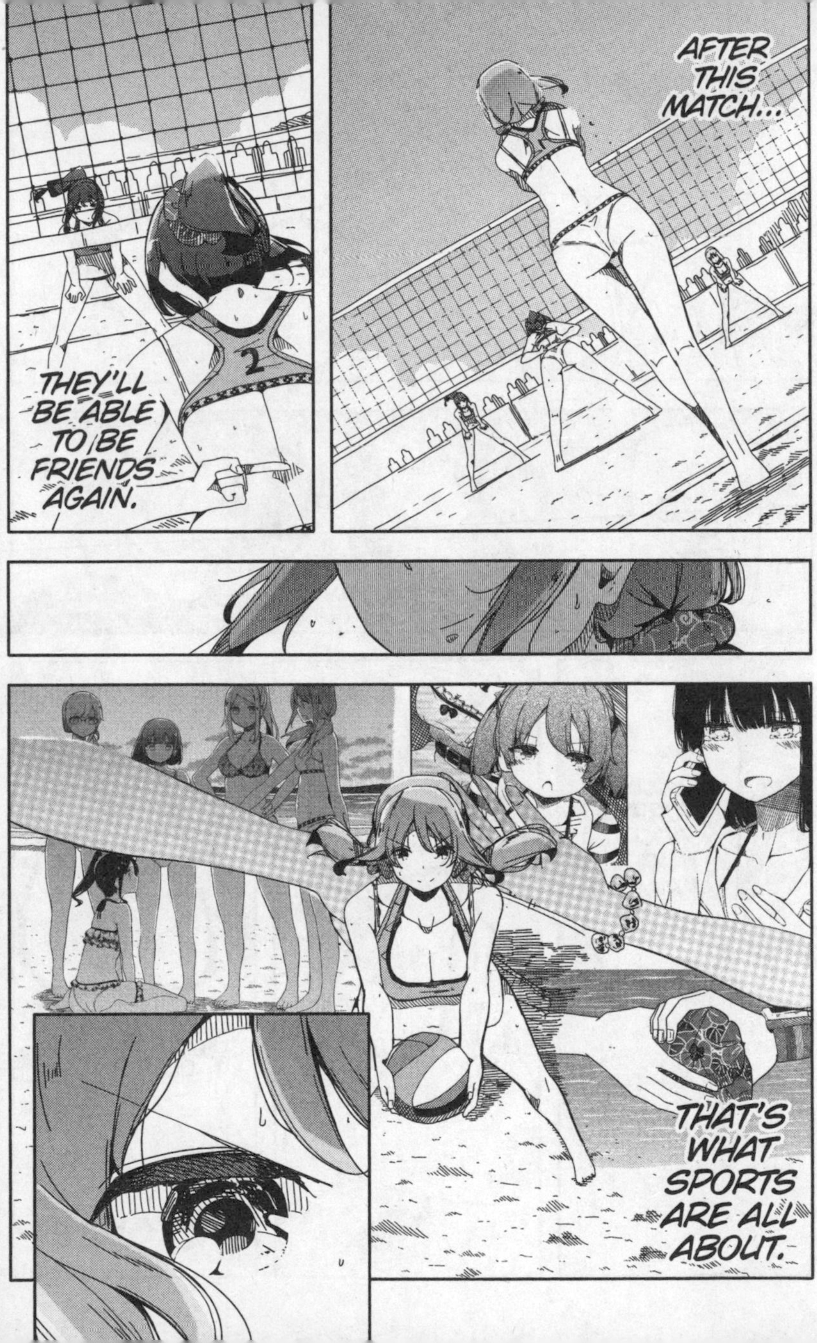
AFTER THIS MATCH...
THEY'LL BE ABLE TO BE FRIENDS AGAIN.
THAT'S WHAT SPORTS ARE ALL ABOUT.

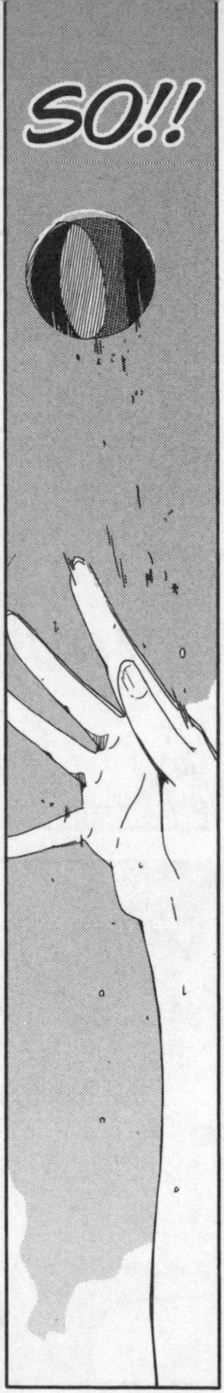
SO!!
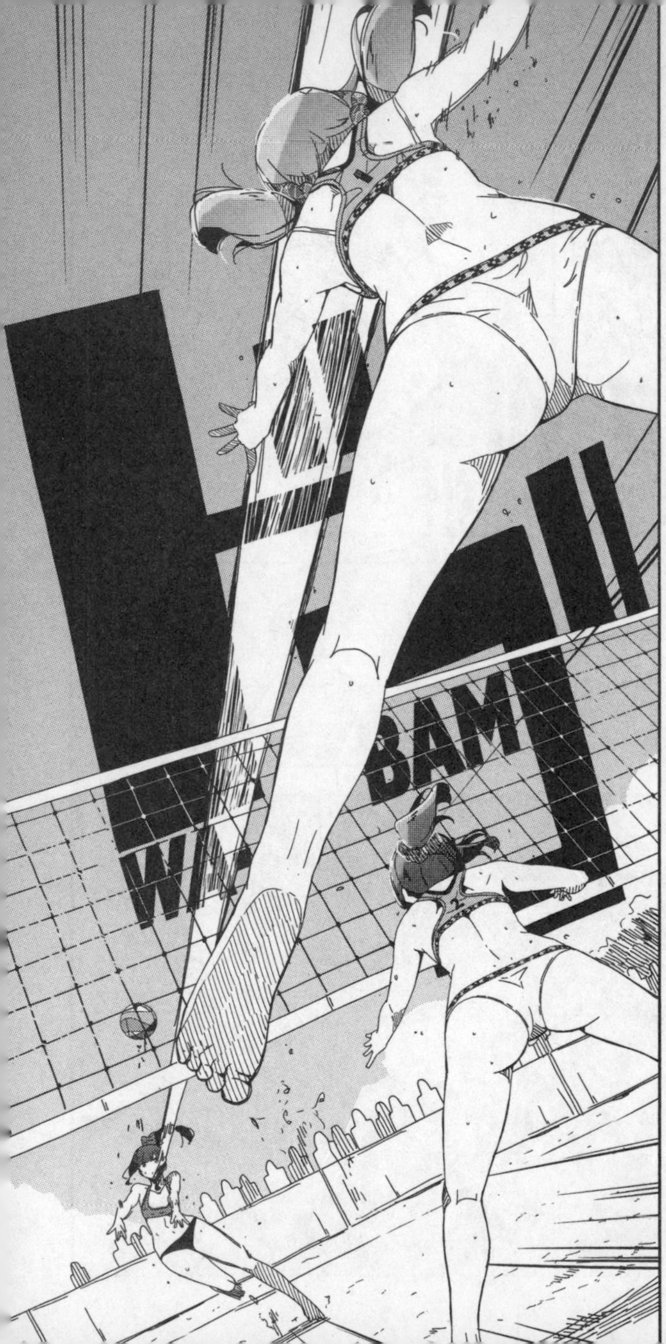
BAM

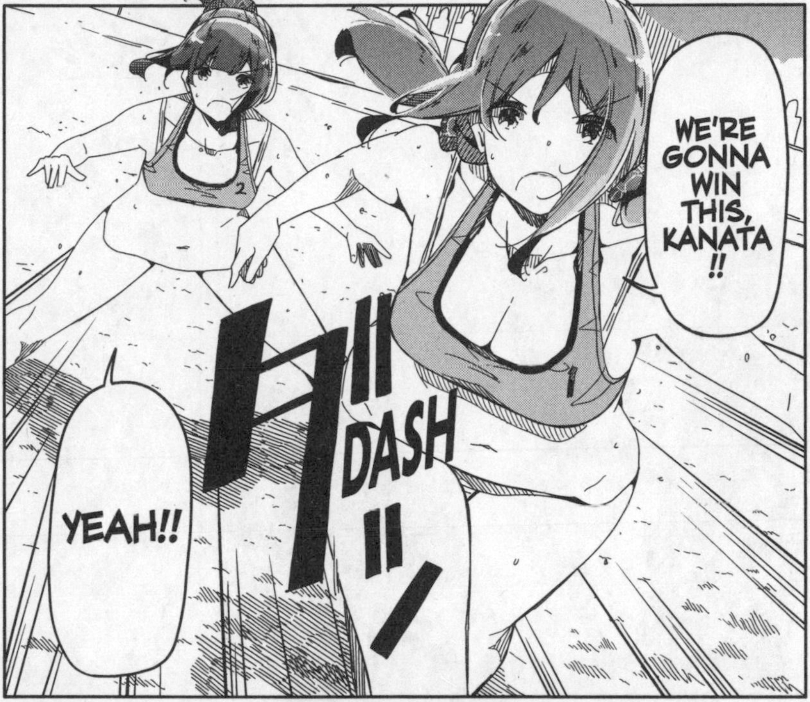
WE'RE GONNA WIN THIS, KANATA!!
DASH
YEAH!!

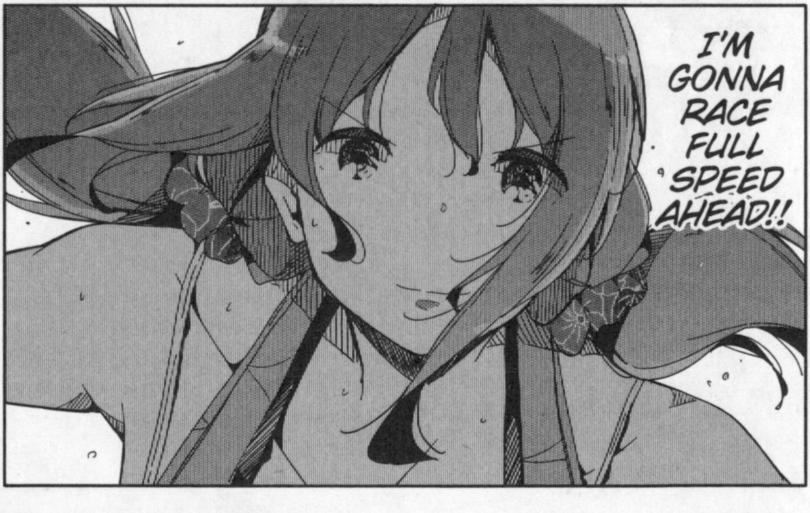
I'M GONNA RACE FULL SPEED AHEAD!!

Harukana★Receive

Presented by Nyoijizai

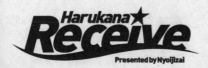

Harukana★Receive

Presented by Nyoijizai

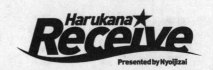

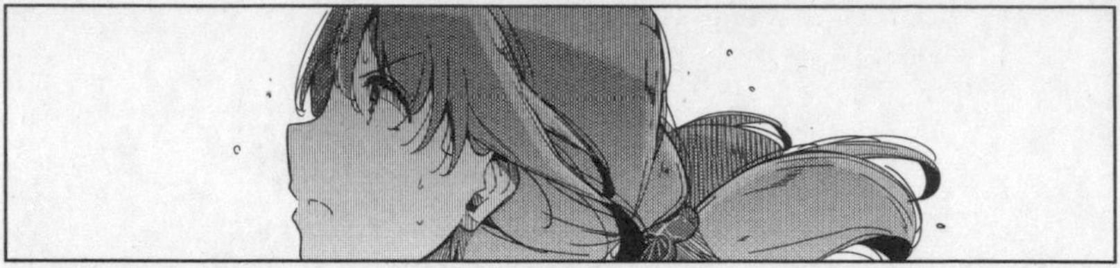

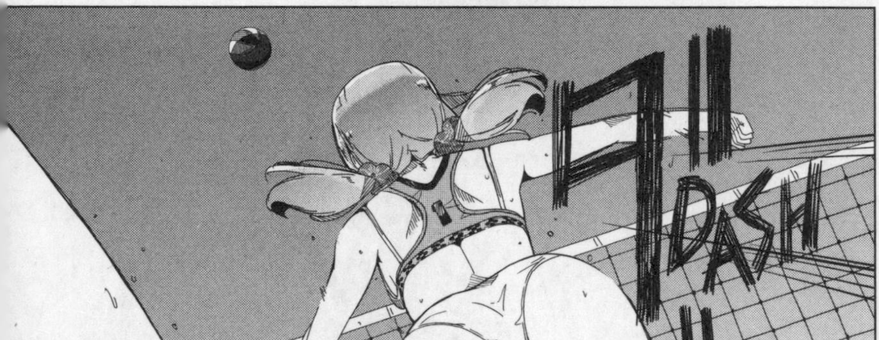
DASH!!

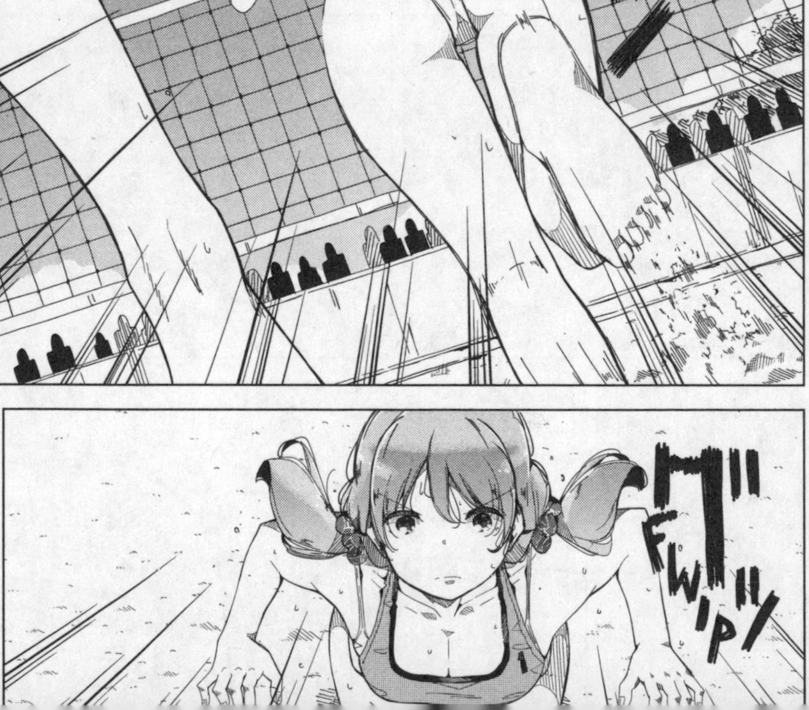
FWIP!!

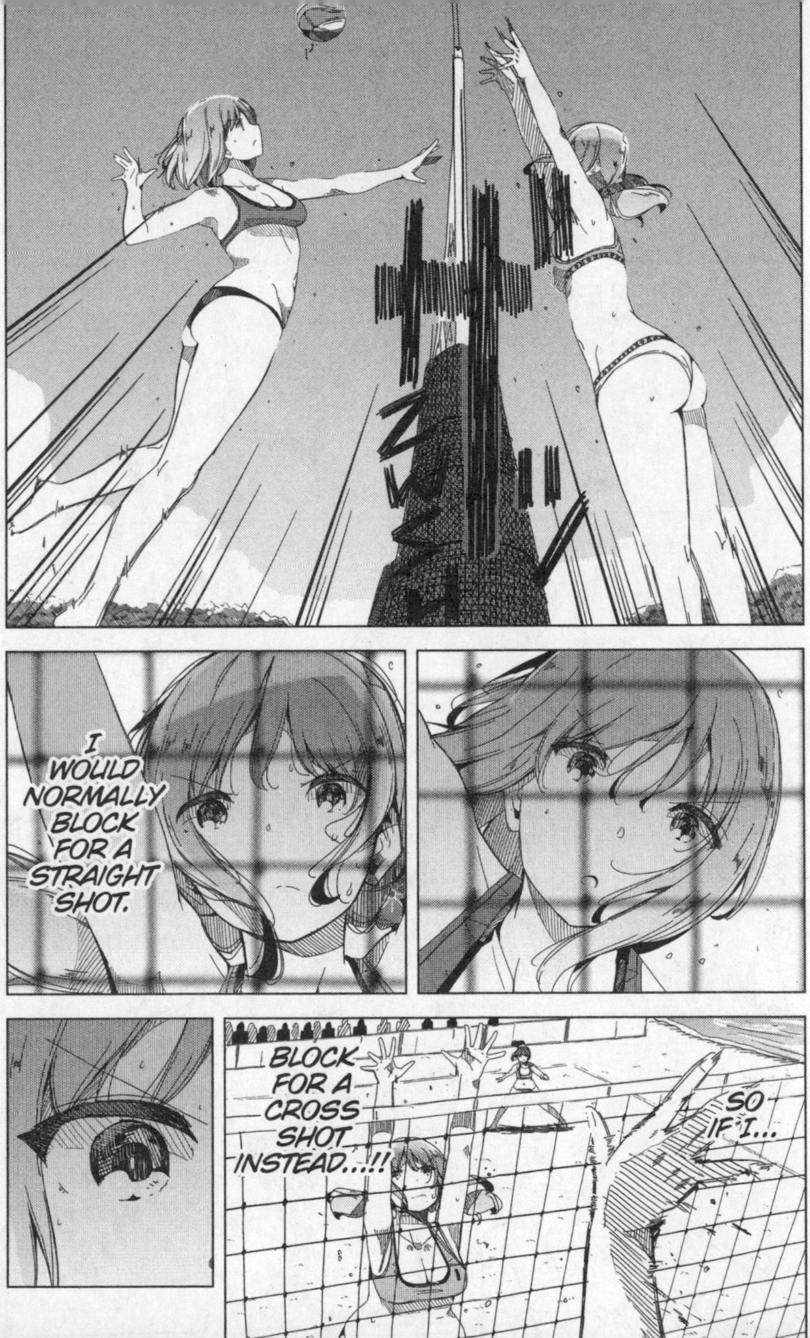
I WOULD NORMALLY BLOCK FOR A STRAIGHT SHOT.
SO IF I...
BLOCK FOR A CROSS SHOT INSTEAD...!!

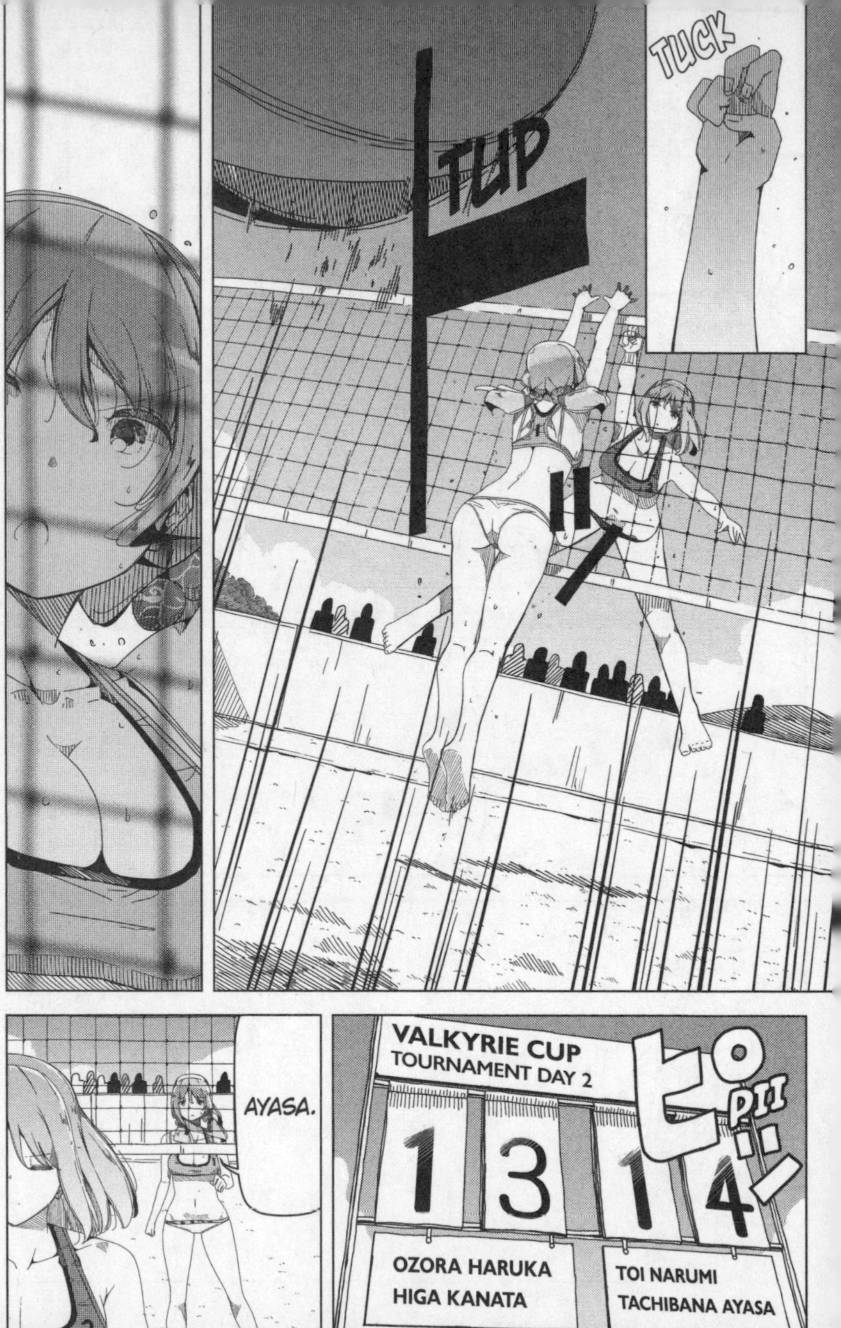
TUCK
TUP
VALKYRIE CUP
TOURNAMENT DAY 2
13
14
OZORA HARUKA
HIGA KANATA
TOI NARUMI
TACHIBANA AYASA
PII
AYASA.

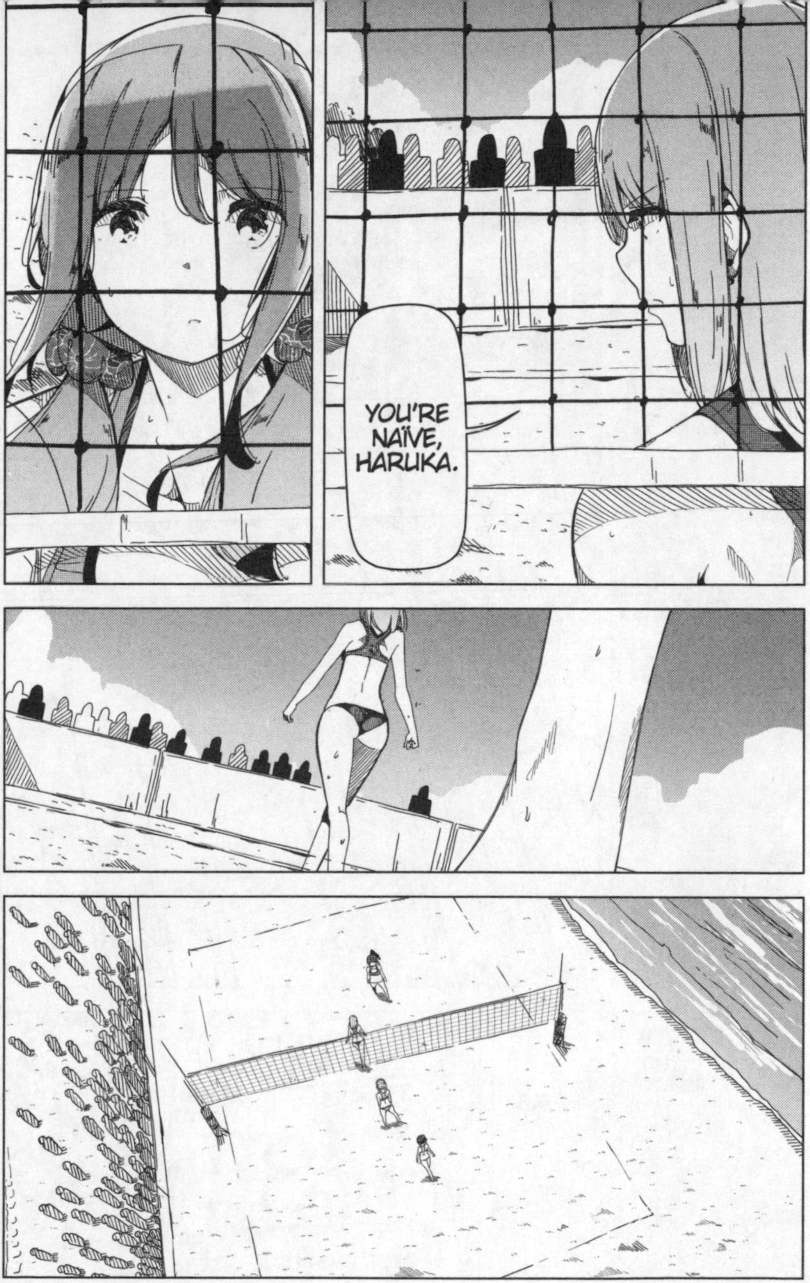
YOU'RE NAÏVE, HARUKA.

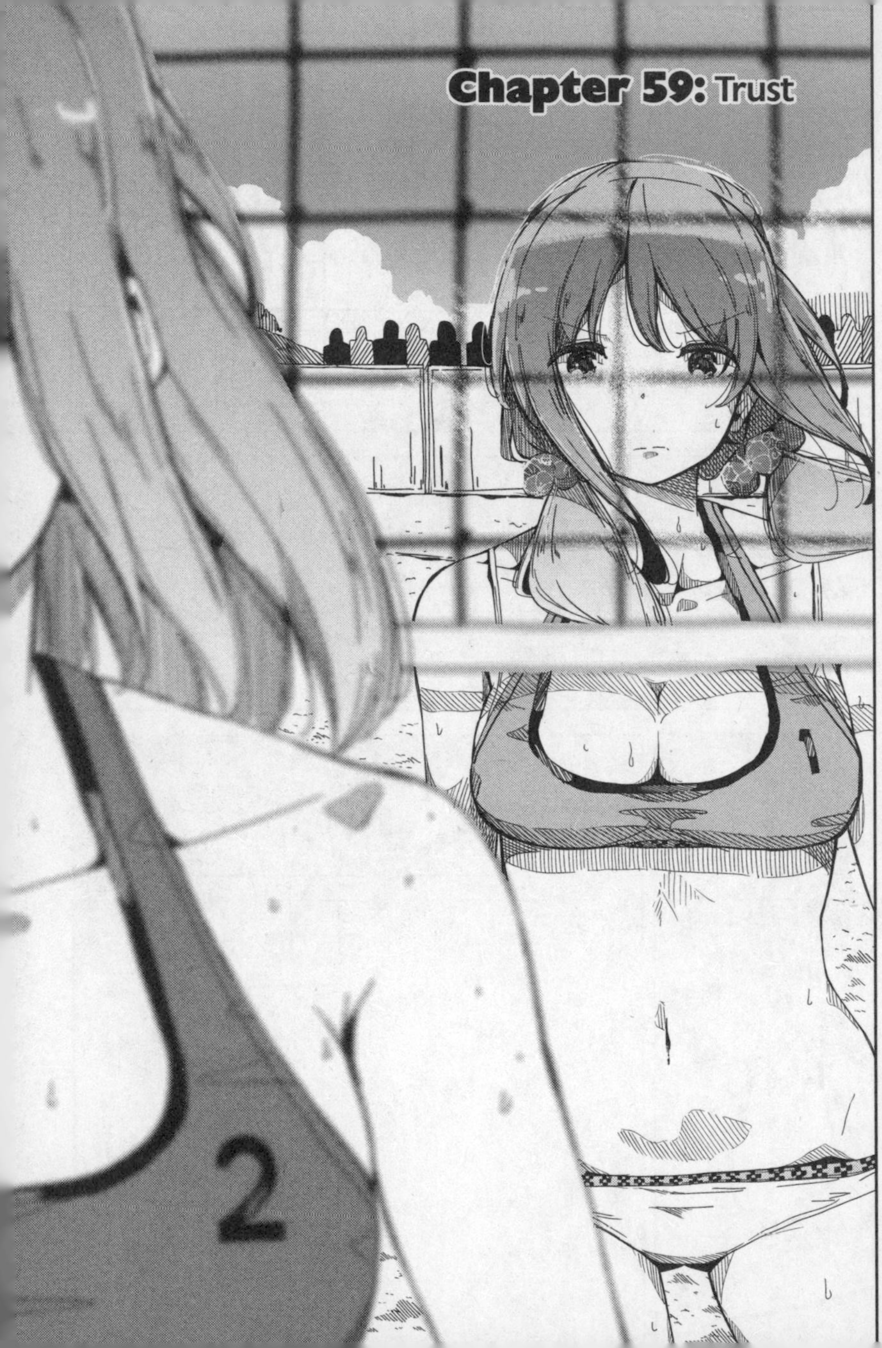
Chapter 59: Trust

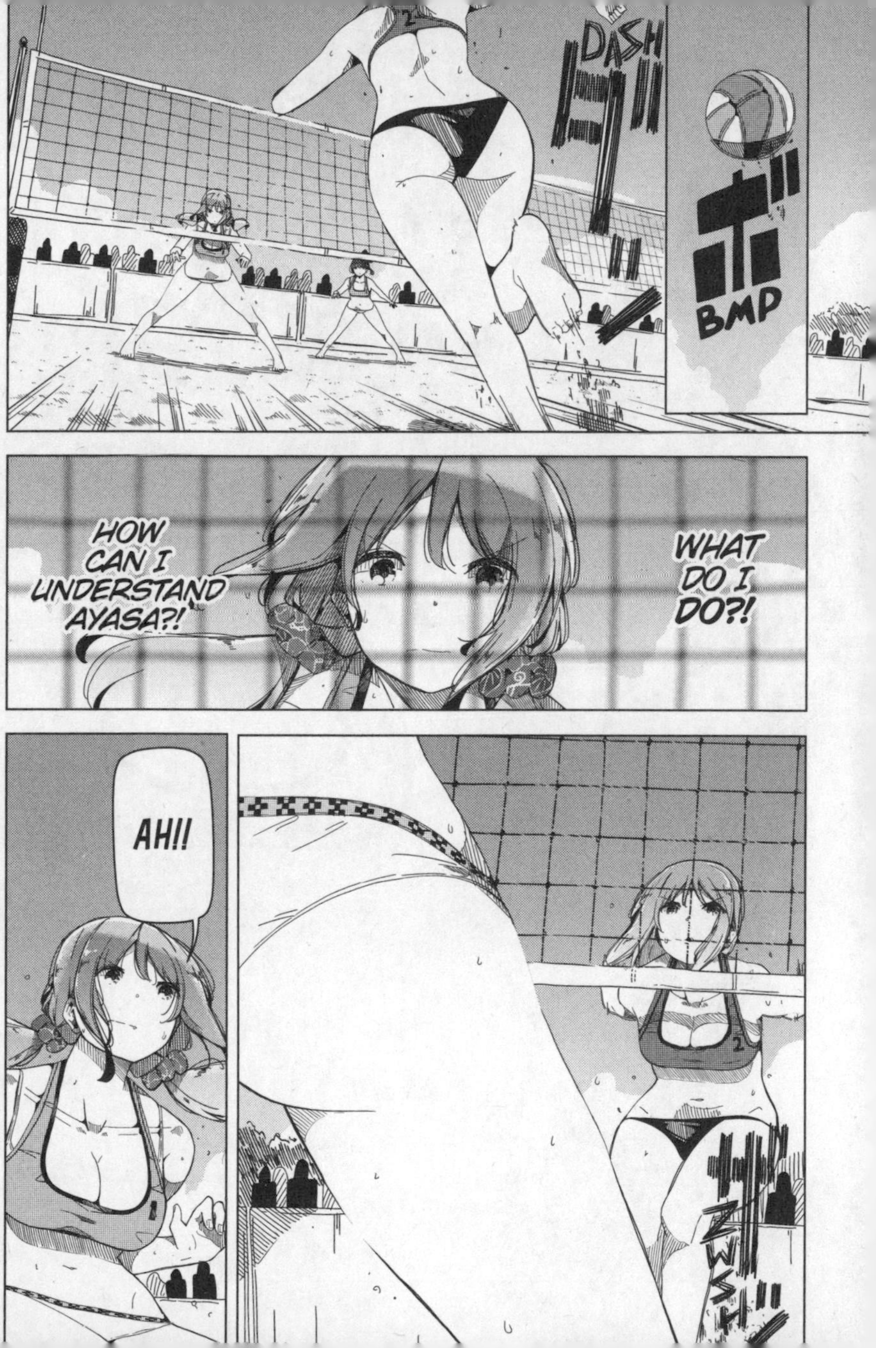
BMP
DASH
WHAT DO I DO?!
HOW CAN I UNDERSTAND AYASA?!
ZWSH
AH!!

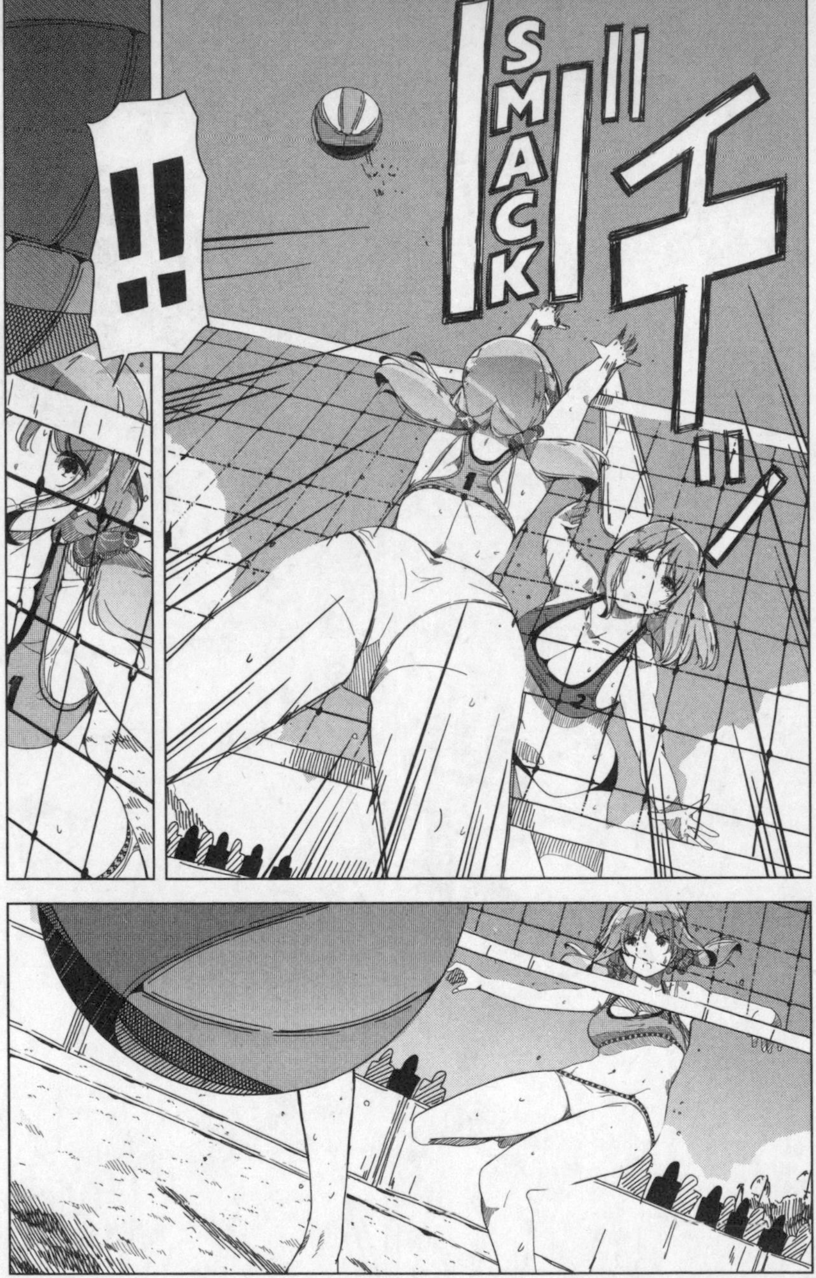
SMACK
!!

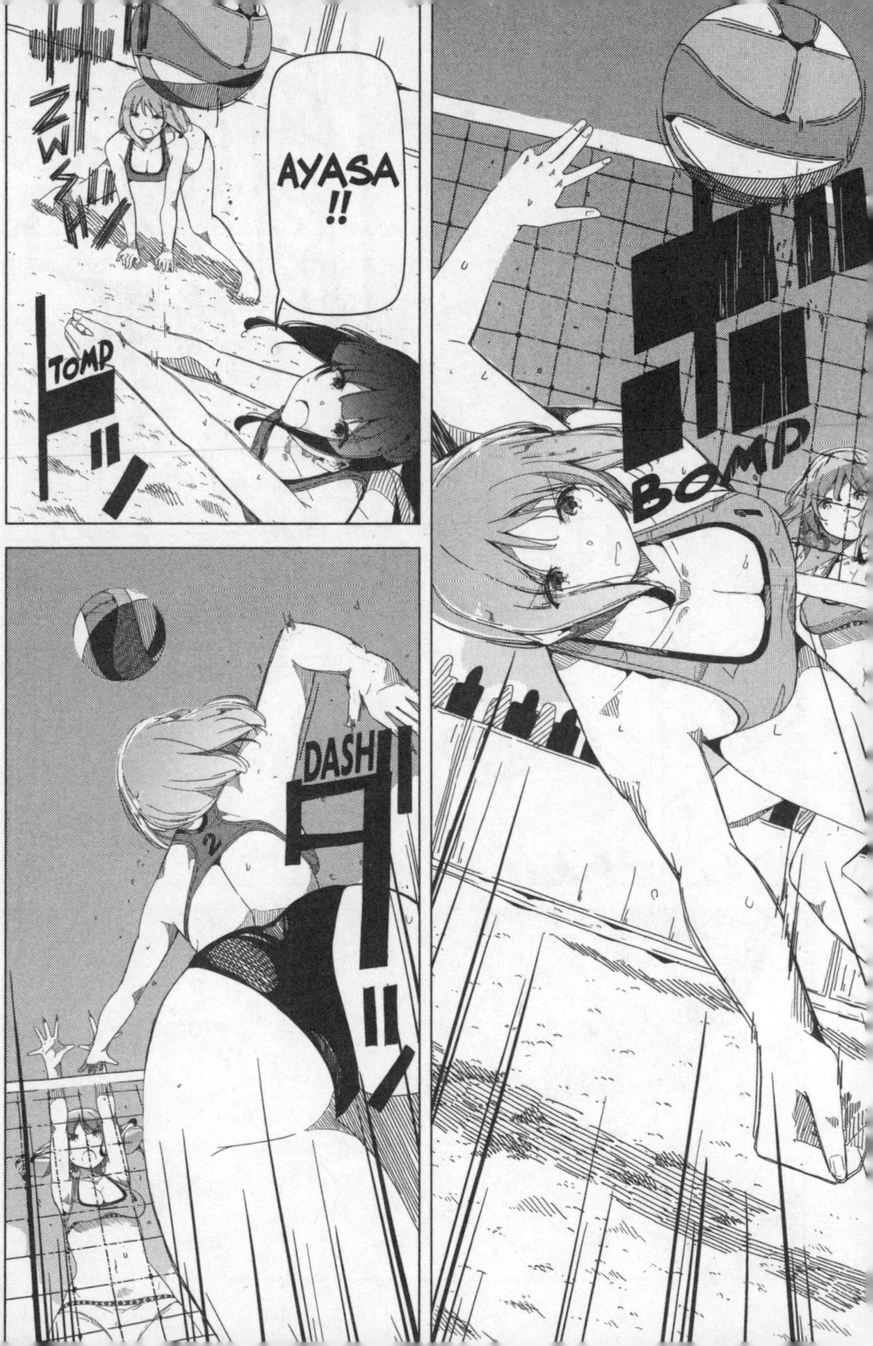
BOMP
ZWSH
AYASA!!
TOMP
DASH

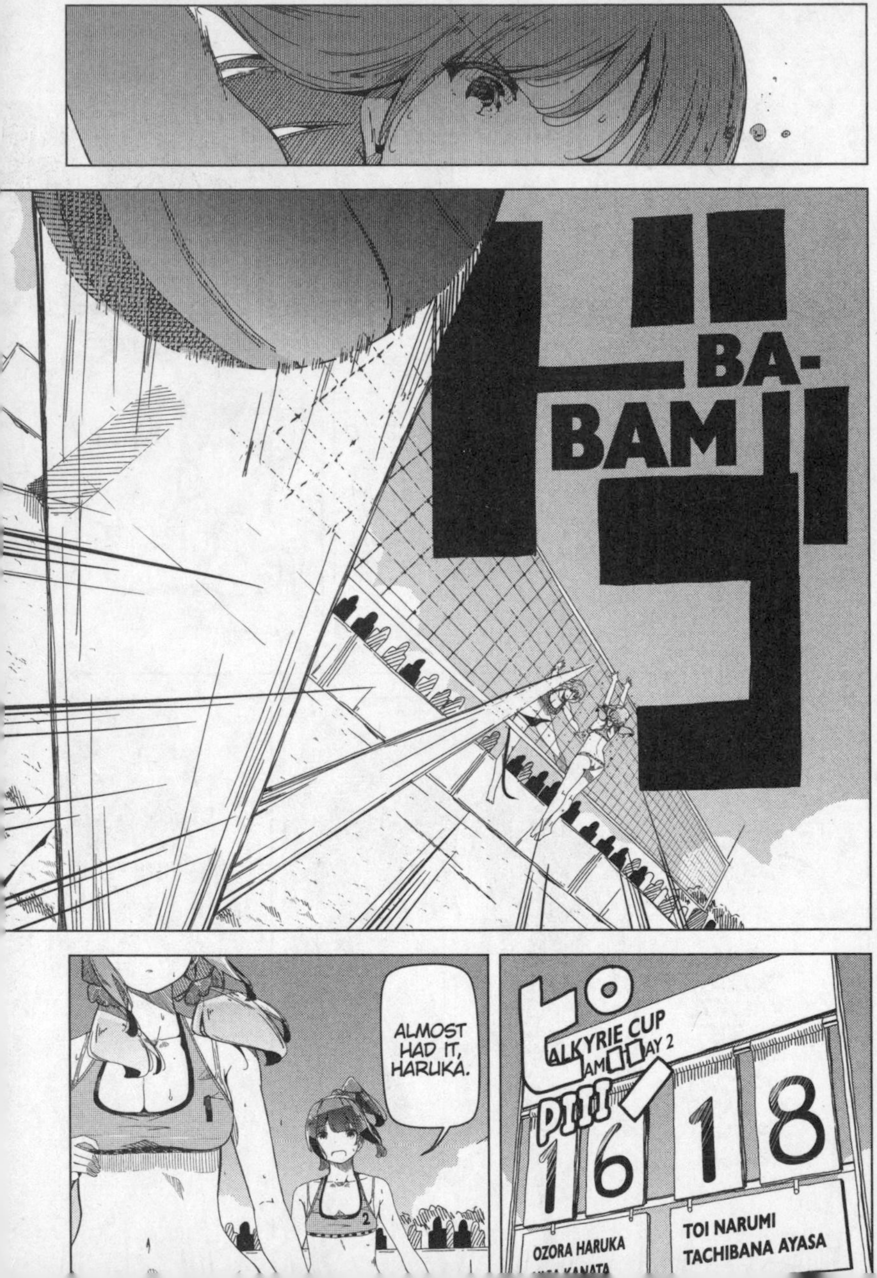
BA-BAM
ALKYRIE CUP
PIII
16
18
TOI NARUMI
TACHIBANA AYASA
OZORA HARUKA
ALMOST HAD IT, HARUKA.

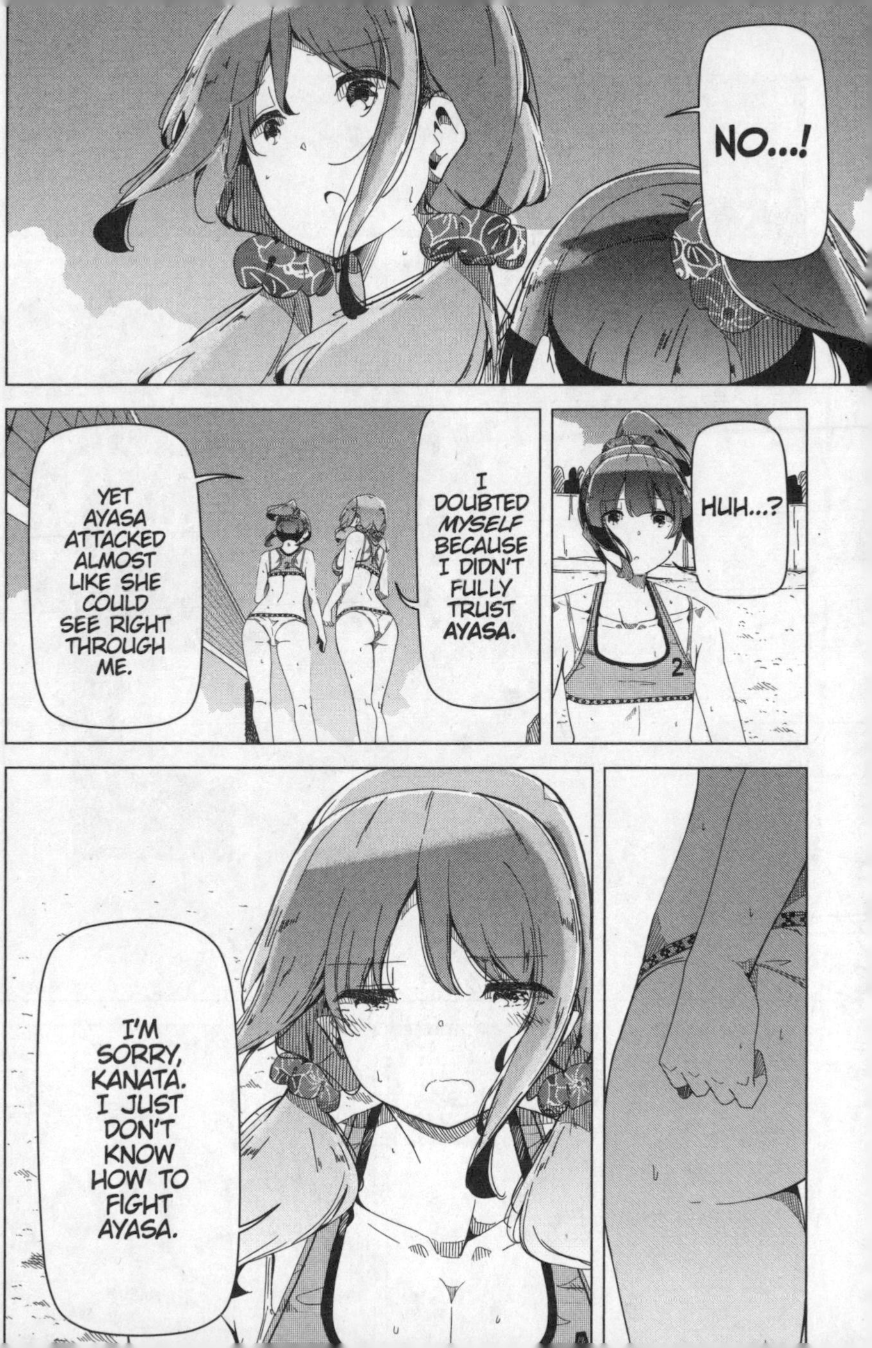
NO...!
HUH...?
I DOUBTED *MYSELF* BECAUSE I DIDN'T FULLY TRUST AYASA.
YET AYASA ATTACKED ALMOST LIKE SHE COULD SEE RIGHT THROUGH ME.
I'M SORRY, KANATA. I JUST DON'T KNOW HOW TO FIGHT AYASA.

HARUKA?

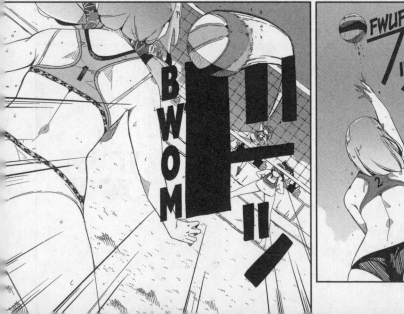

BWOM

FWUF

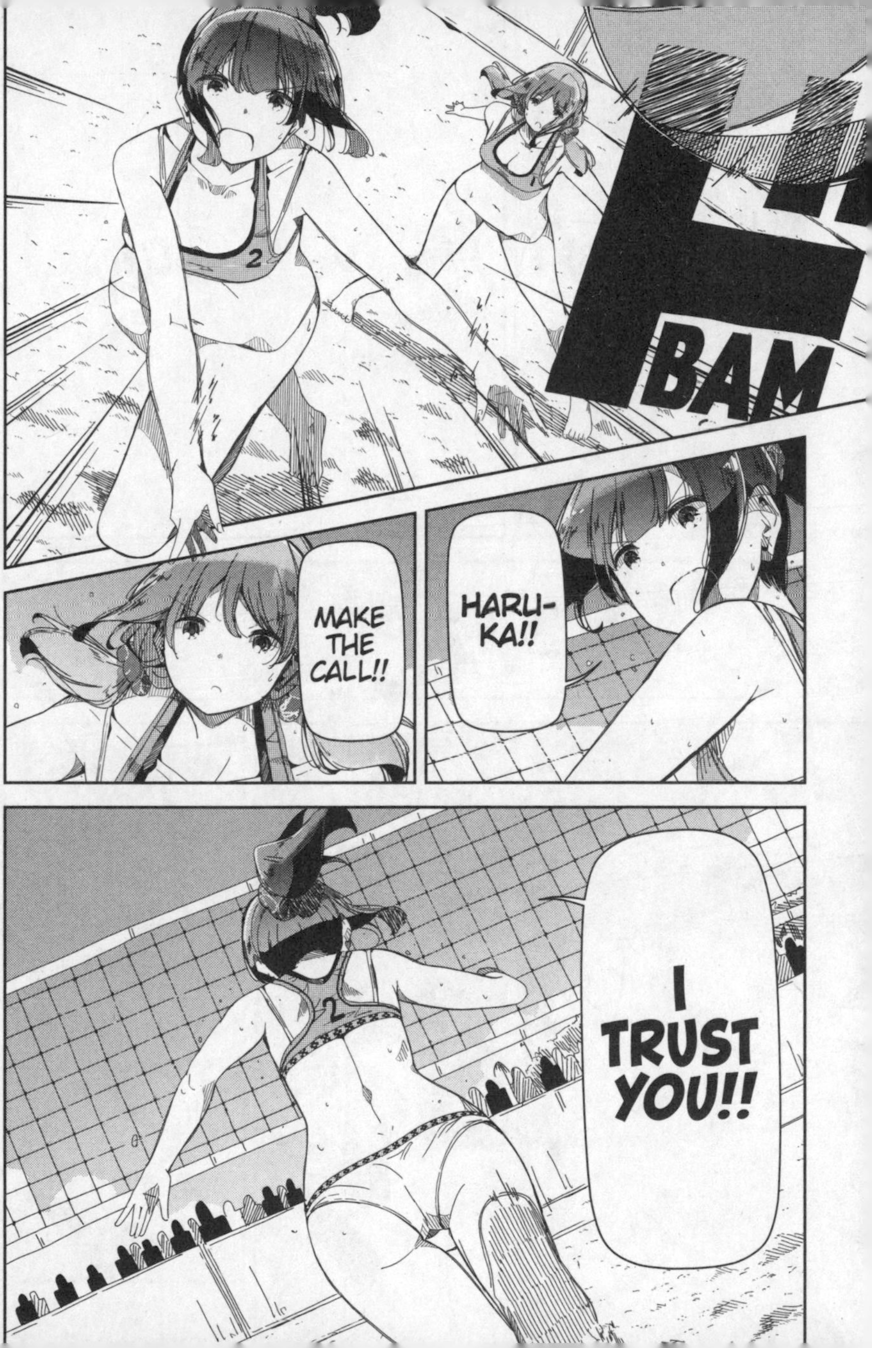
BAM
HARU-KA!!
MAKE THE CALL!!
I TRUST YOU!!

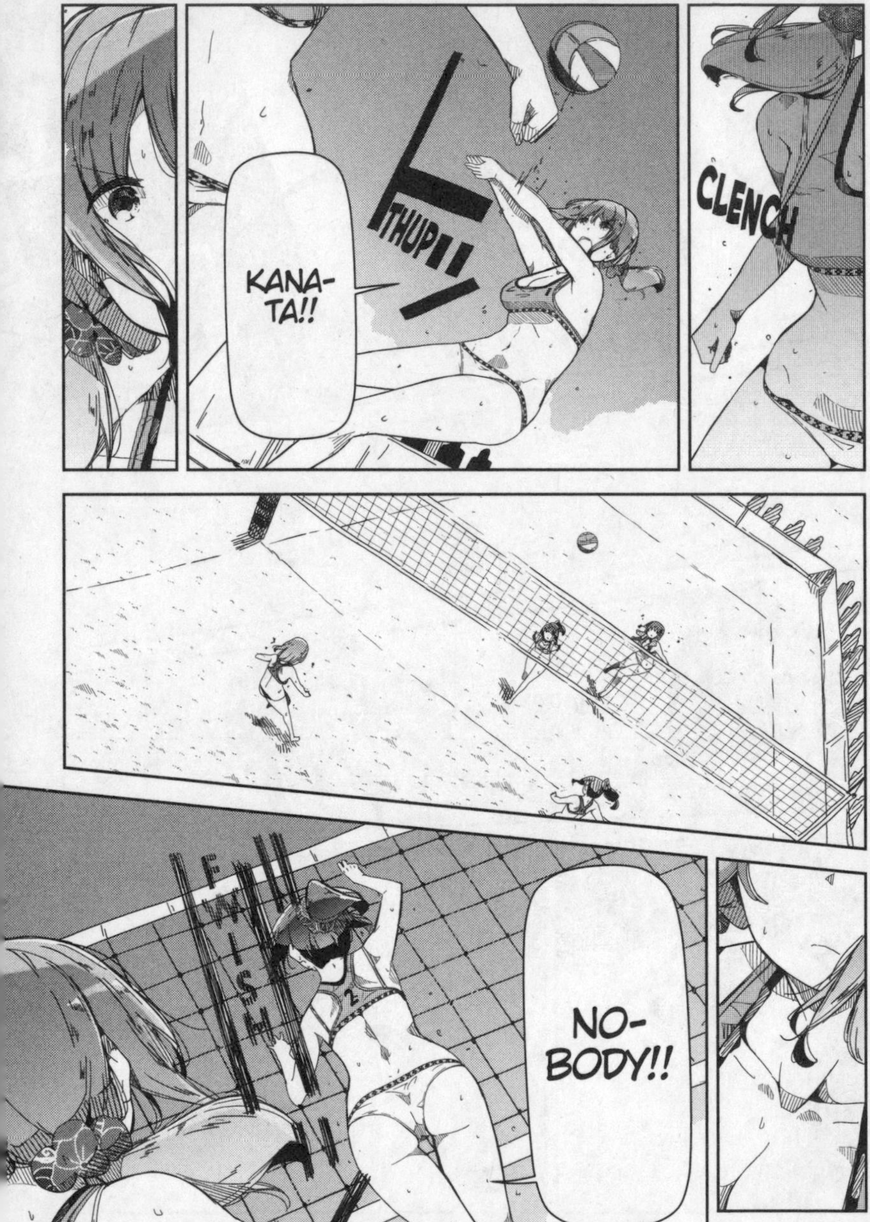
CLENCH
THUP
KANA-TA!!
FWISH
NO-BODY!!

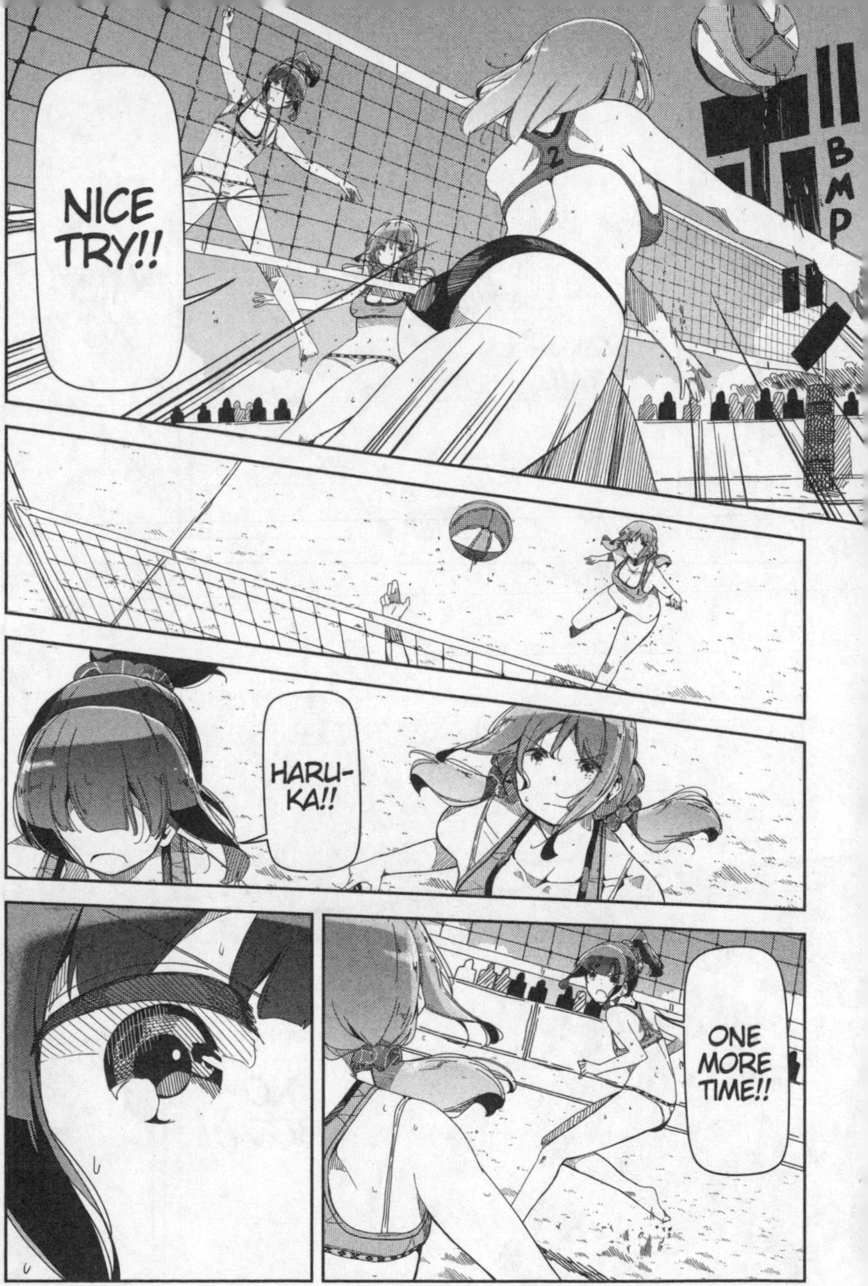
BMP
NICE TRY!!
HARUKA!!
ONE MORE TIME!!

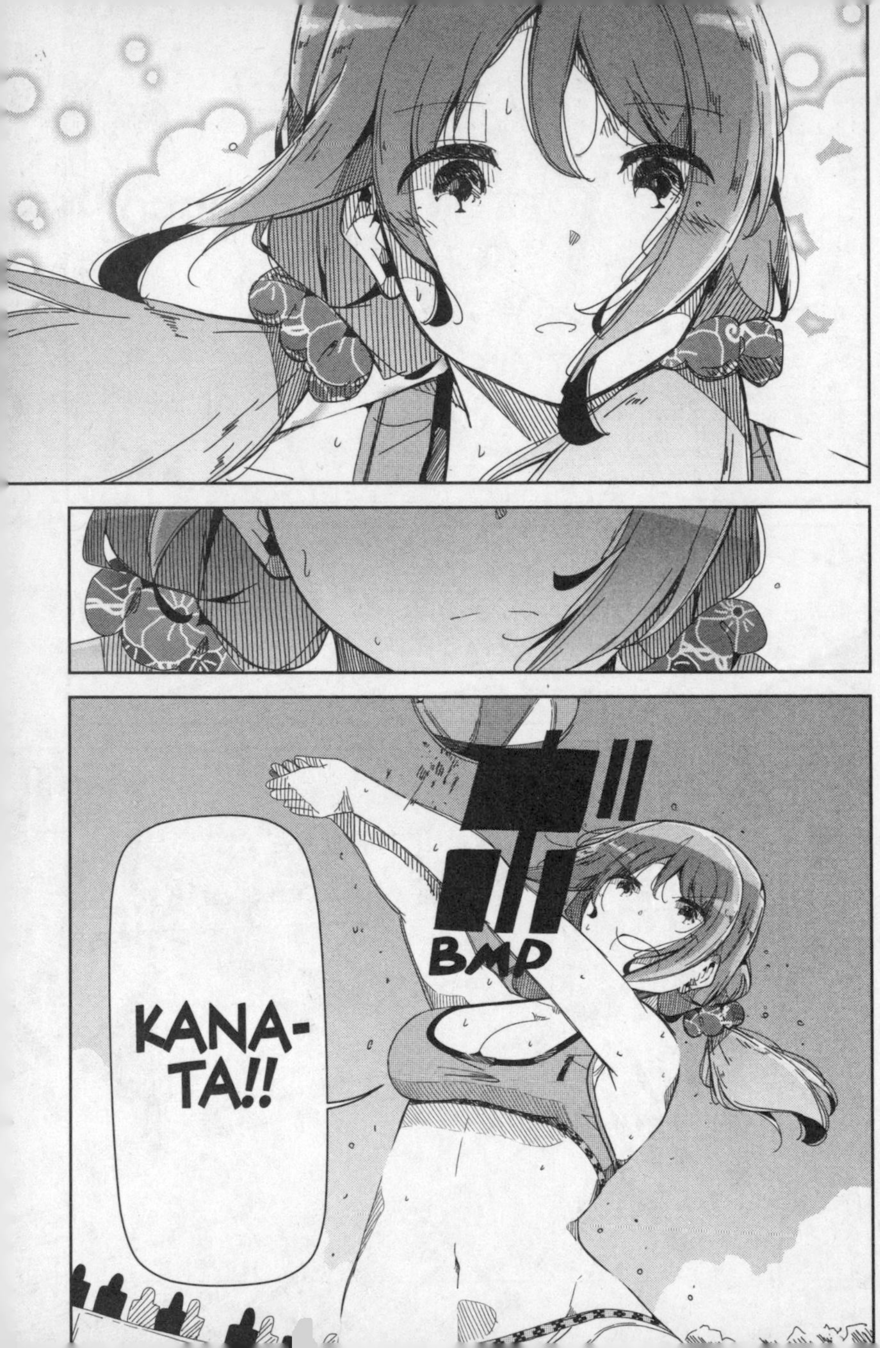

BMP
KANA-
TA!!

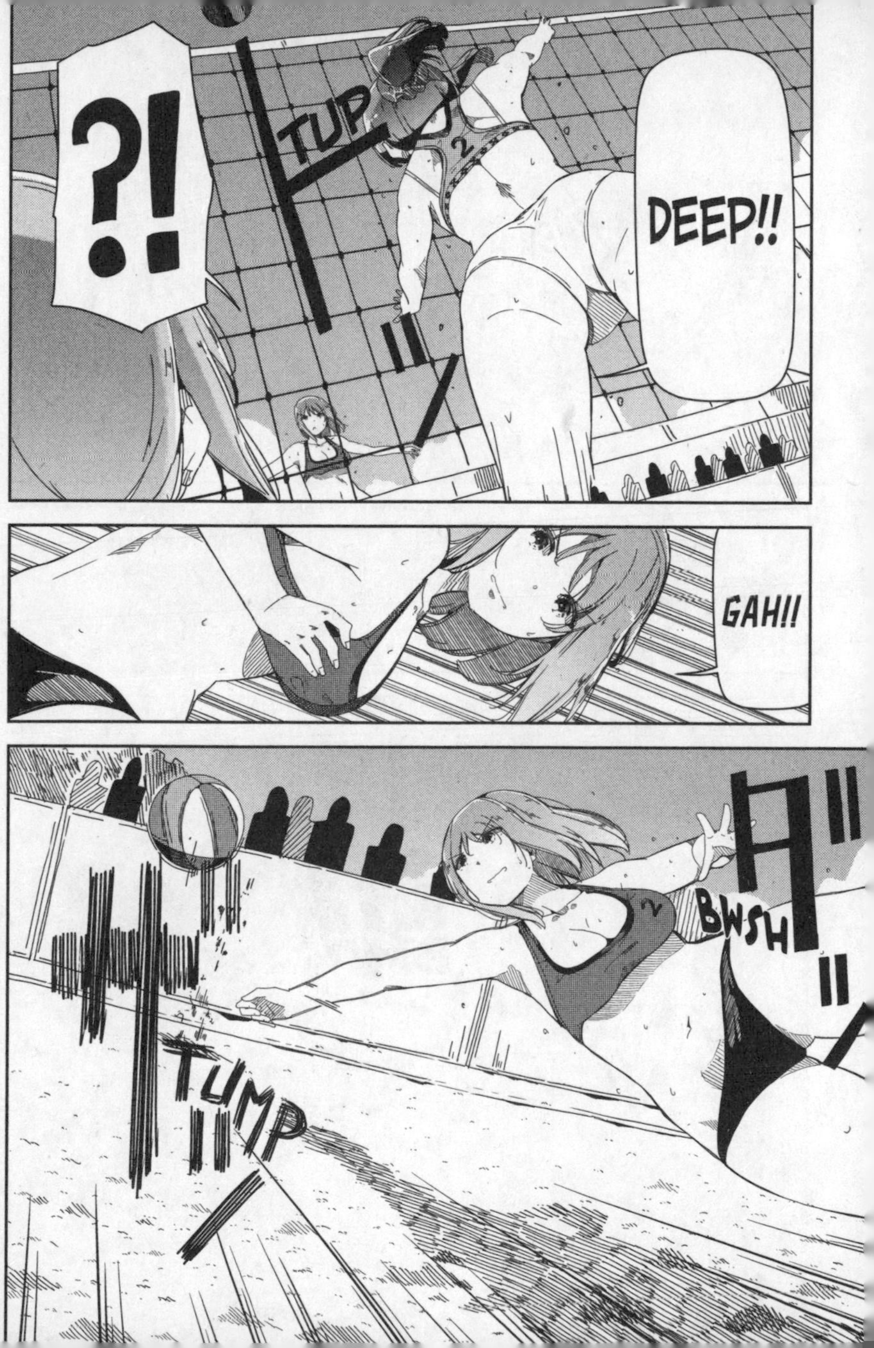
DEEP!!
TUP
?!
GAH!!
BWSH
TUMP

PHEW!

NICE
ONE,
KANATA!

ピ°
P!!

VALKYRIE
TOURNAMENT DAY 2

1	7		1	8
OZORA HARUKA			TOI NARUMI	
HIGA KANATA			TACHIBANA AYASA	

HAPH!

?!

SMAK

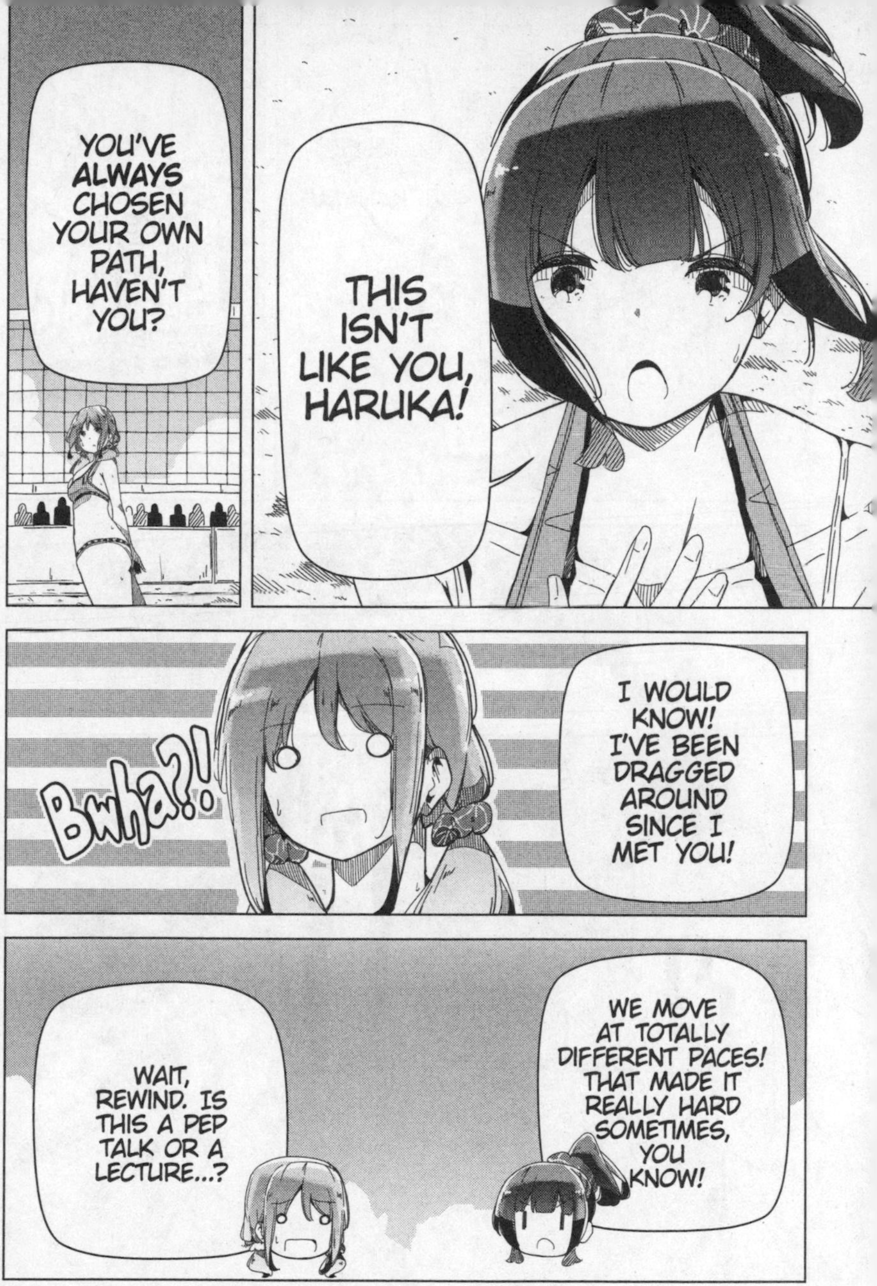
THIS ISN'T LIKE YOU, HARUKA!
YOU'VE ALWAYS CHOSEN YOUR OWN PATH, HAVEN'T YOU?
I WOULD KNOW! I'VE BEEN DRAGGED AROUND SINCE I MET YOU!
Bwha?!
WE MOVE AT TOTALLY DIFFERENT PACES! THAT MADE IT REALLY HARD SOMETIMES, YOU KNOW!
WAIT, REWIND. IS THIS A PEP TALK OR A LECTURE...?

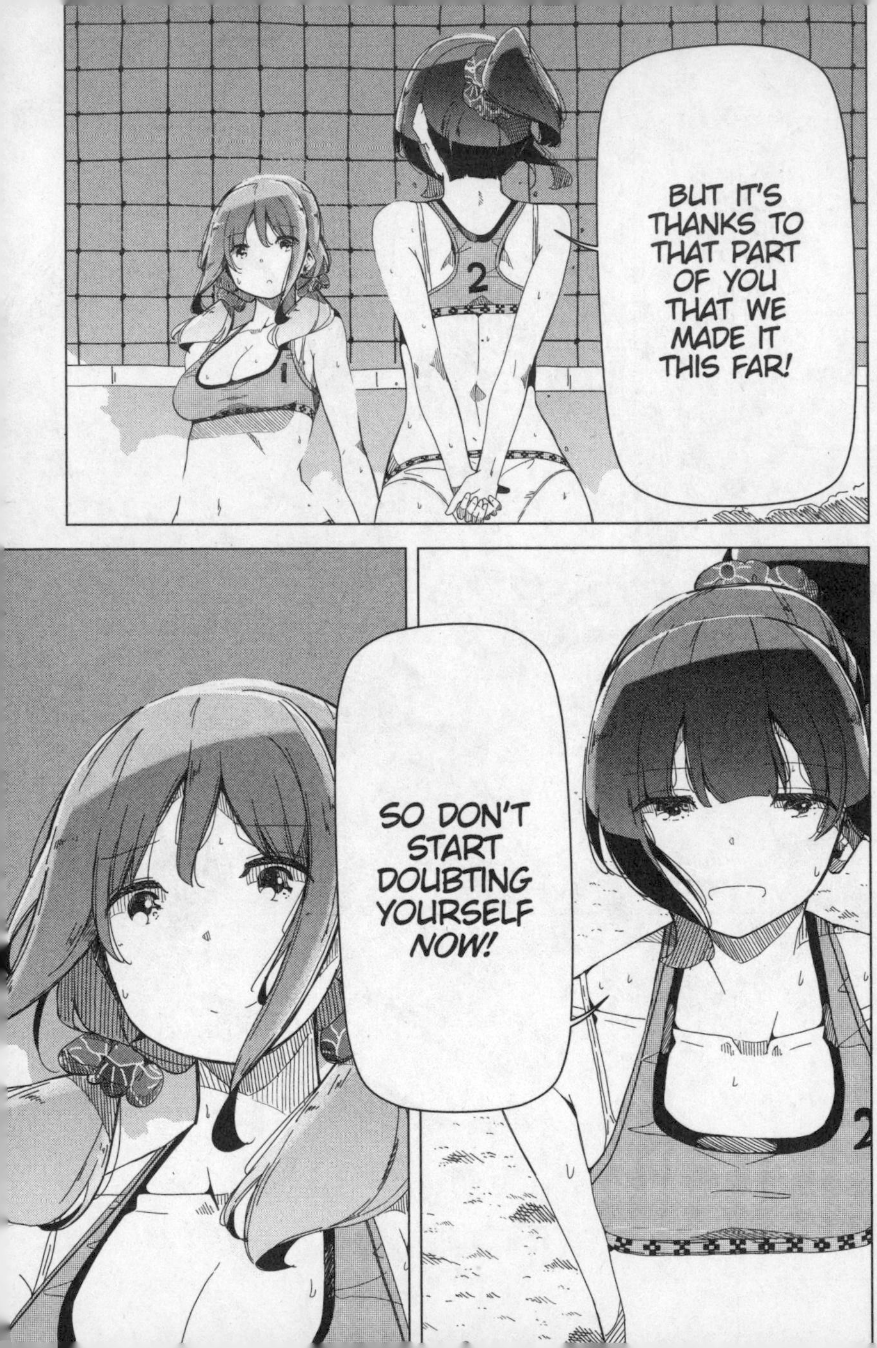
BUT IT'S THANKS TO THAT PART OF YOU THAT WE MADE IT THIS FAR!
2
SO DON'T START DOUBTING YOURSELF *NOW!*

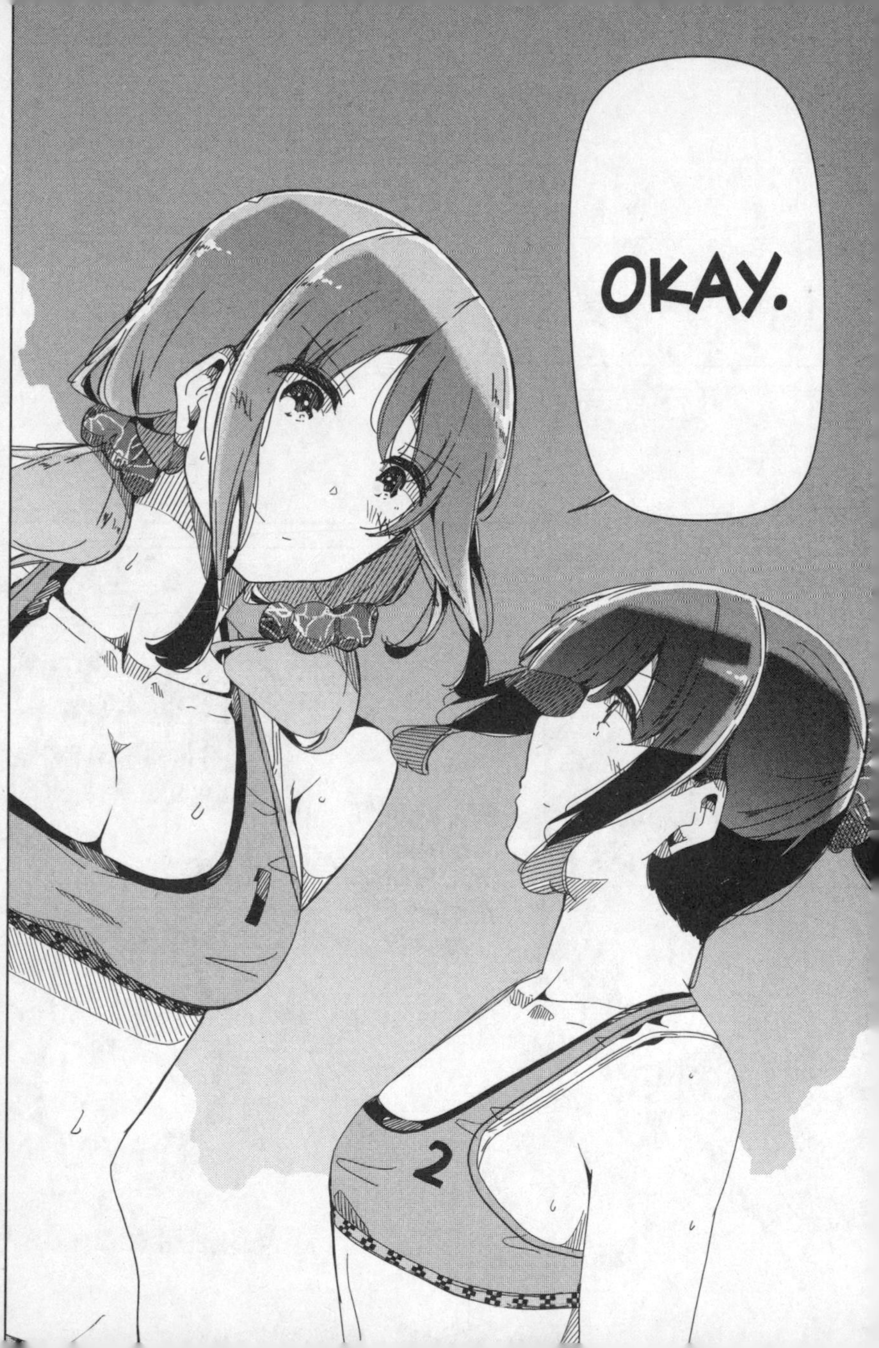
OKAY.
1
2

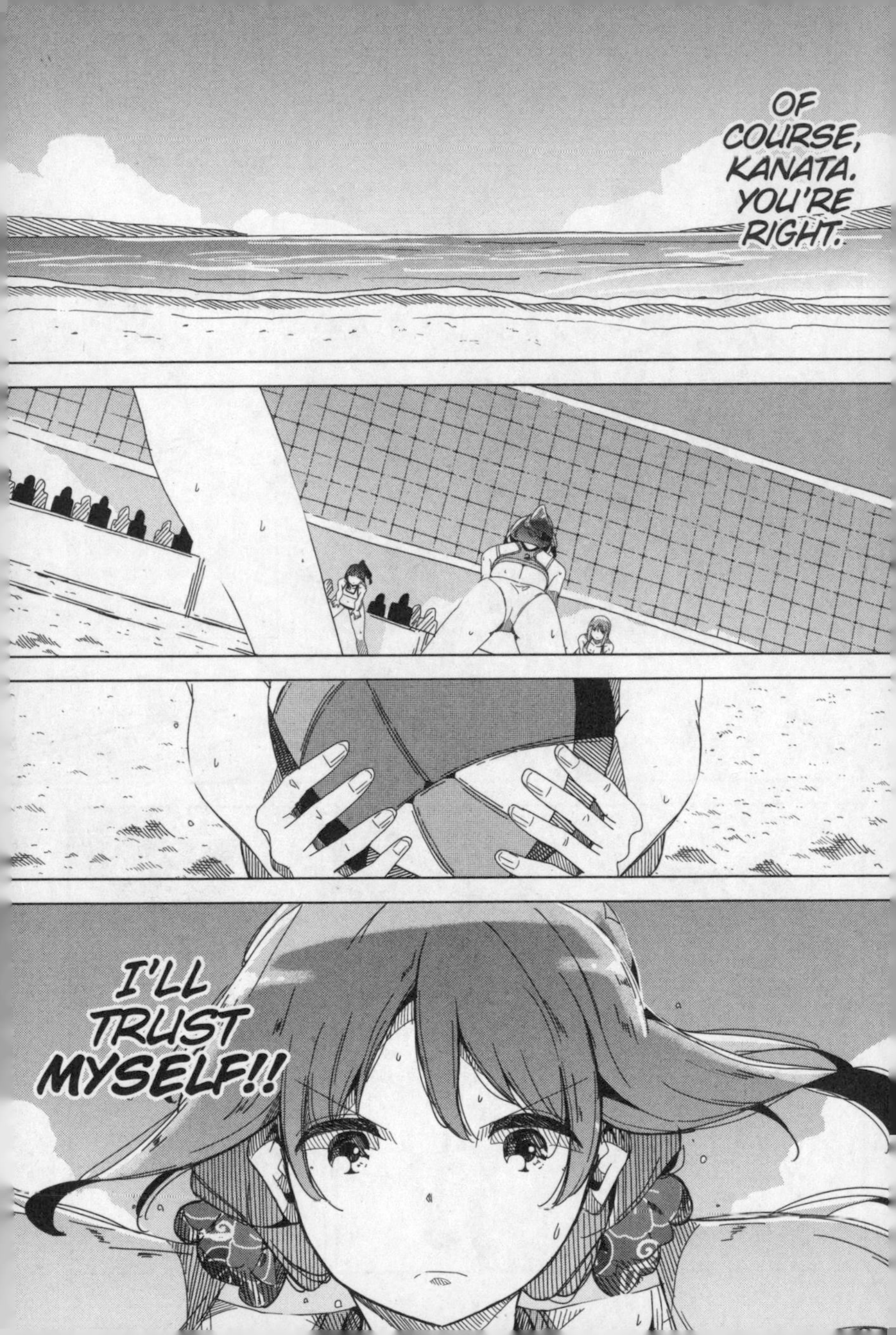
OF COURSE, KANATA. YOU'RE RIGHT.
I'LL TRUST MYSELF!!

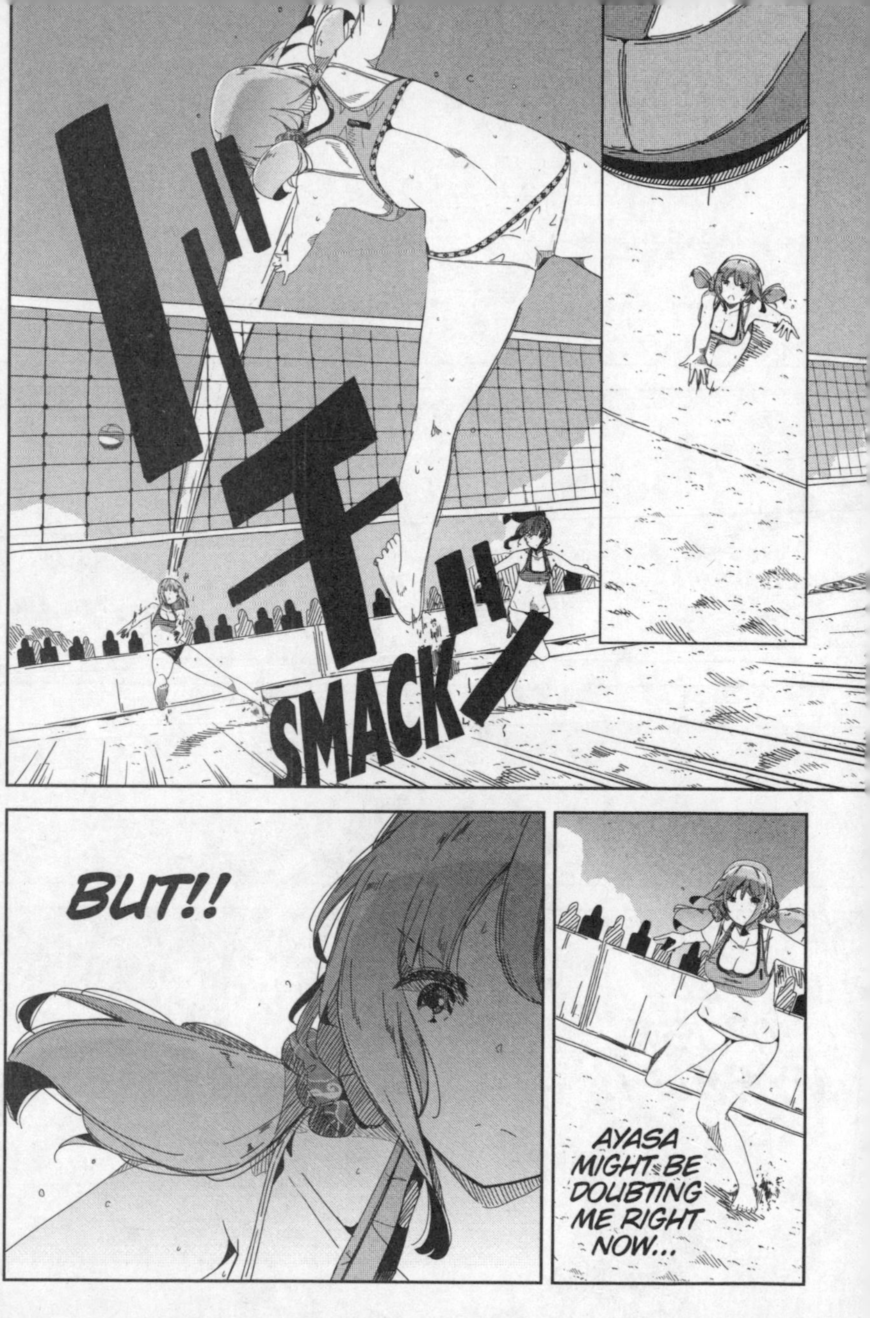
SMACK
AYASA MIGHT BE DOUBTING ME RIGHT NOW...
BUT!!

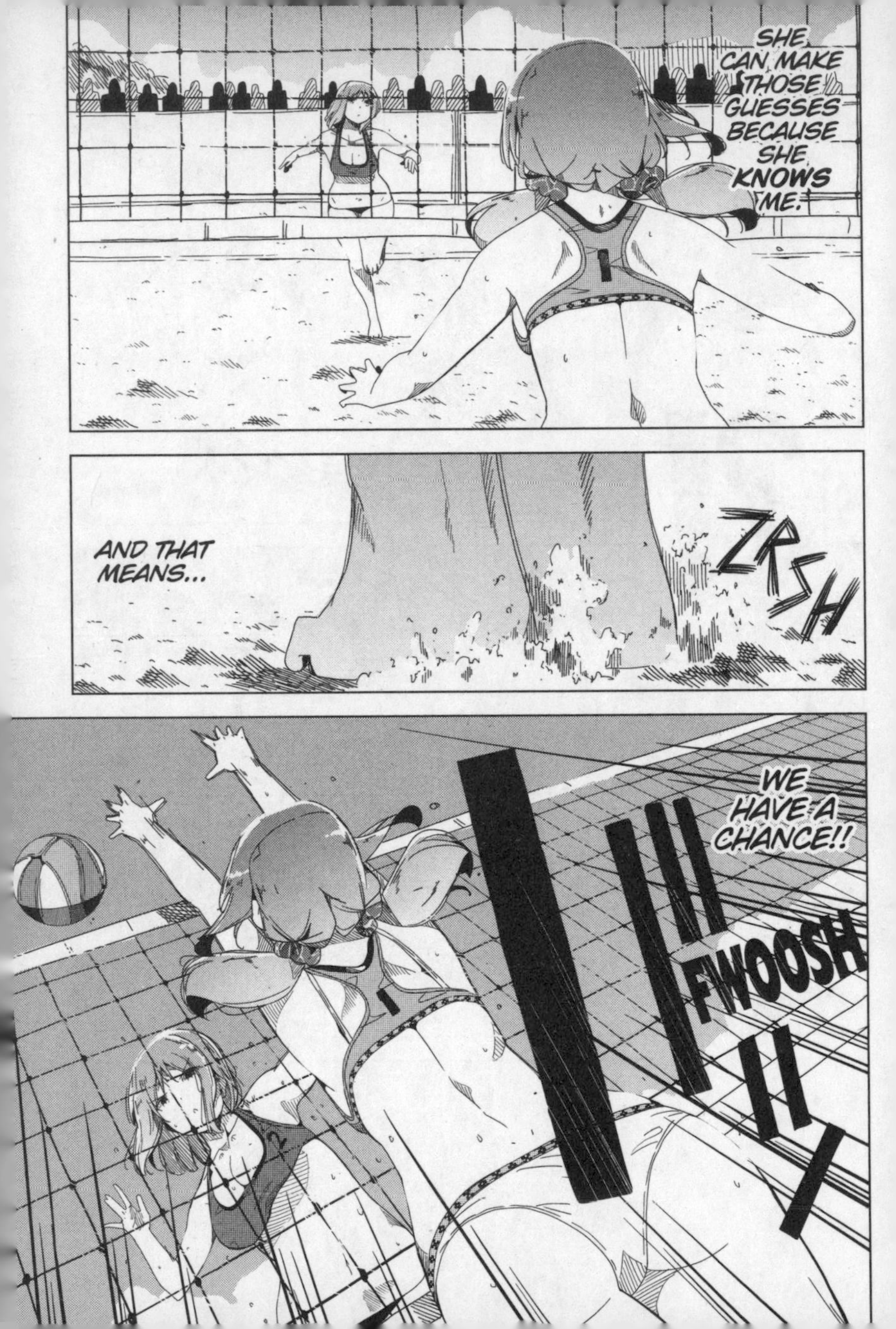
SHE CAN MAKE THOSE GUESSES BECAUSE SHE KNOWS ME.
ZRSH
AND THAT MEANS...
WE HAVE A CHANCE!!
FWOOSH

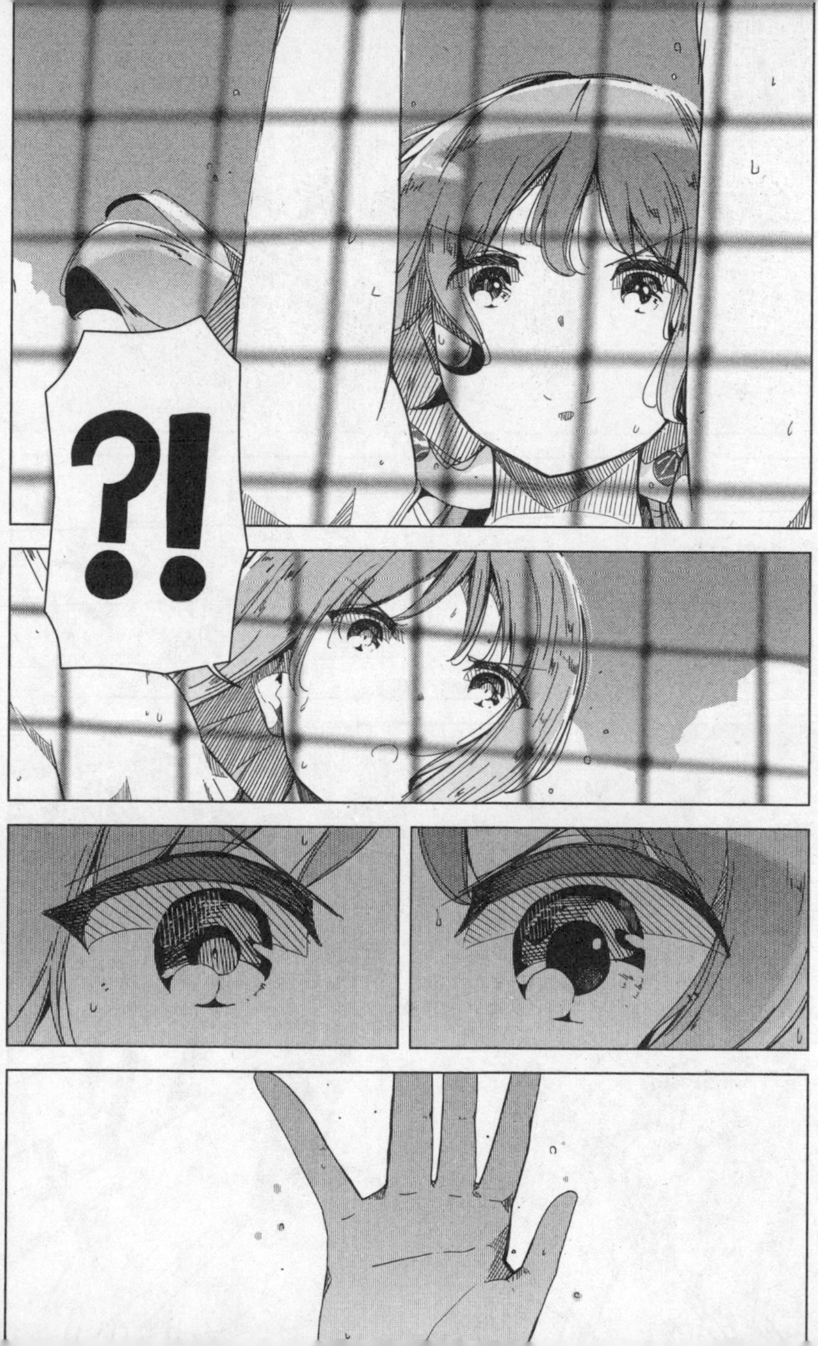
?!

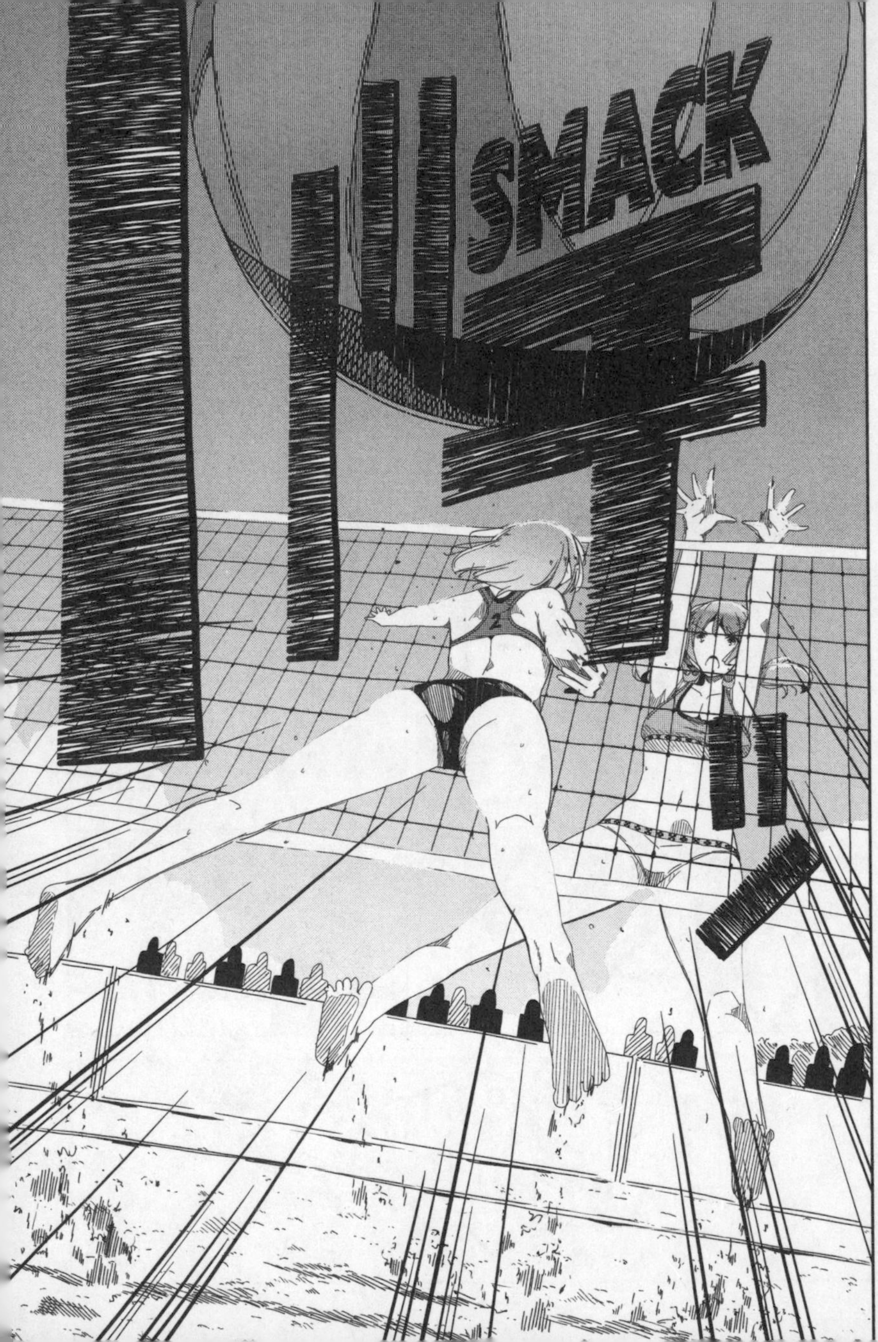
SMACK

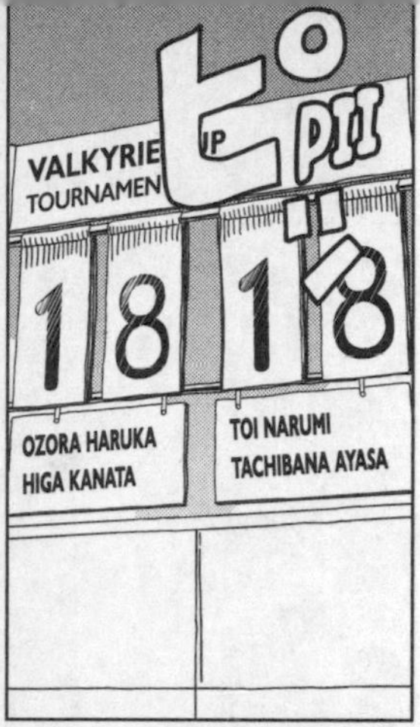
VALKYRIE UP
TOURNAMEN
ピッ PII
18
18
OZORA HARUKA
HIGA KANATA
TOI NARUMI
TACHIBANA AYASA
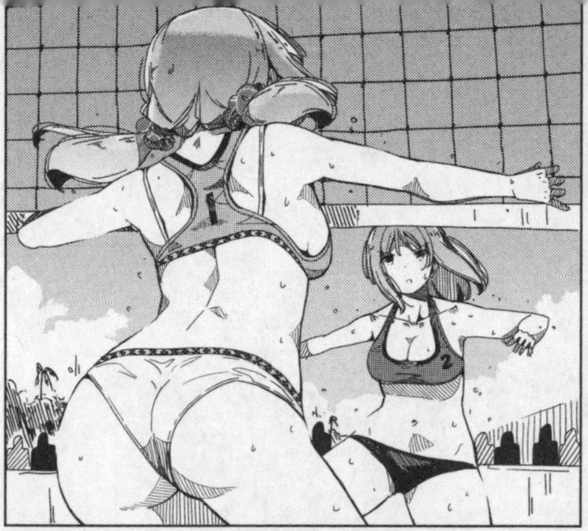
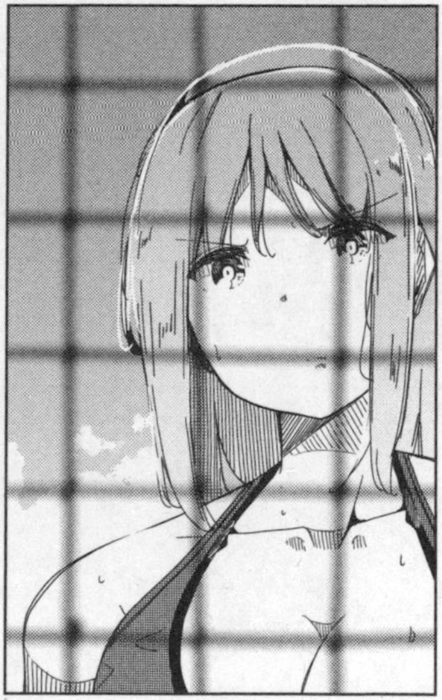
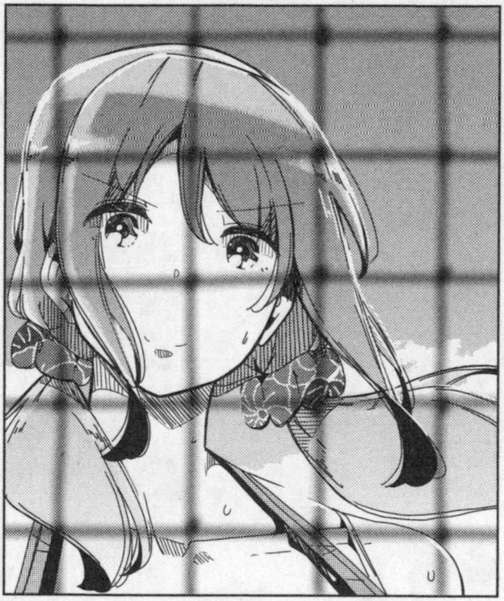
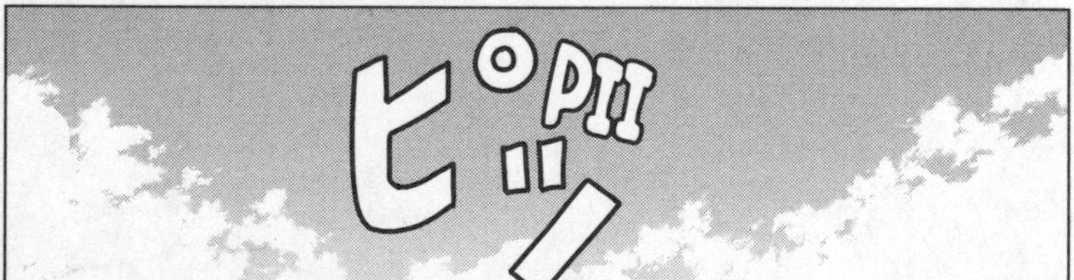
ピッ PII

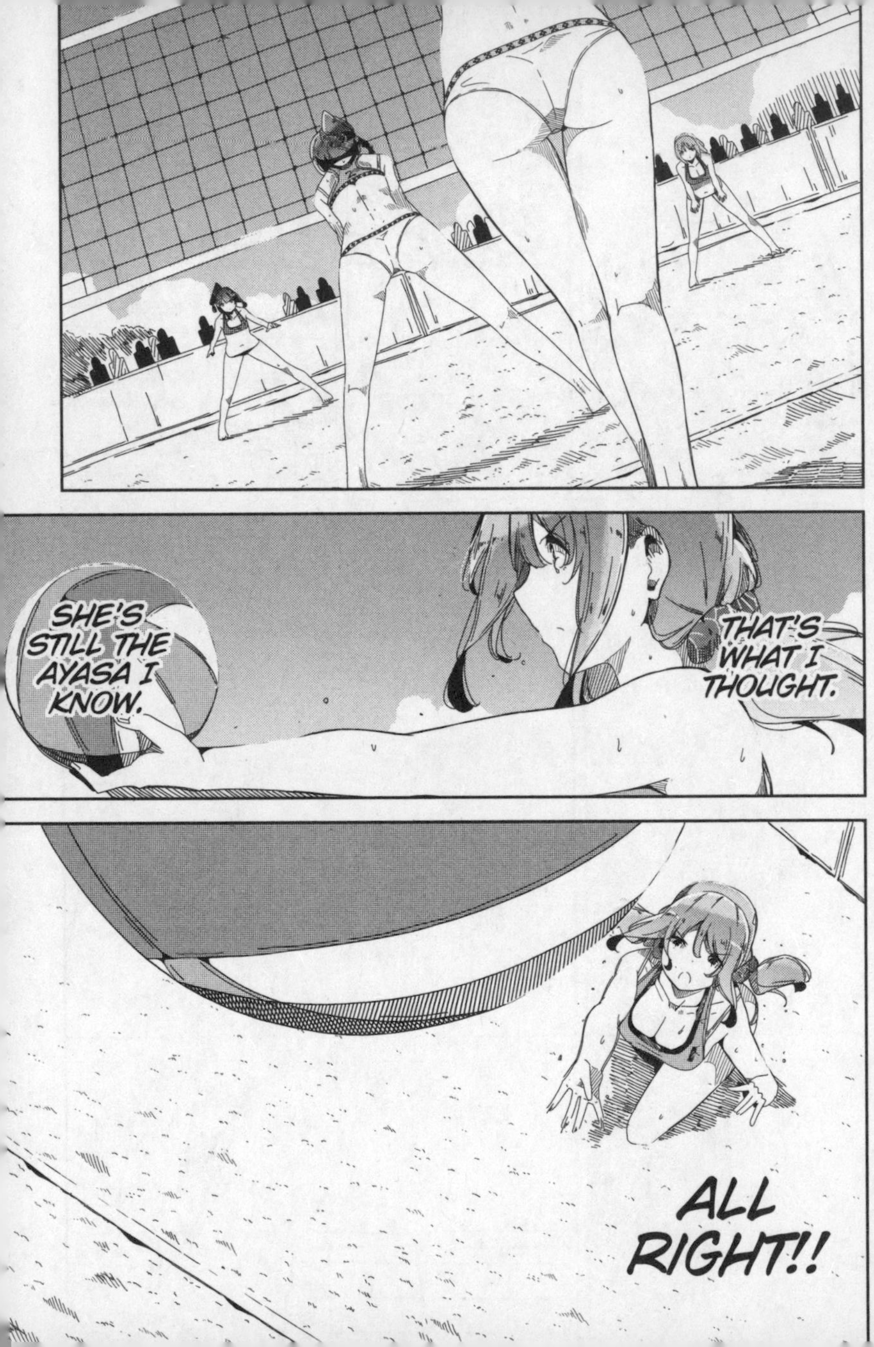
THAT'S WHAT I THOUGHT.
SHE'S STILL THE AYASA I KNOW.
ALL RIGHT!!

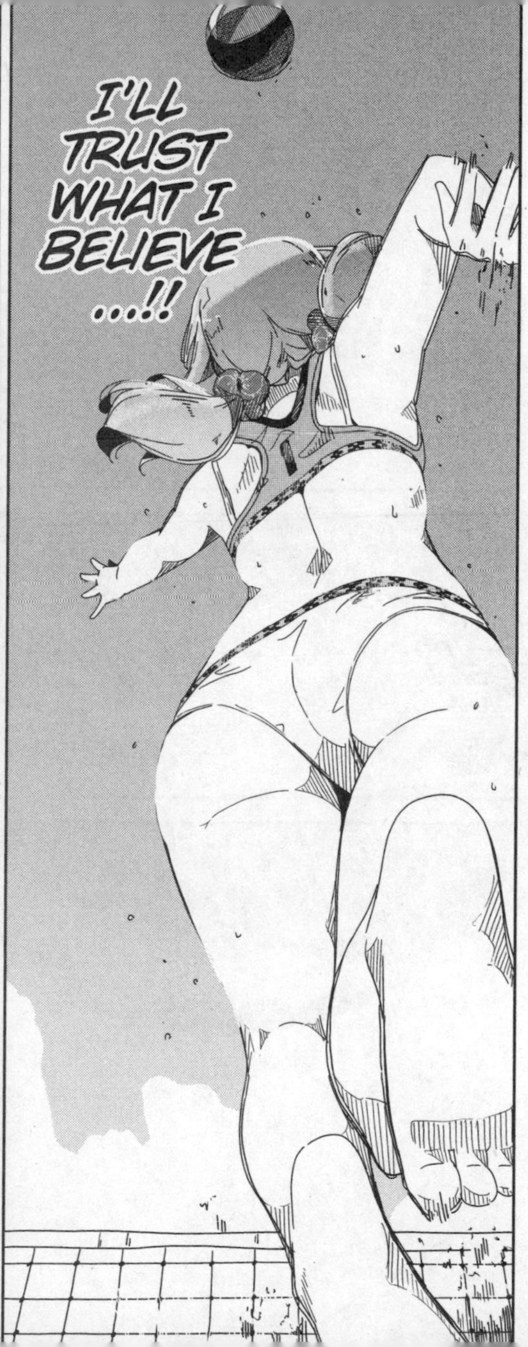
I'LL TRUST WHAT I BELIEVE ...!!
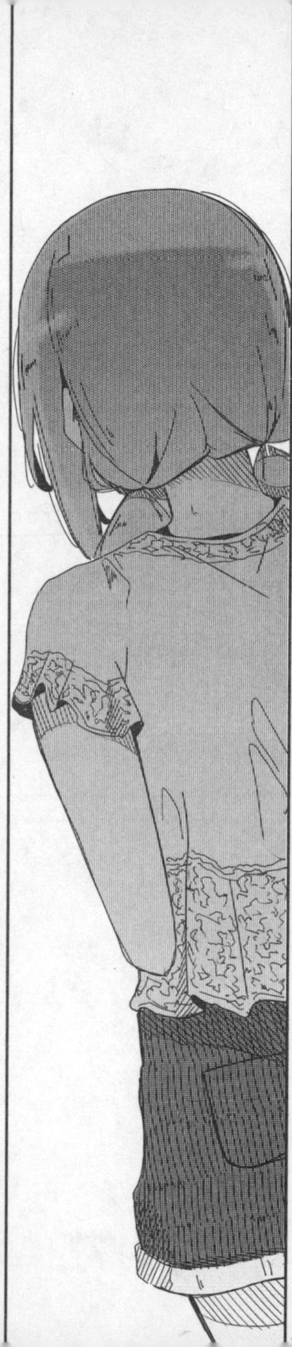

Presented by Nyoijizai

Harukana Receive

Presented by Nyoijizai

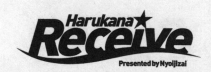

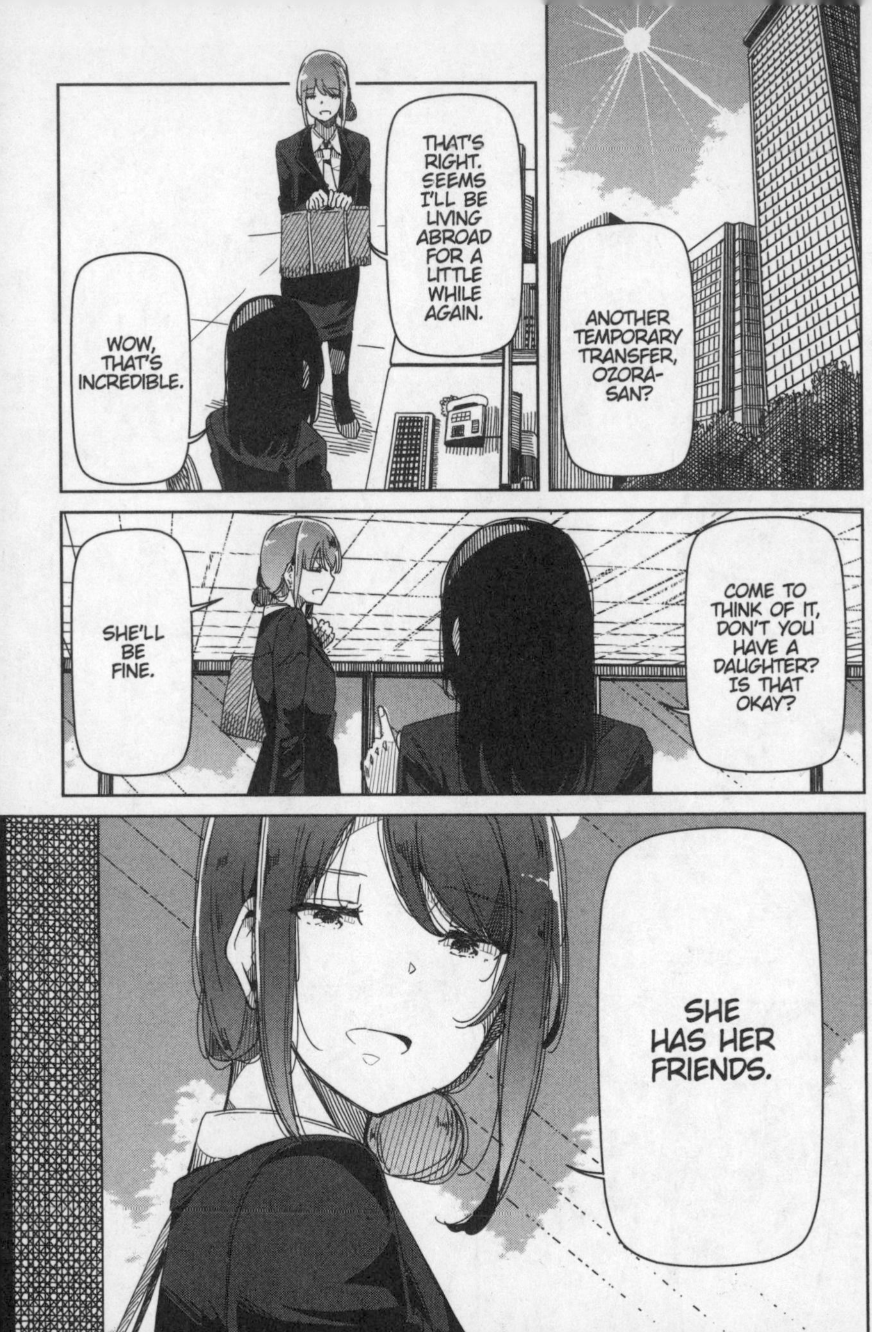
ANOTHER TEMPORARY TRANSFER, OZORA-SAN?
THAT'S RIGHT. SEEMS I'LL BE LIVING ABROAD FOR A LITTLE WHILE AGAIN.
WOW, THAT'S INCREDIBLE.
COME TO THINK OF IT, DON'T YOU HAVE A DAUGHTER? IS THAT OKAY?
SHE'LL BE FINE.
SHE HAS HER FRIENDS.

Chapter 60: Haruka and Kanata

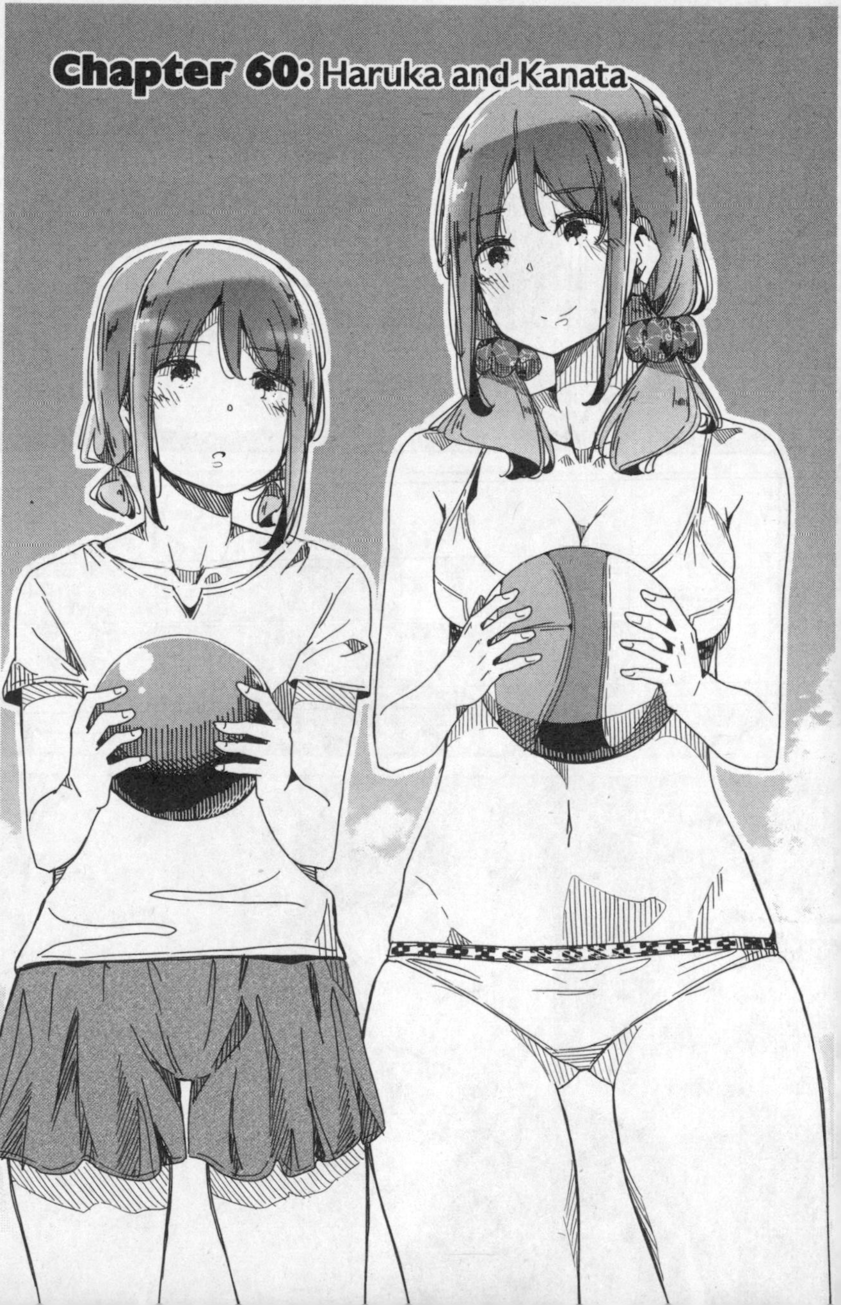

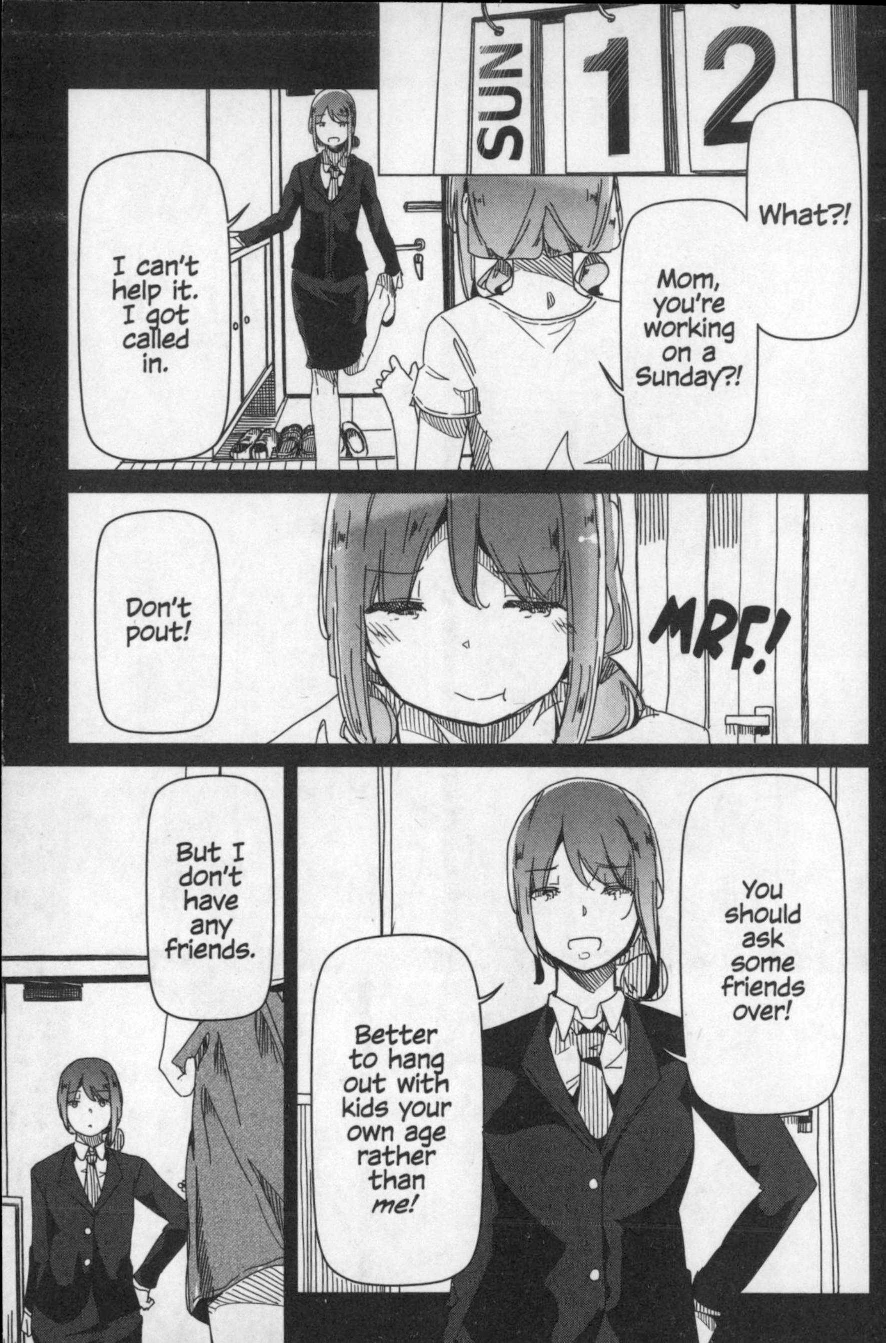
SUN 12
What?!
Mom, you're working on a Sunday?!
I can't help it. I got called in.
MRF!
Don't pout!
You should ask some friends over!
Better to hang out with kids your own age rather than *me!*
But I don't have any friends.

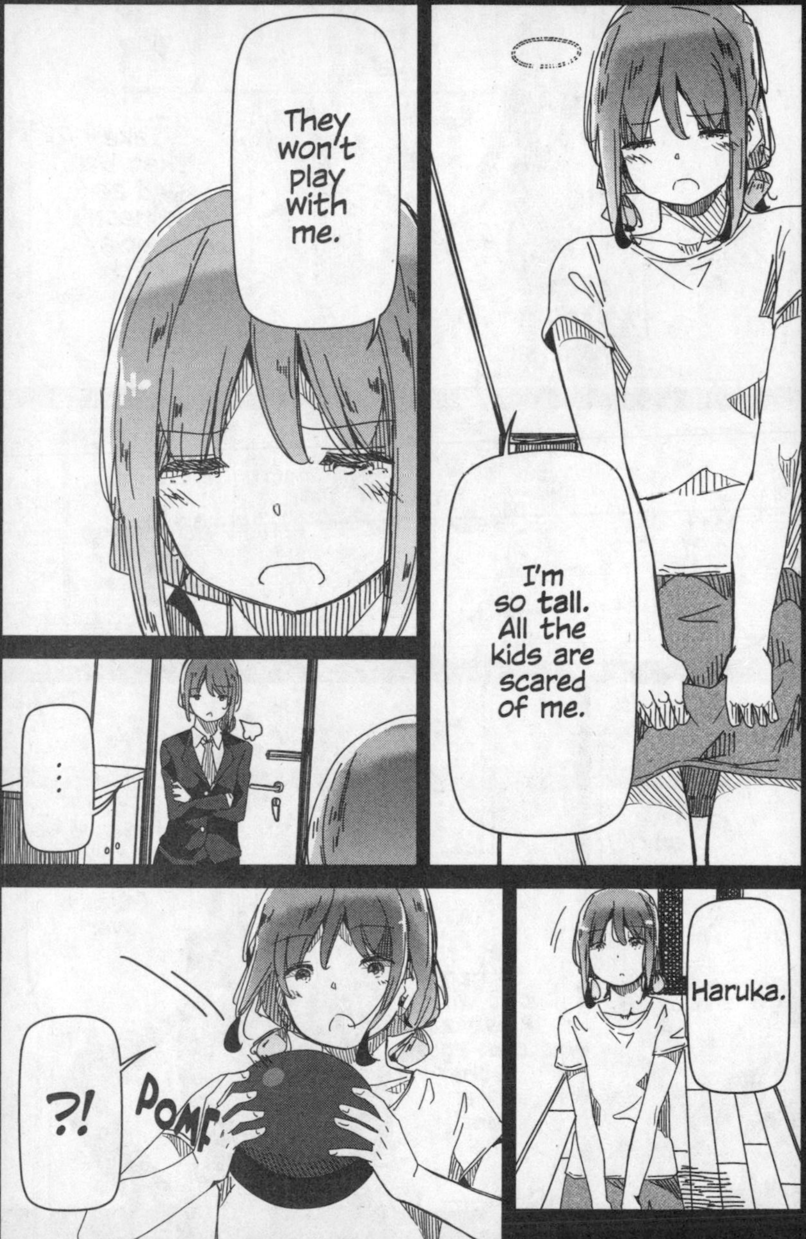
I'm so tall. All the kids are scared of me.
They won't play with me.
...
Haruka.
?!
POMF

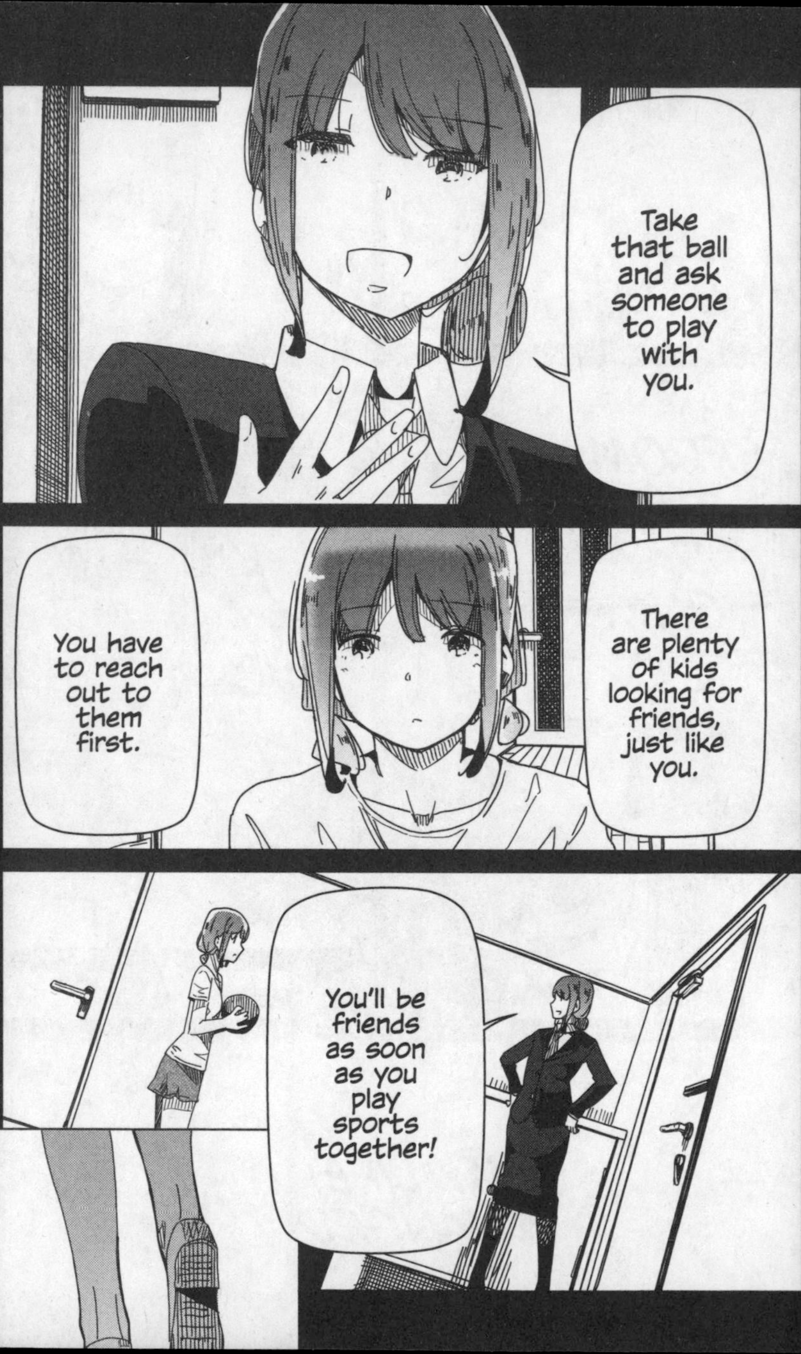
Take that ball and ask someone to play with you.
There are plenty of kids looking for friends, just like you.
You have to reach out to them first.
You'll be friends as soon as you play sports together!

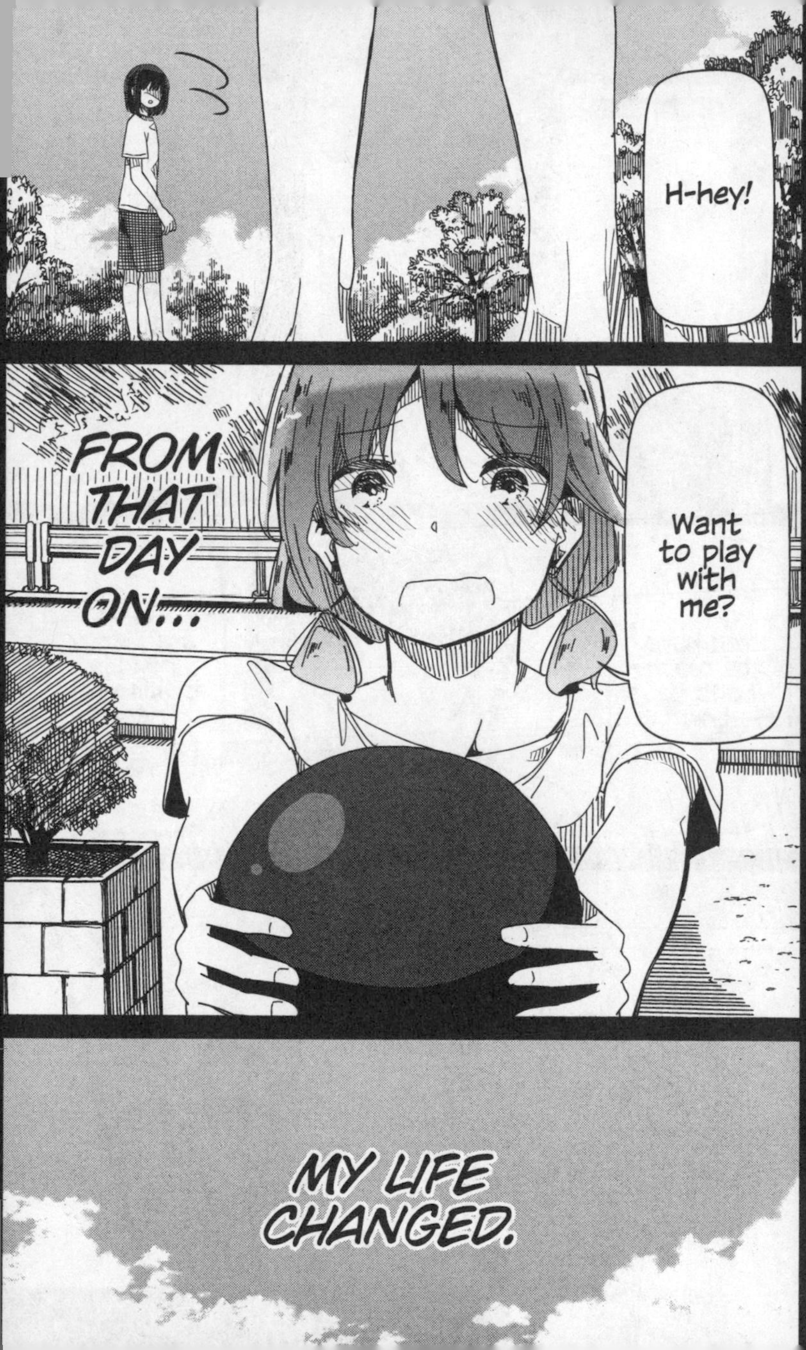
H-hey!
Want to play with me?
FROM THAT DAY ON...
MY LIFE CHANGED.

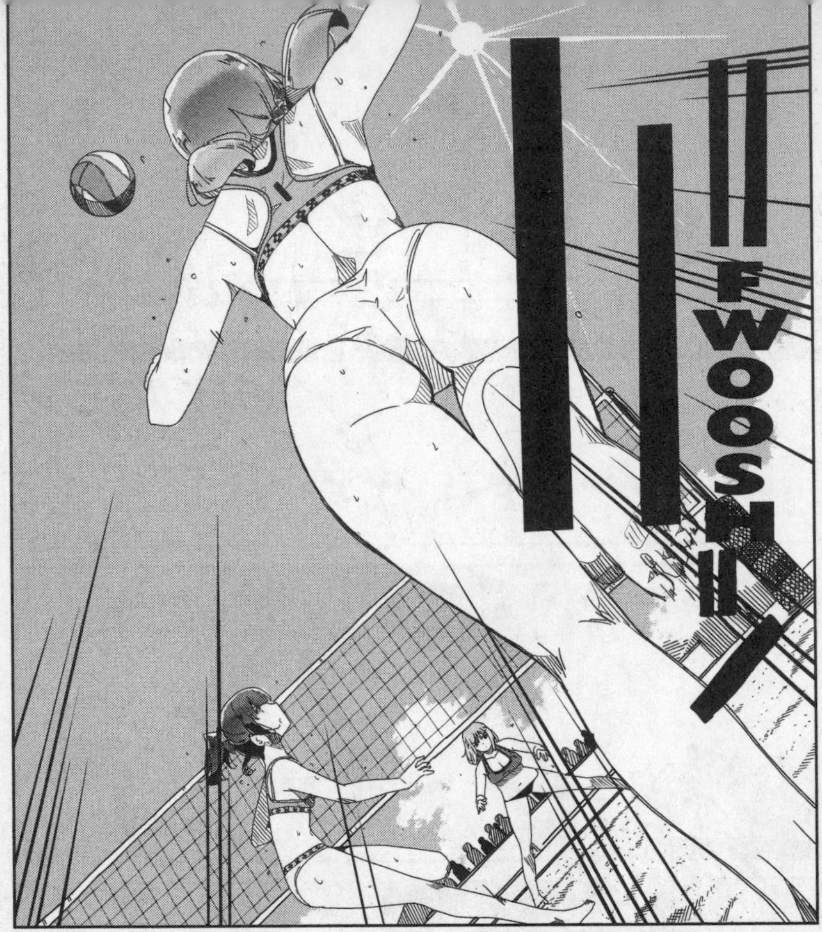
FWOOSH
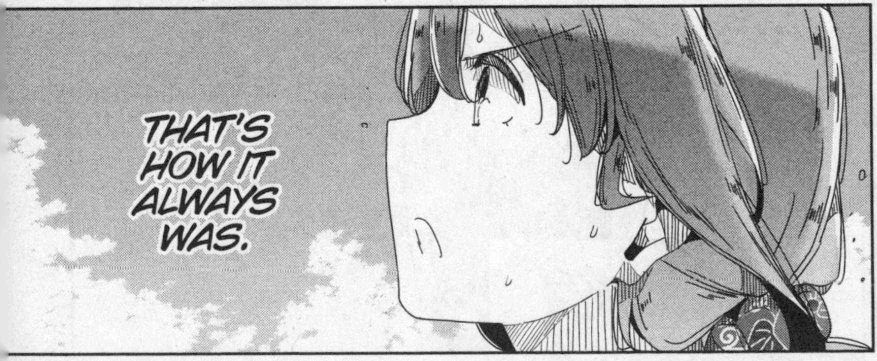
THAT'S HOW IT ALWAYS WAS.

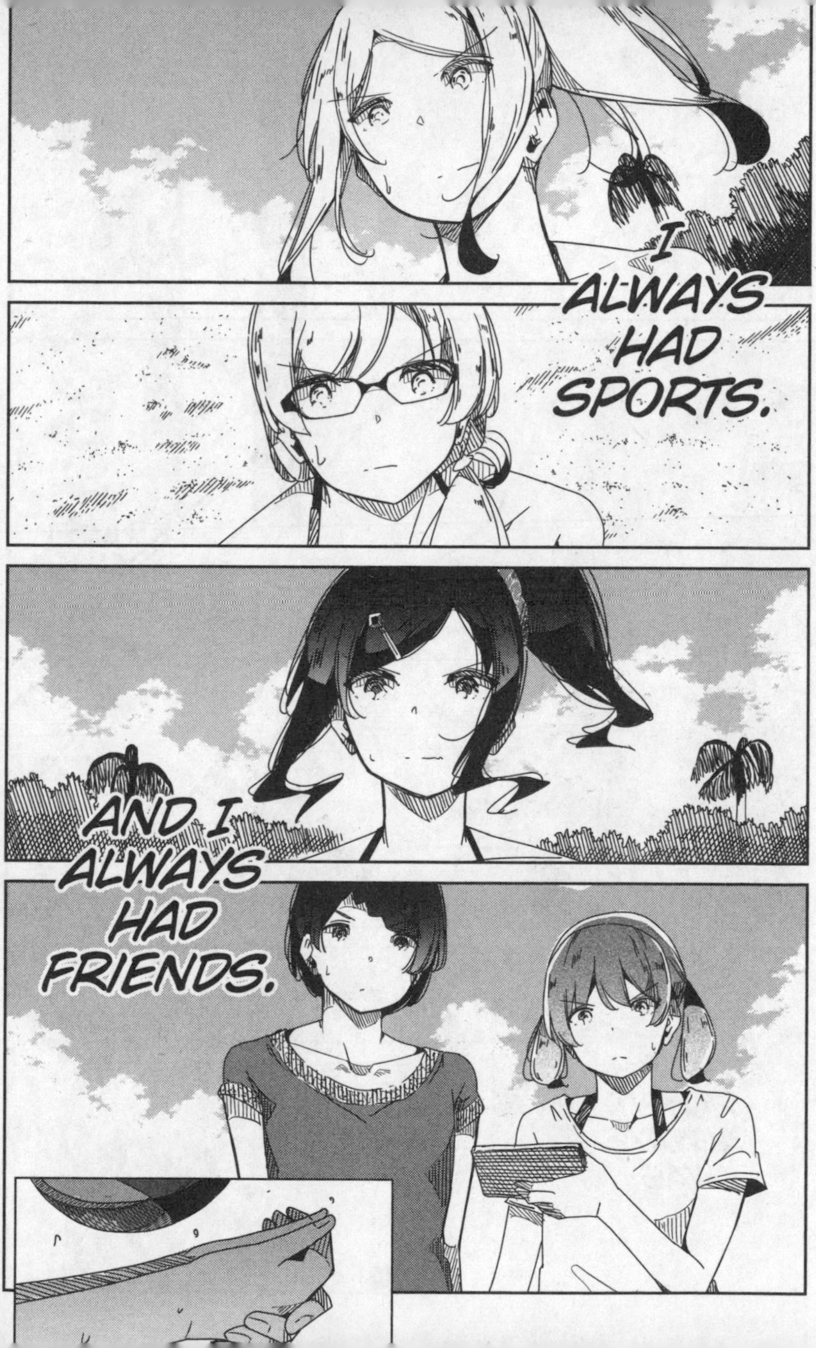
I ALWAYS HAD SPORTS.
AND I ALWAYS HAD FRIENDS.

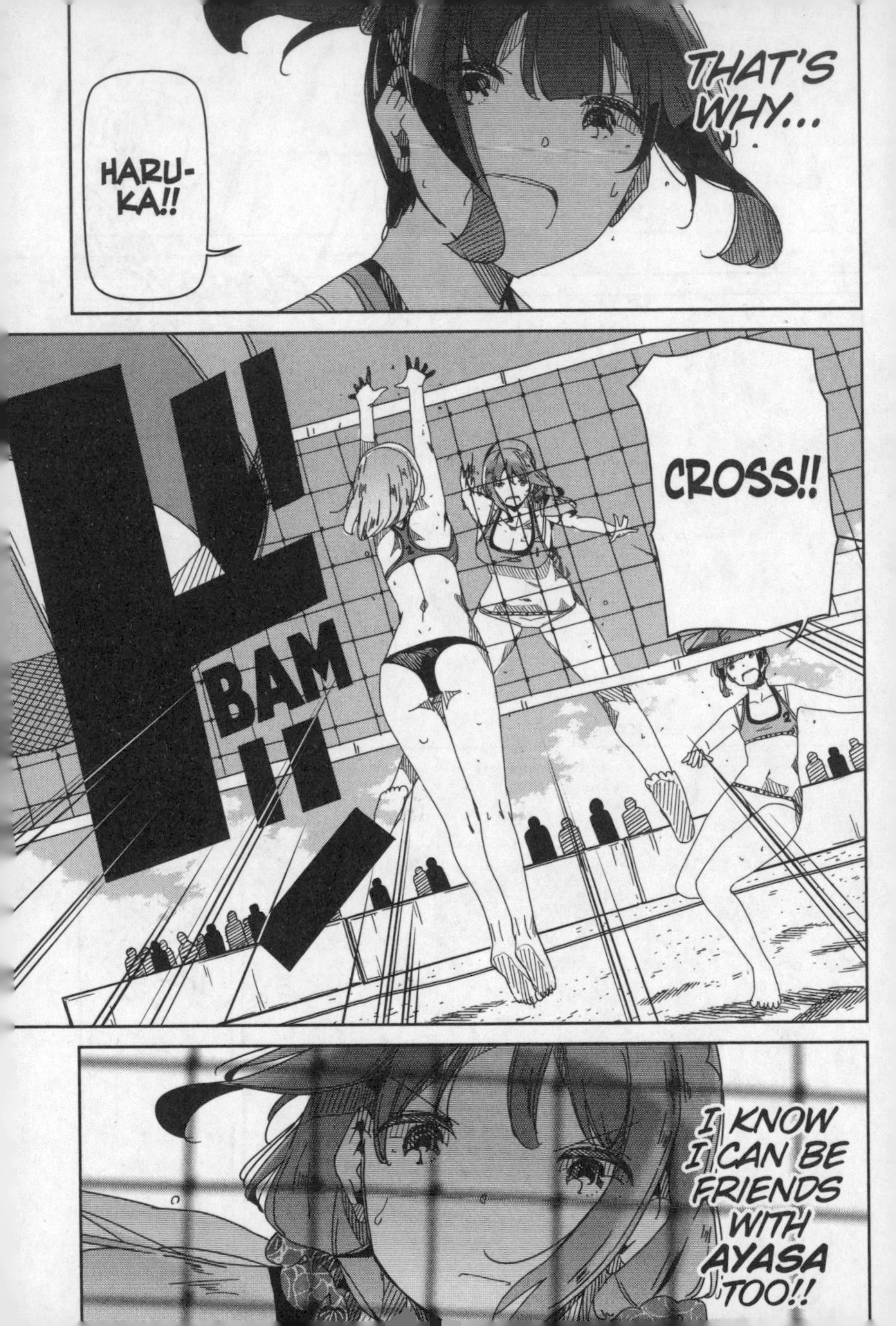
THAT'S WHY...
HARU-KA!!
CROSS!!
BAM!!
I KNOW I CAN BE FRIENDS WITH AYASA TOO!!

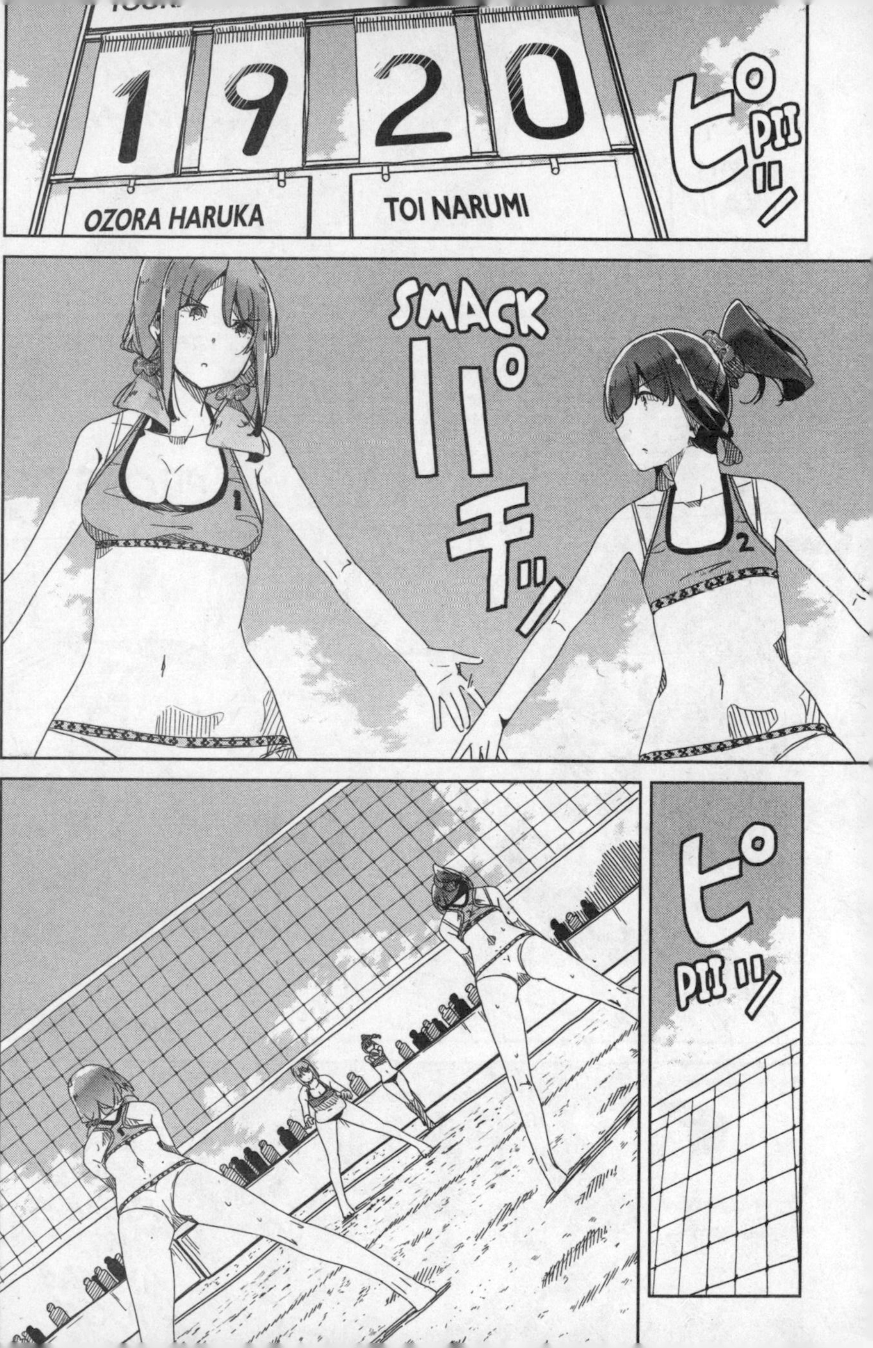
ピッ
PII
19
20
OZORA HARUKA
TOI NARUMI
SMACK
パーチッ
ピッ
PII

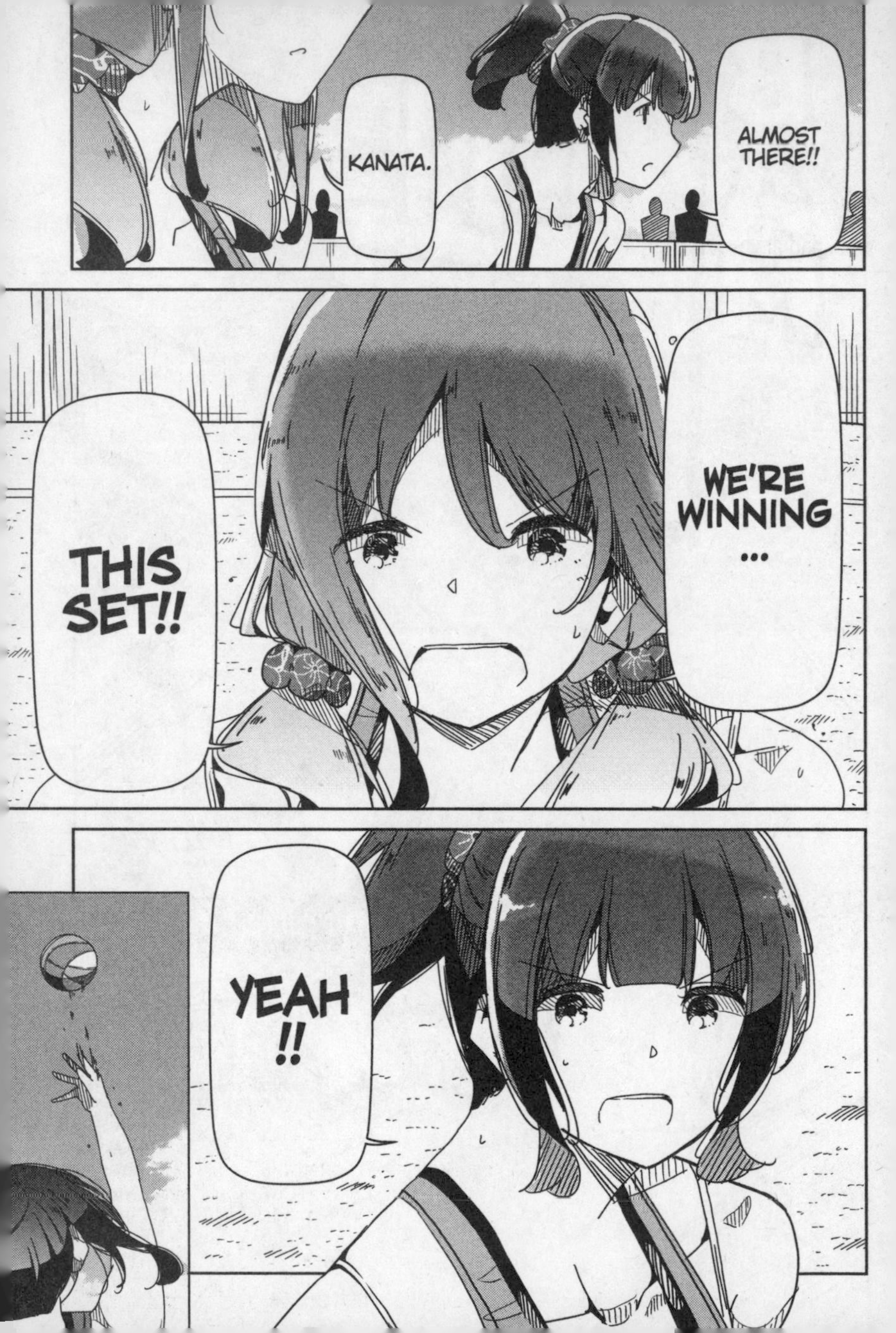
ALMOST THERE!!
KANATA.
WE'RE WINNING ...
THIS SET!!
YEAH !!

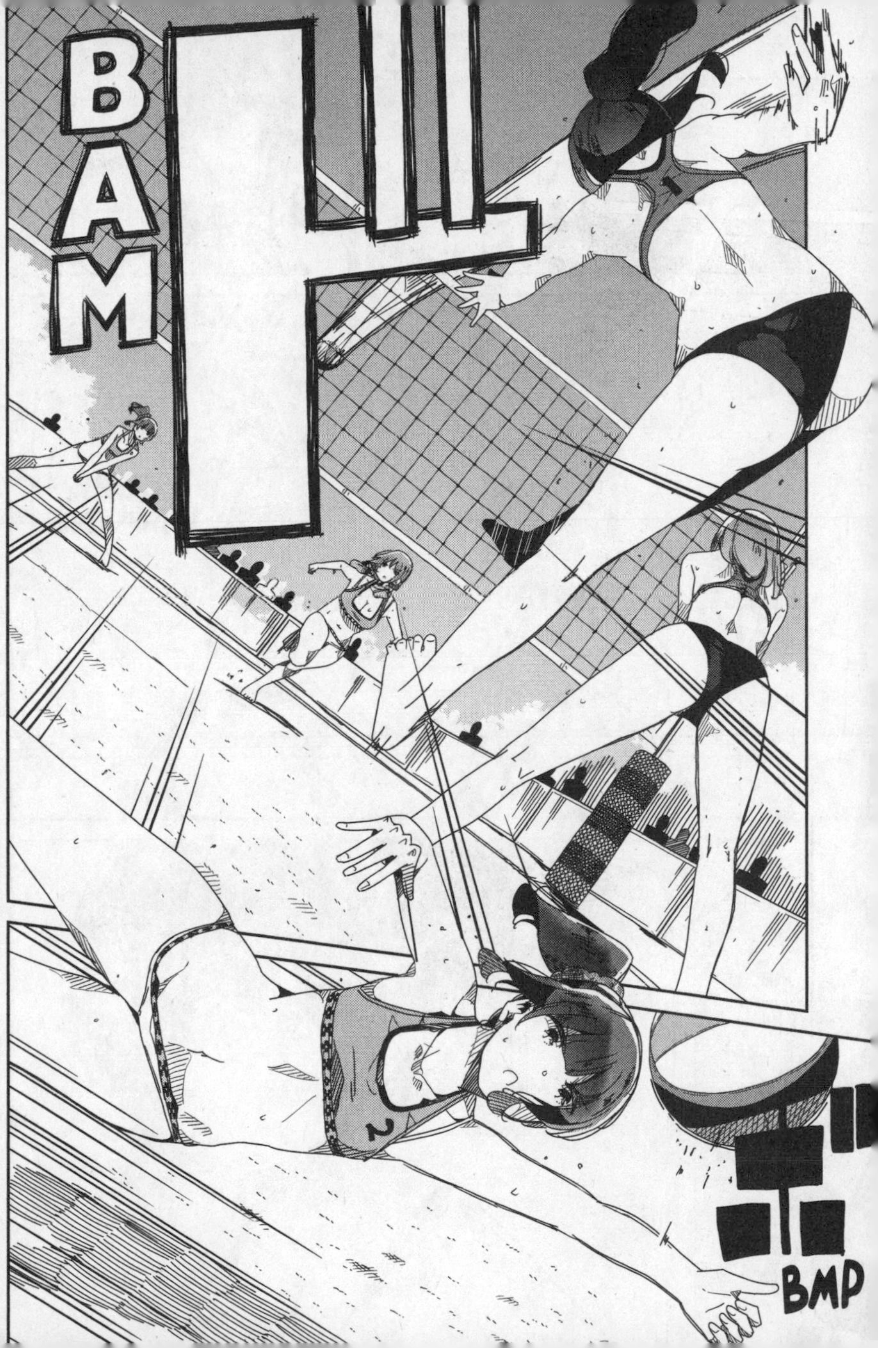
BAM
BMP

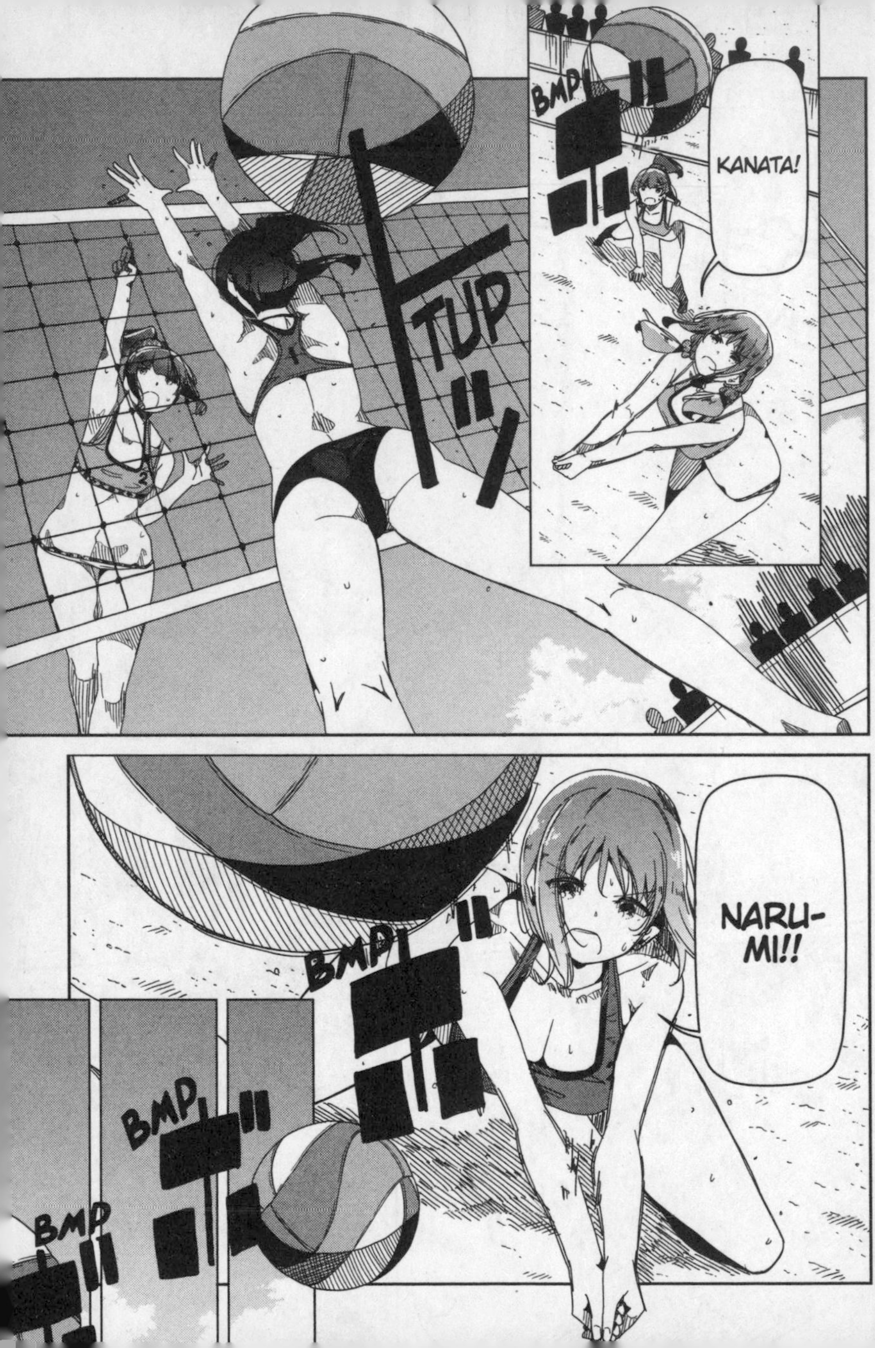

BMP!!
KANATA!
TUP!!
NARU-MI!!
BMP!!
BMP!!
BMP!!

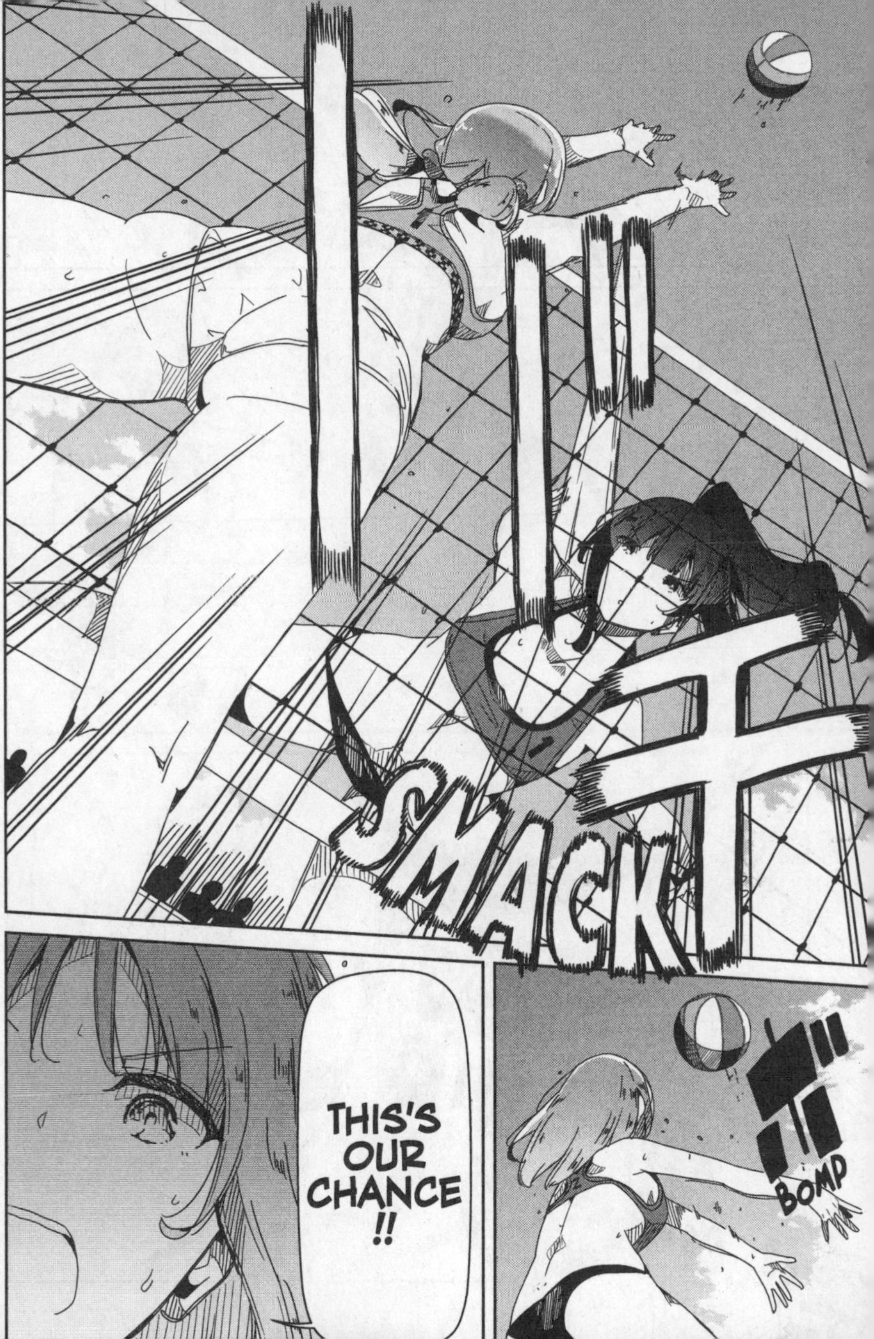
SMACK
BOMP
THIS'S OUR CHANCE !!

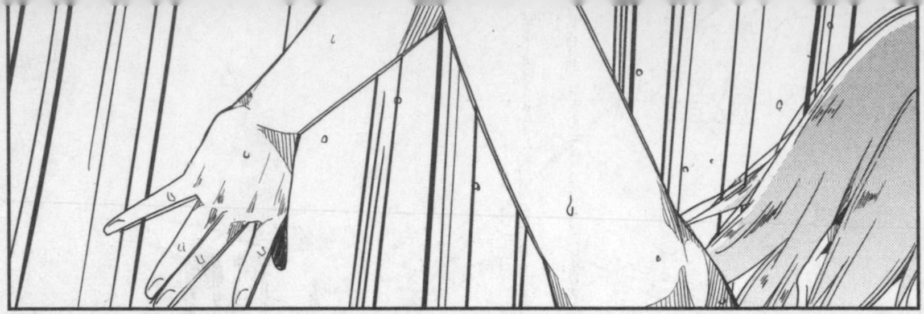

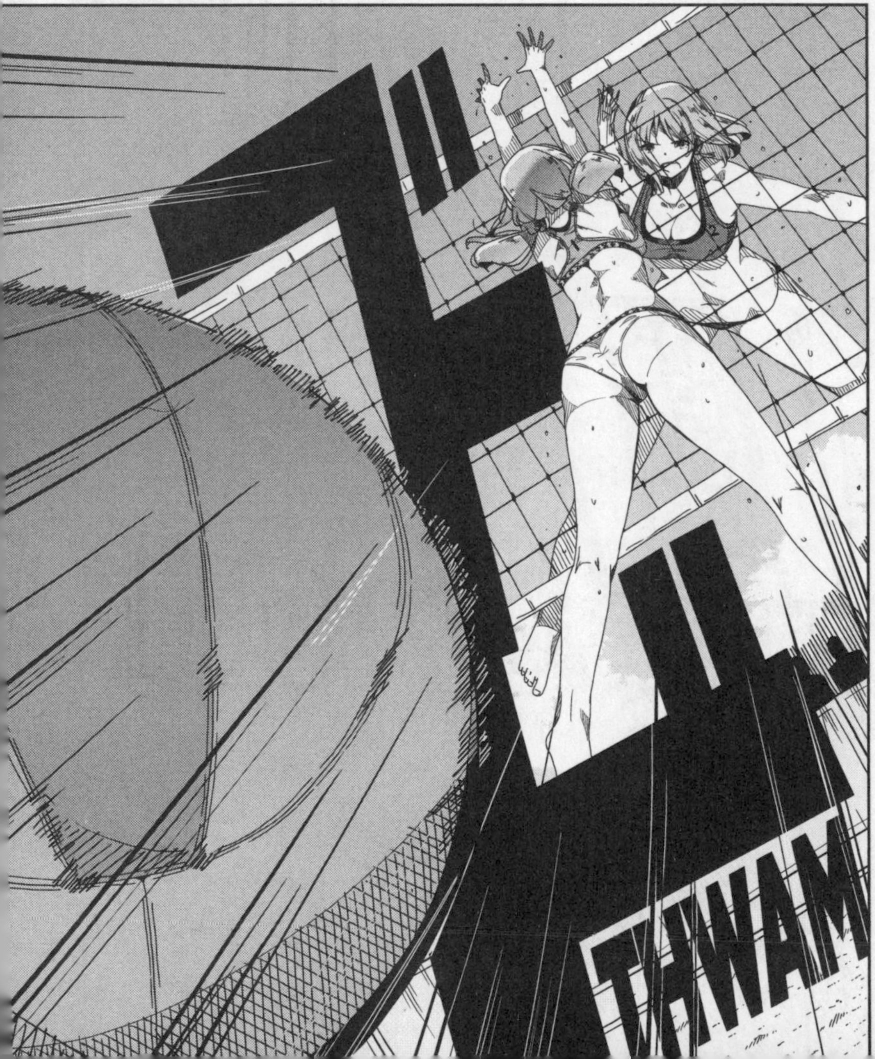
THWAM

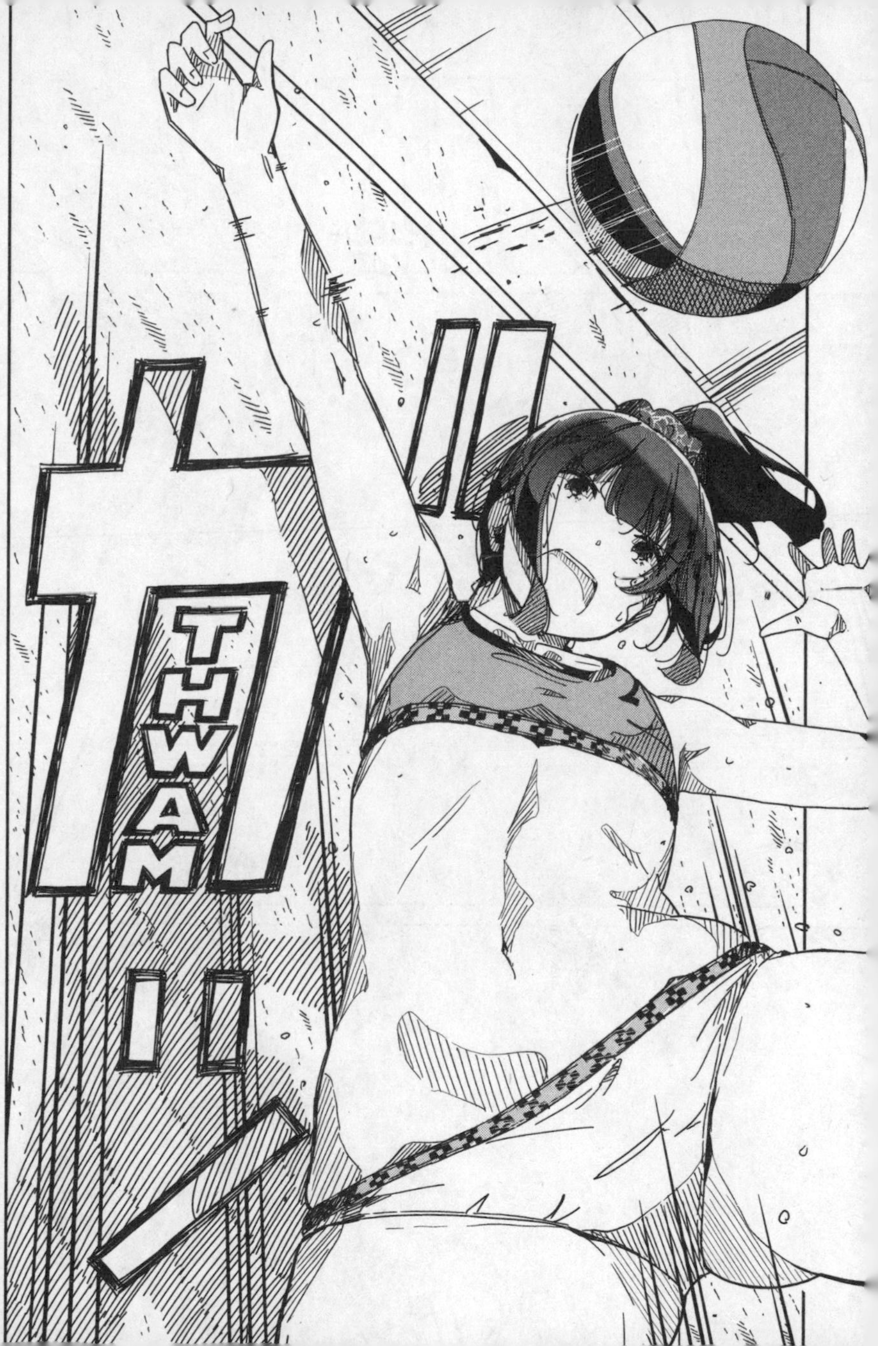
THWAM

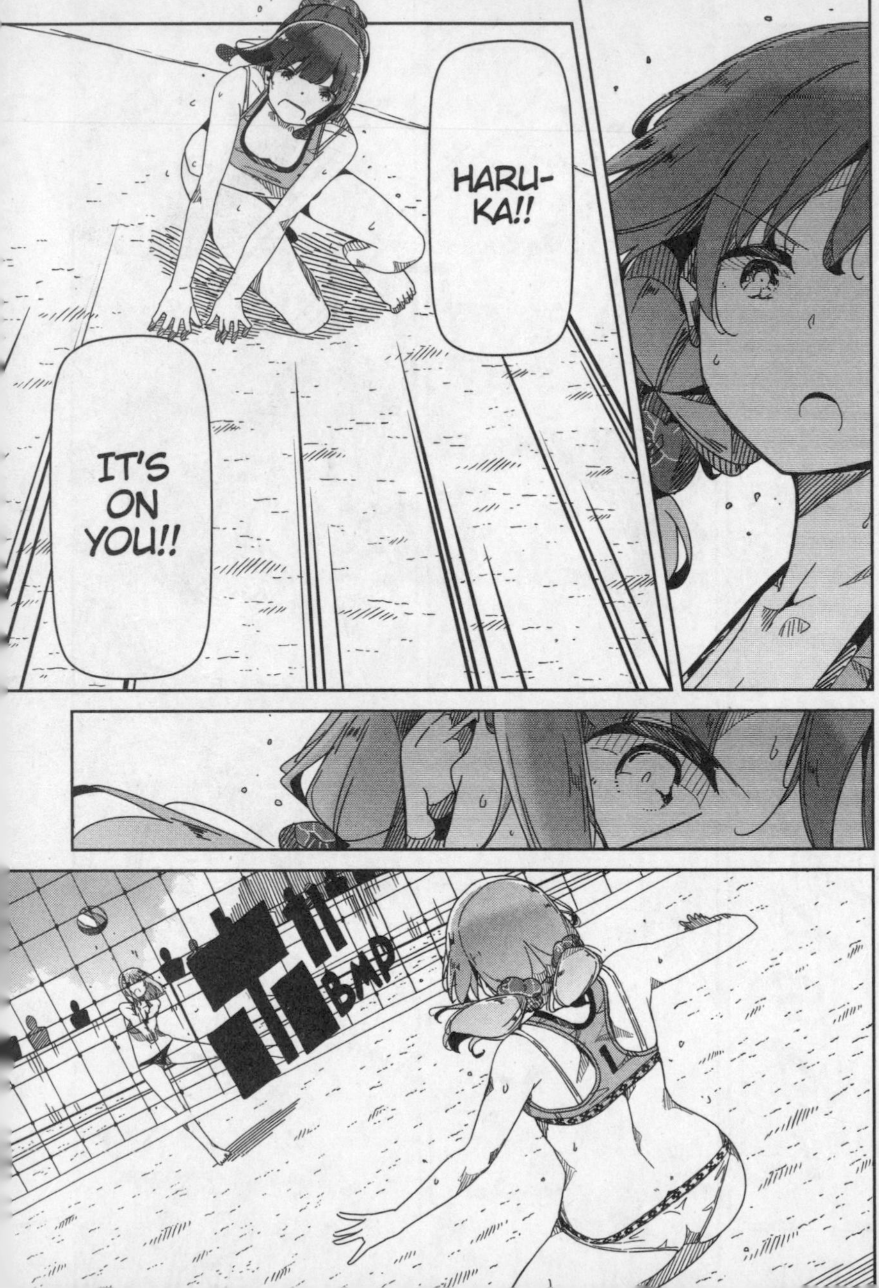
HARU-KA!!
IT'S ON YOU!!
BMP

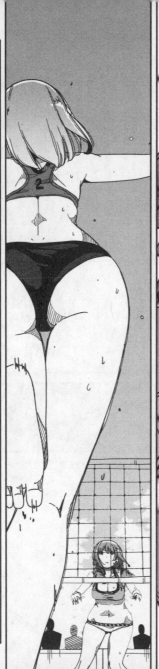

AYASA!

THIS IS AYASA'S CLEANEST CHANCE YET!!

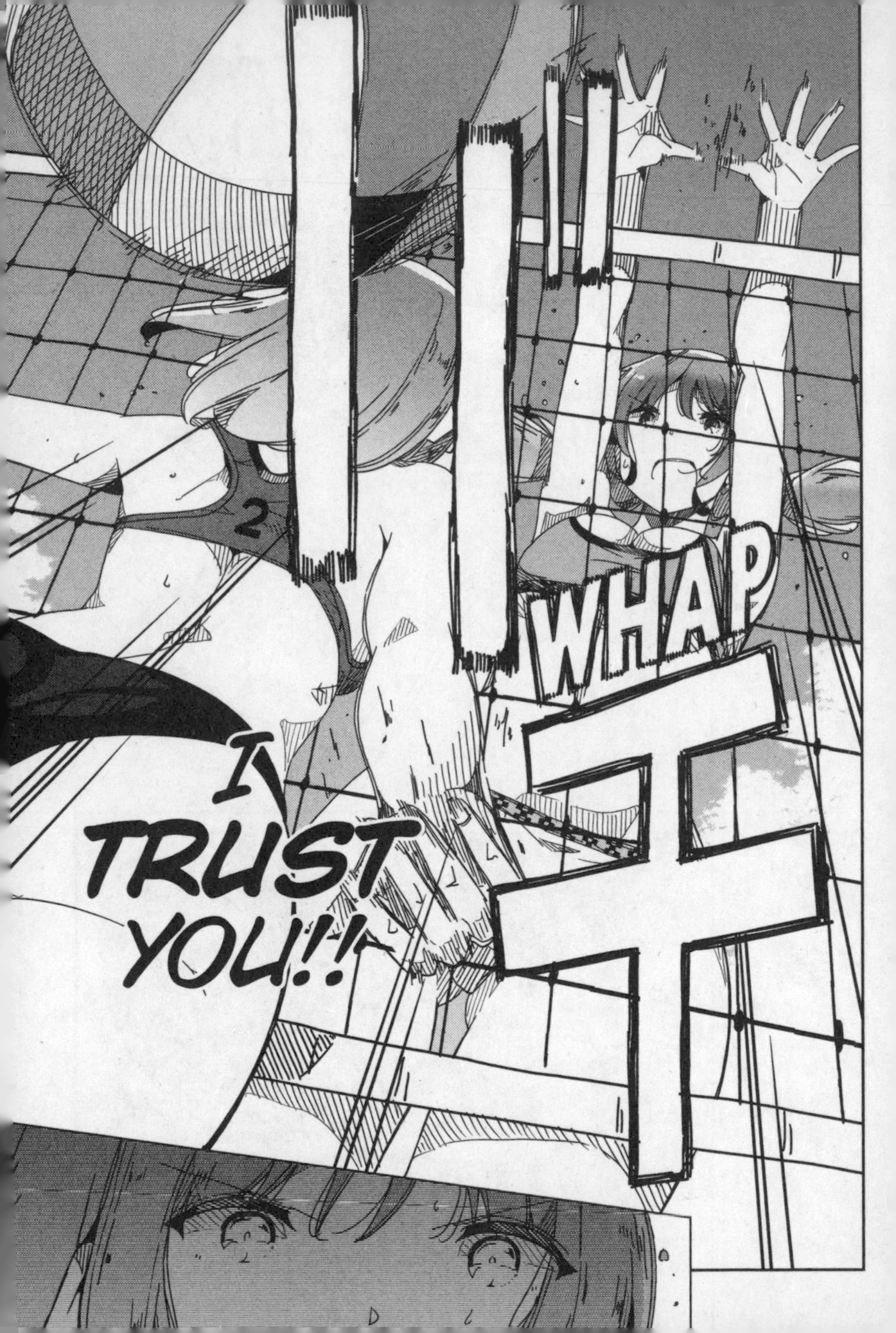
WHAP
I TRUST YOU!!

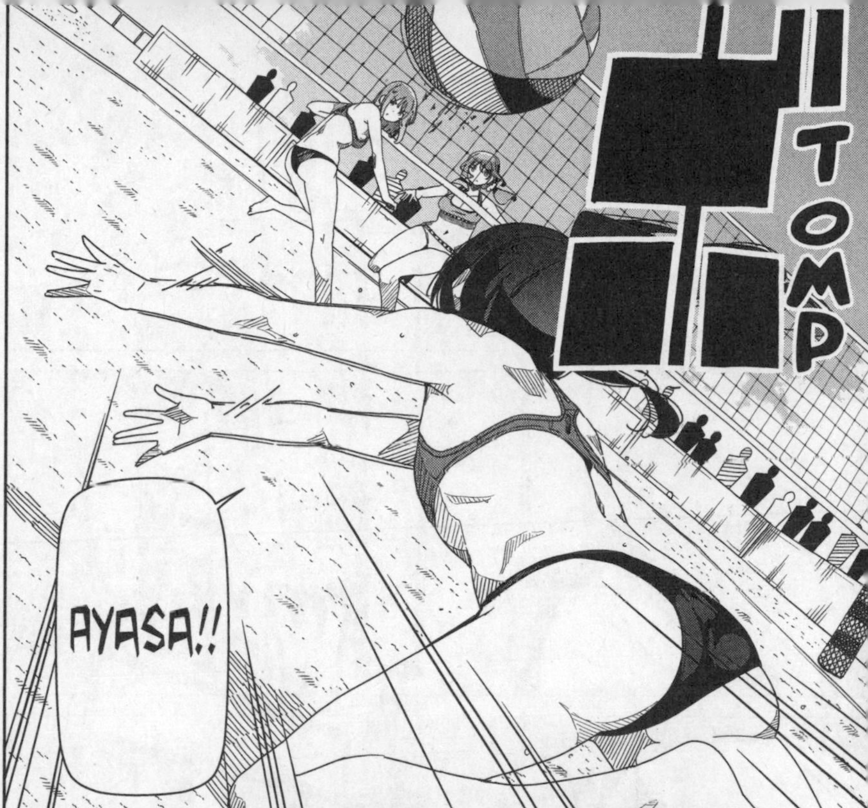
STOMP
AYASA!!
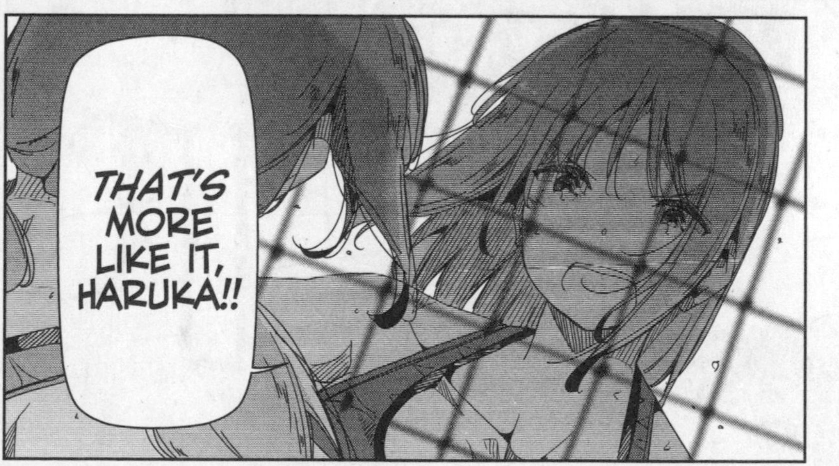
THAT'S MORE LIKE IT, HARUKA!!

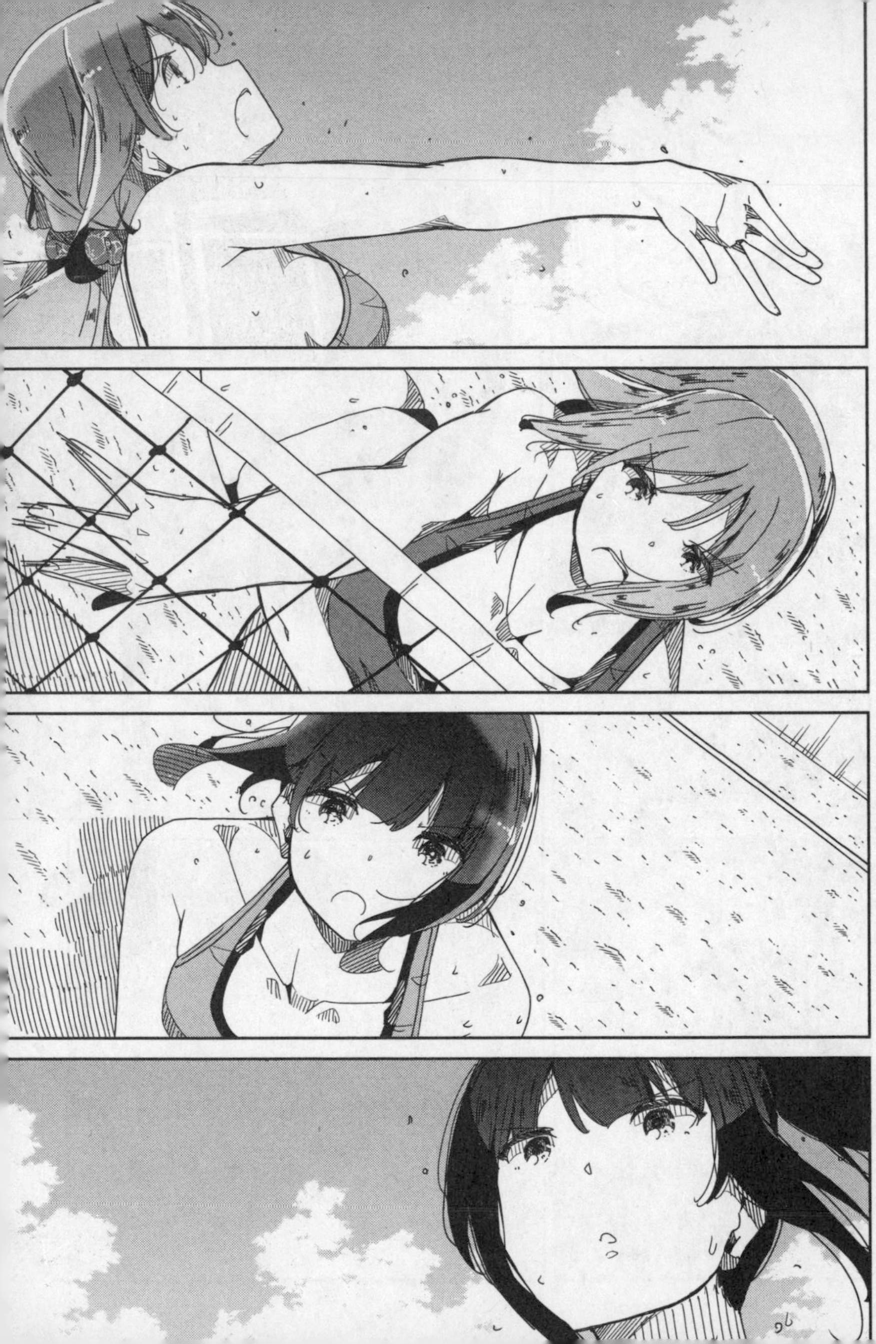

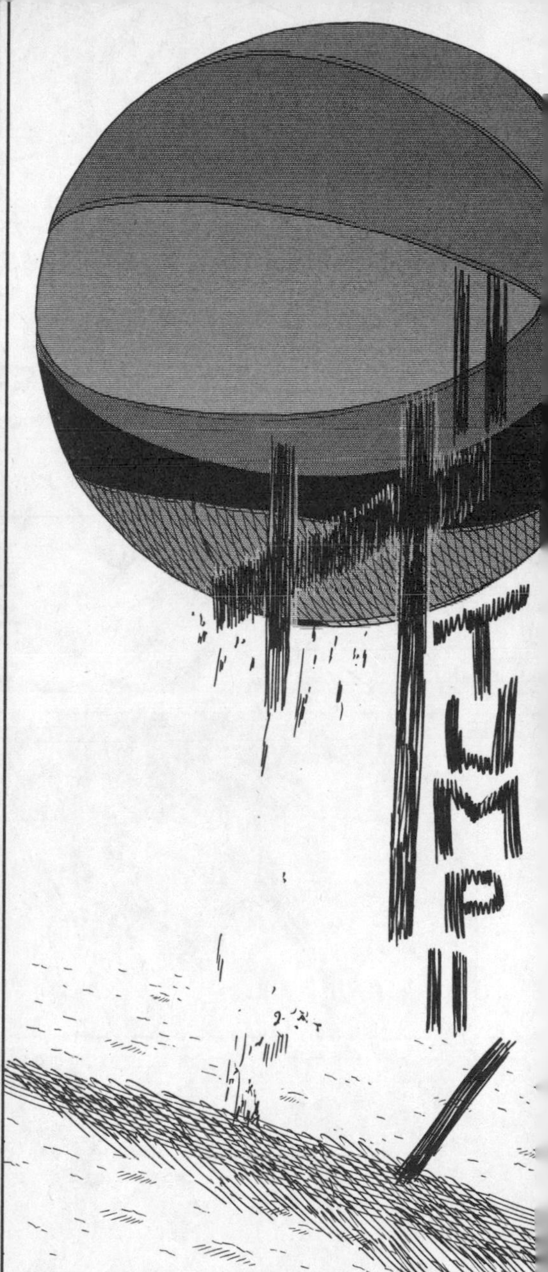
TUMP!!
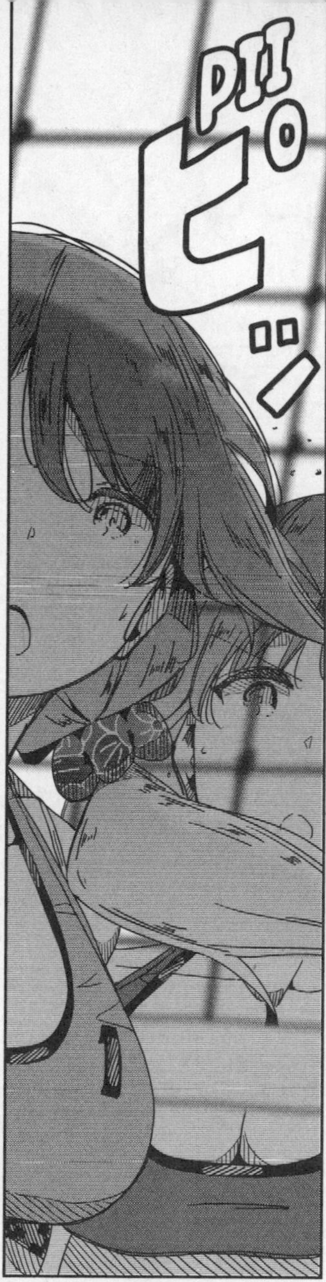
PII
ピッ

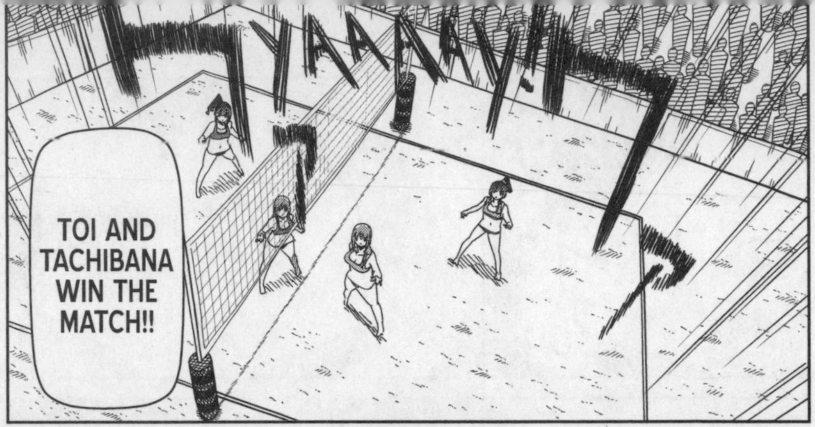
TOI AND TACHIBANA WIN THE MATCH!!

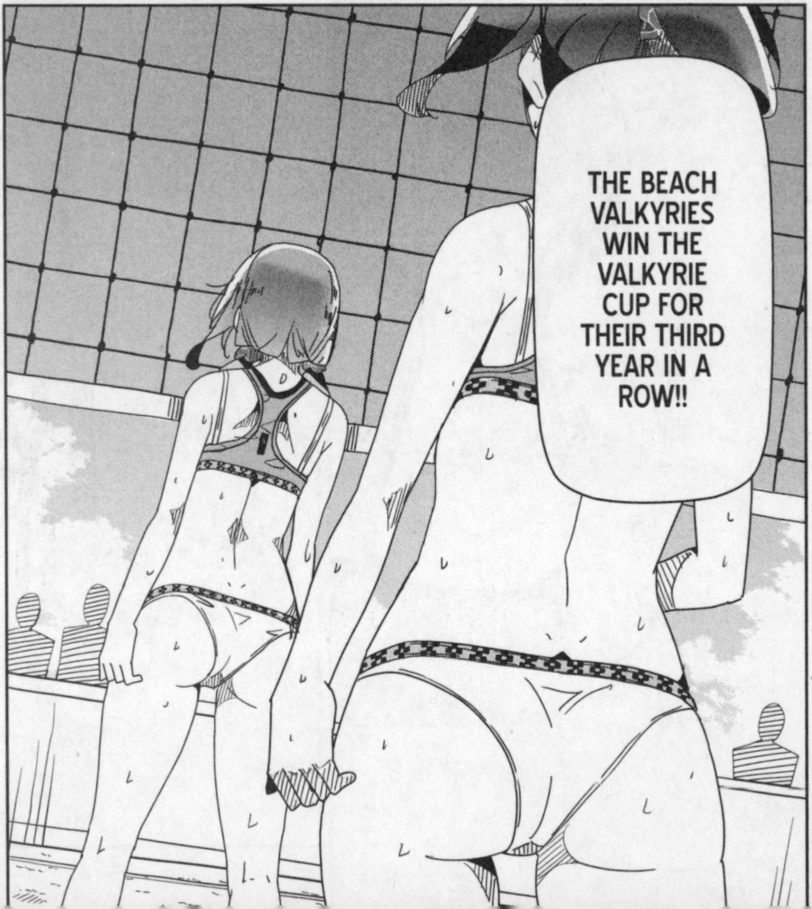
THE BEACH VALKYRIES WIN THE VALKYRIE CUP FOR THEIR THIRD YEAR IN A ROW!!

HARUKA.

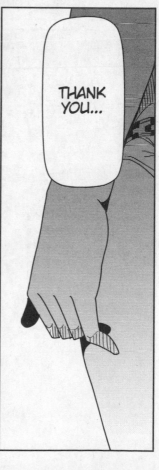

THANK YOU...

FOR GETTING ME THIS FAR.

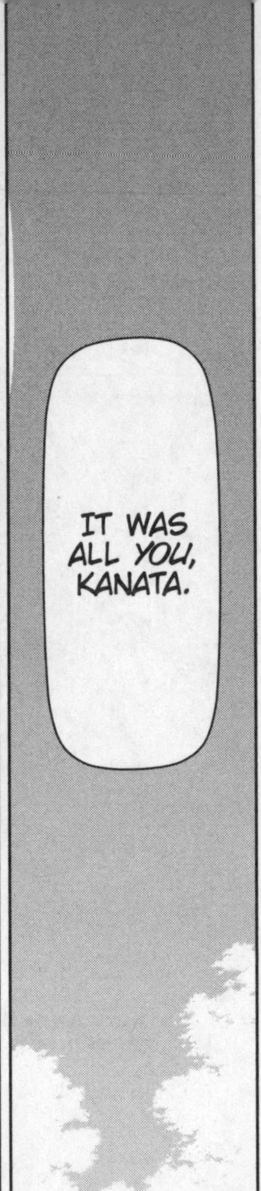
IT WAS ALL YOU, KANATA.
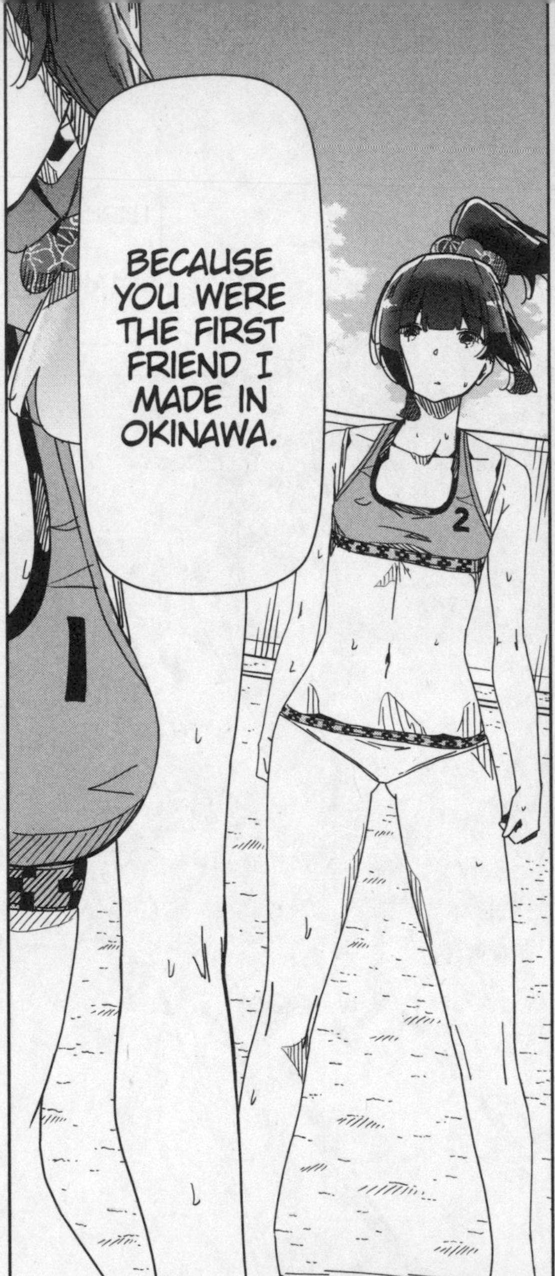
BECAUSE YOU WERE THE FIRST FRIEND I MADE IN OKINAWA.

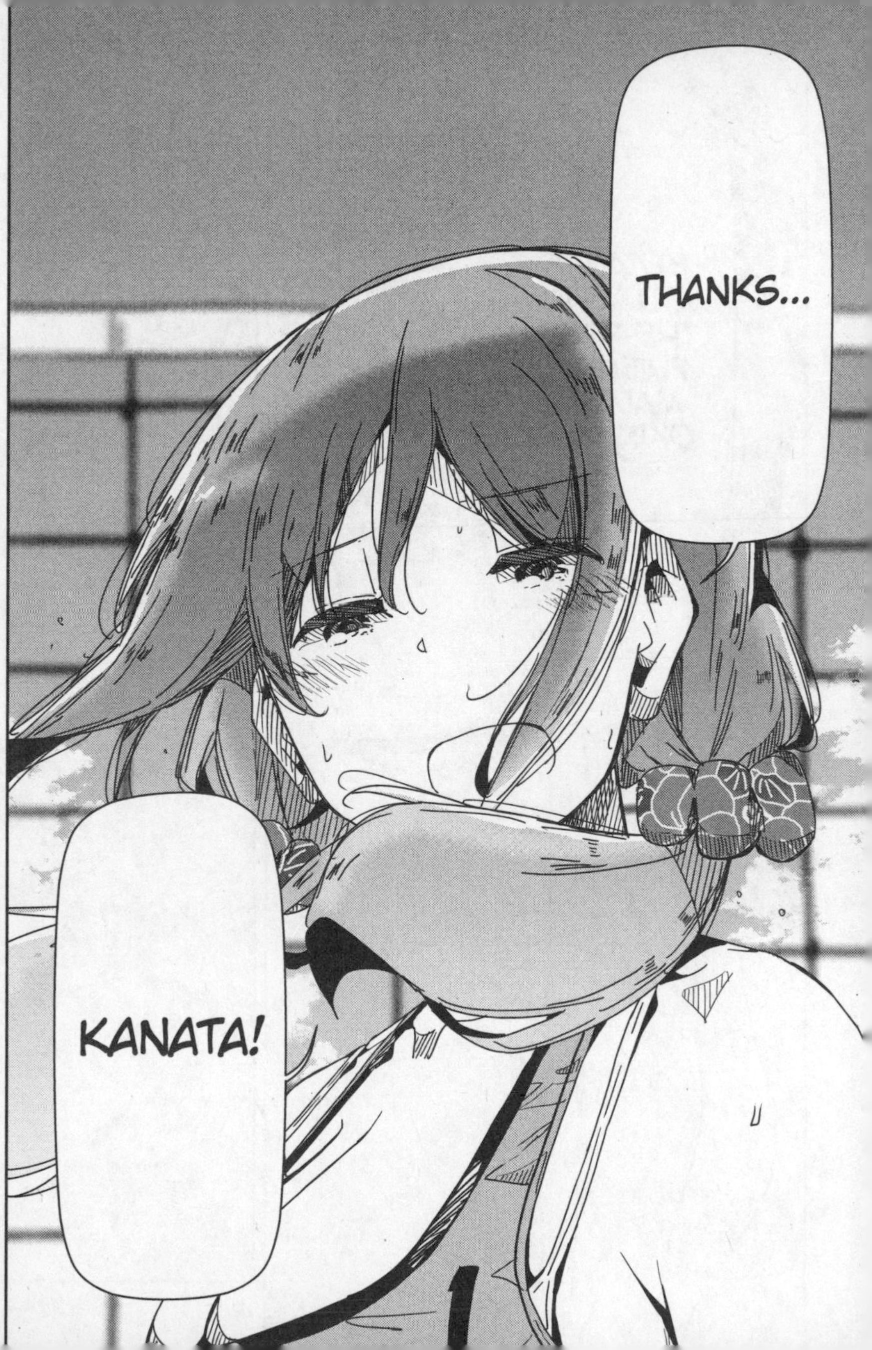
THANKS...
KANATA!

Harukana★Receive

Presented by Nyoijizai

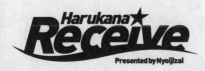

Harukana Receive

Presented by Nyoijizai

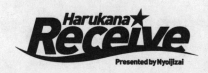

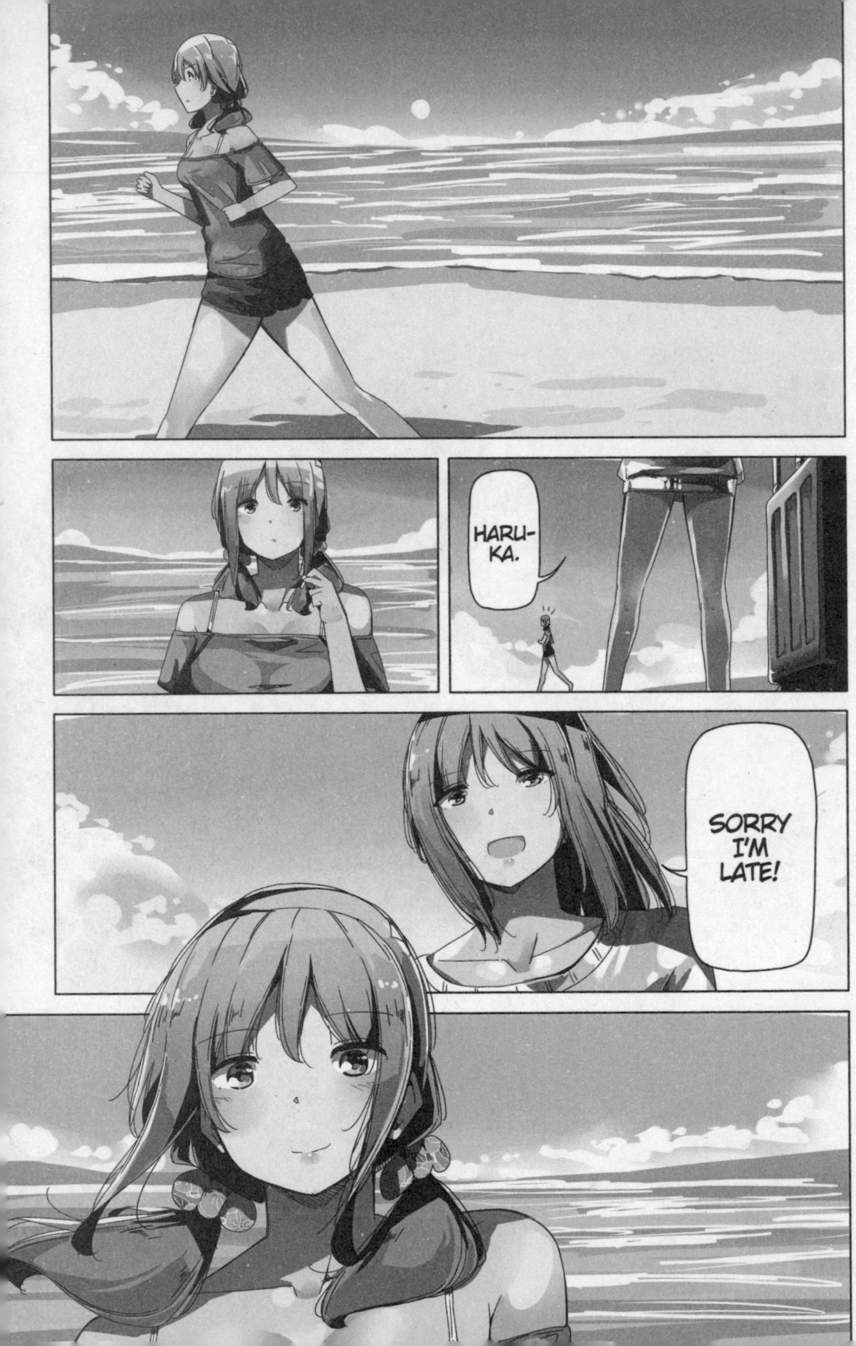
HARU-
KA.
SORRY
I'M
LATE!

Chapter 61: Harukana Receive

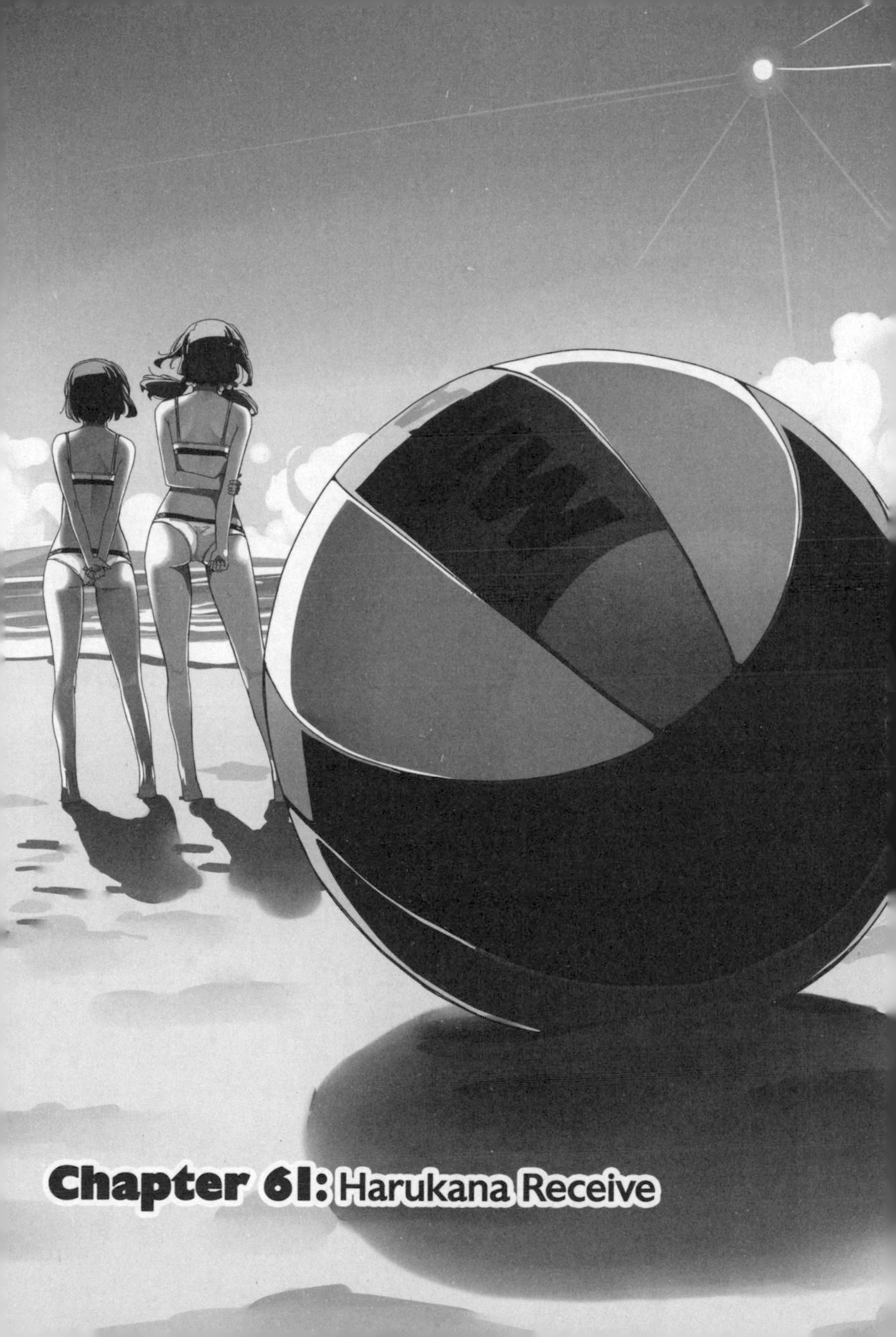

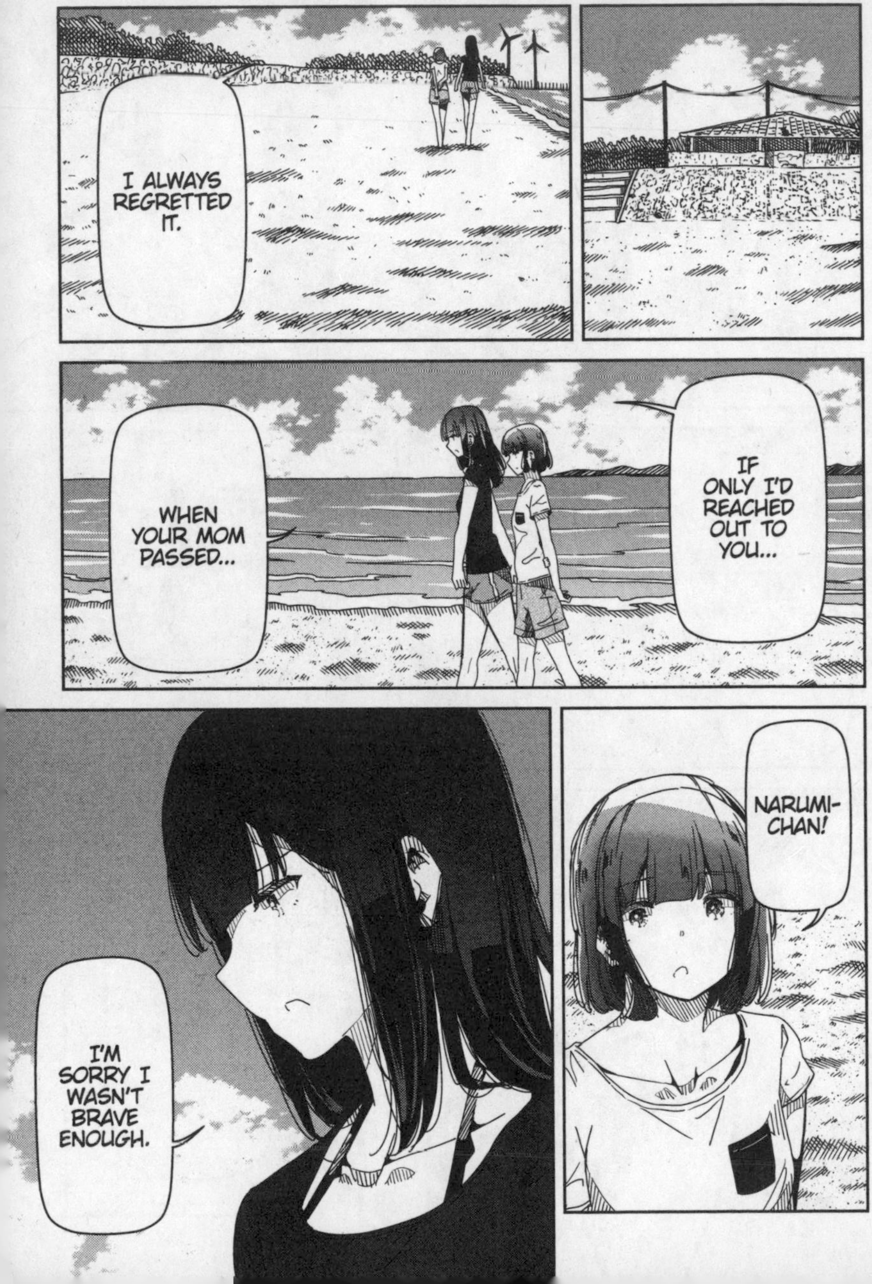
I ALWAYS REGRETTED IT.
IF ONLY I'D REACHED OUT TO YOU...
WHEN YOUR MOM PASSED...
NARUMI-CHAN!
I'M SORRY I WASN'T BRAVE ENOUGH.

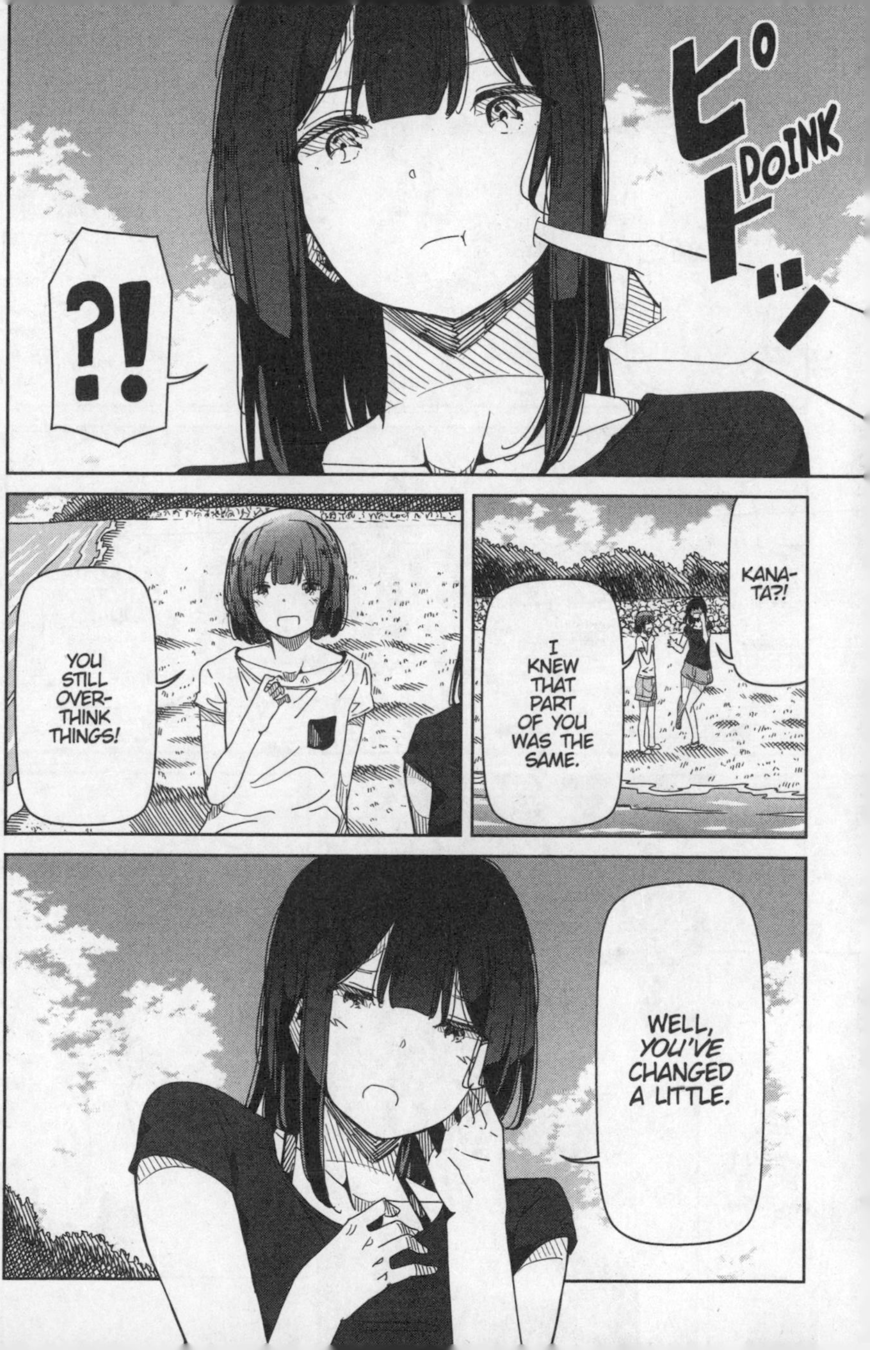
ピ
POINK
ト
ッ
?!
KANA-TA?!
I KNEW THAT PART OF YOU WAS THE SAME.
YOU STILL OVER-THINK THINGS!
WELL, *YOU'VE* CHANGED A LITTLE.

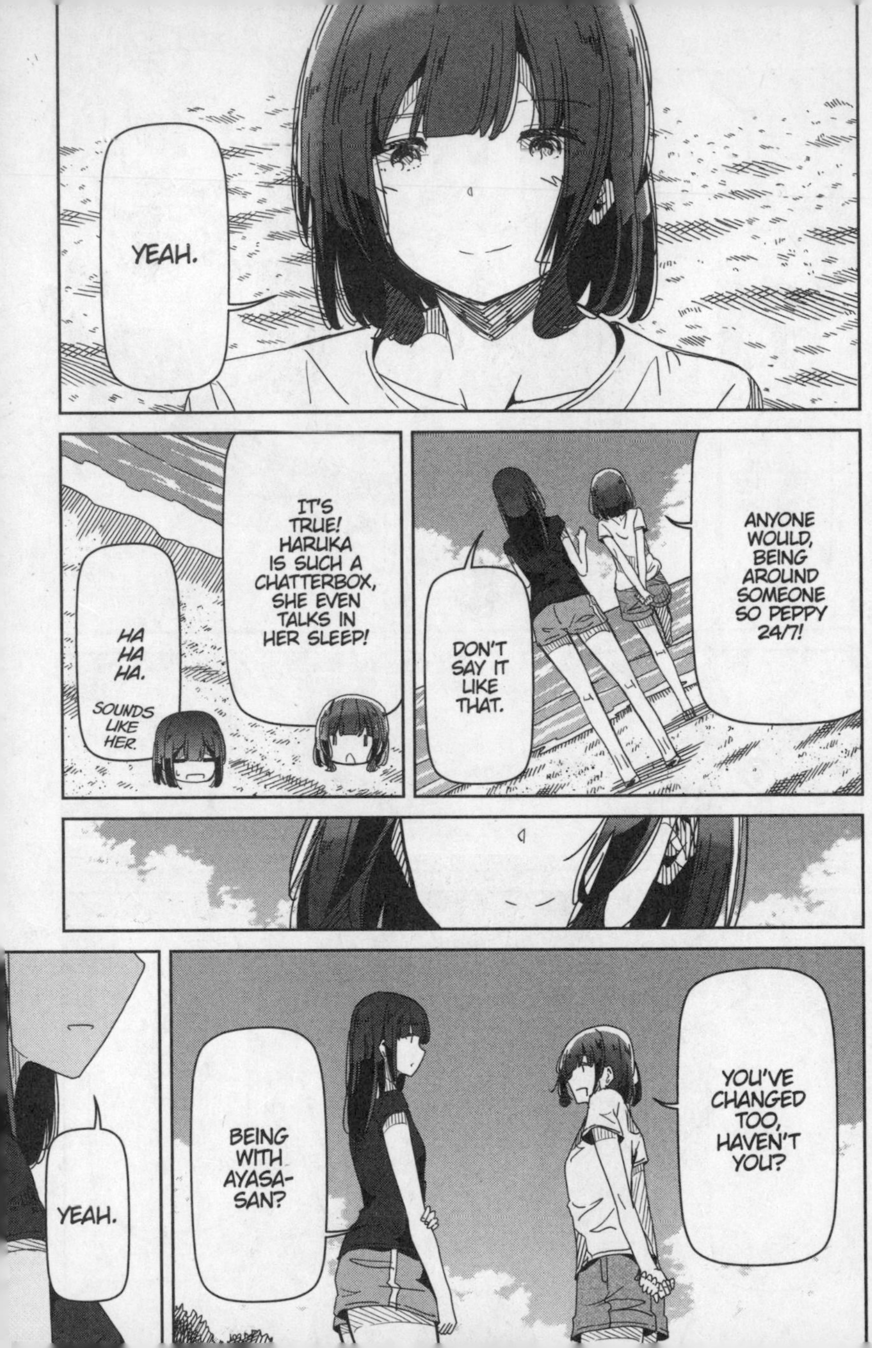
YEAH.
ANYONE WOULD, BEING AROUND SOMEONE SO PEPPY 24/7!
DON'T SAY IT LIKE THAT.
IT'S TRUE! HARUKA IS SUCH A CHATTERBOX, SHE EVEN TALKS IN HER SLEEP!
HA HA HA.
SOUNDS LIKE HER.
YOU'VE CHANGED TOO, HAVEN'T YOU?
BEING WITH AYASA-SAN?
YEAH.

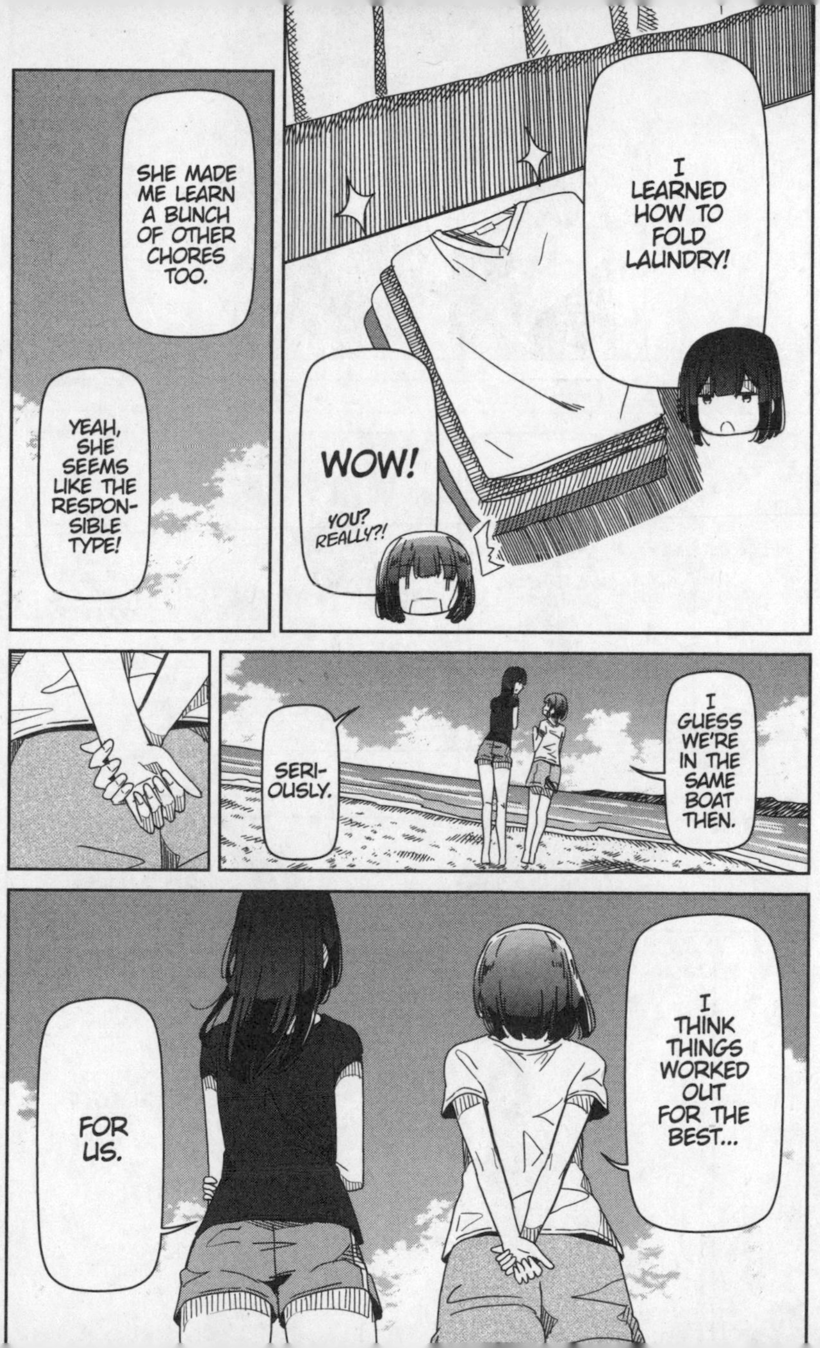
I LEARNED HOW TO FOLD LAUNDRY!
WOW!
YOU? REALLY?!
SHE MADE ME LEARN A BUNCH OF OTHER CHORES TOO.
YEAH, SHE SEEMS LIKE THE RESPON-SIBLE TYPE!
I GUESS WE'RE IN THE SAME BOAT THEN.
SERI-OUSLY.
I THINK THINGS WORKED OUT FOR THE BEST...
FOR US.

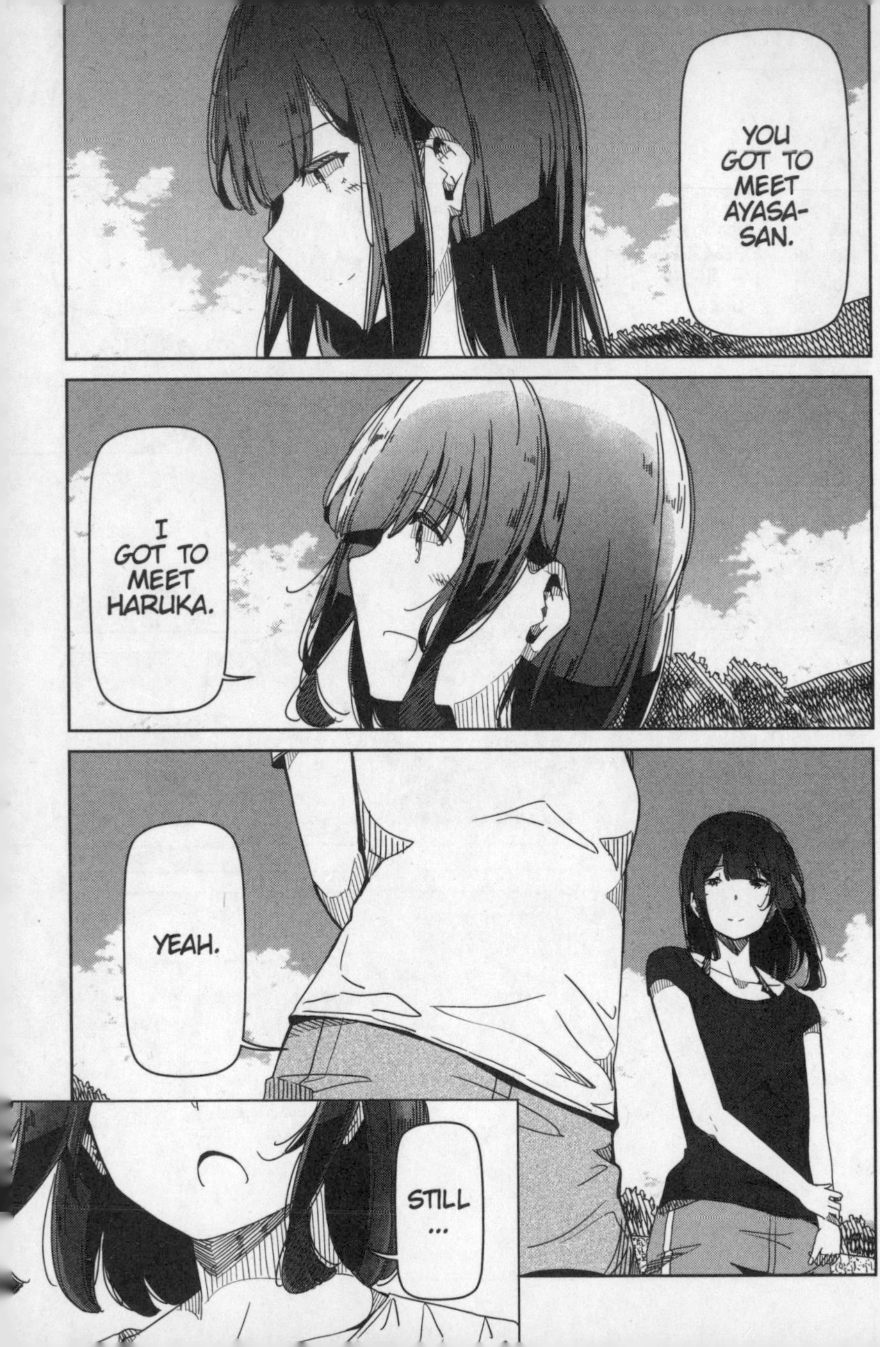
YOU GOT TO MEET AYASA-SAN.
I GOT TO MEET HARUKA.
YEAH.
STILL ...

I'M THE ONE WHO SHOULD APOLOGIZE.

I'M SORRY.

I CLOSED MYSELF OFF AND RAN AWAY ON YOU.

I'M REALLY SORRY.

KANATA...

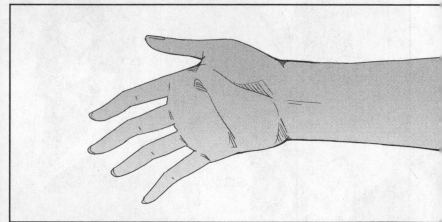

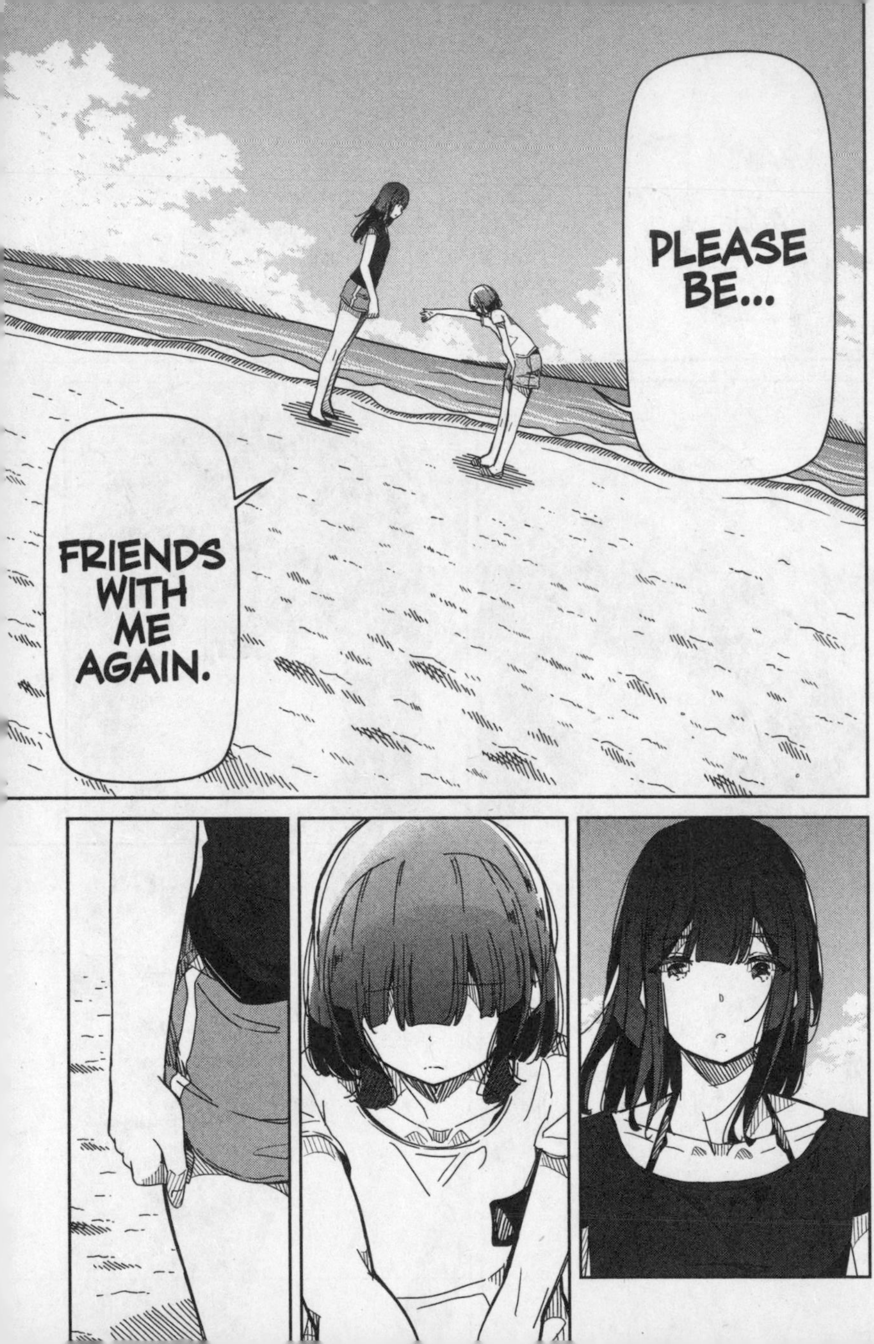
PLEASE BE...
FRIENDS WITH ME AGAIN.

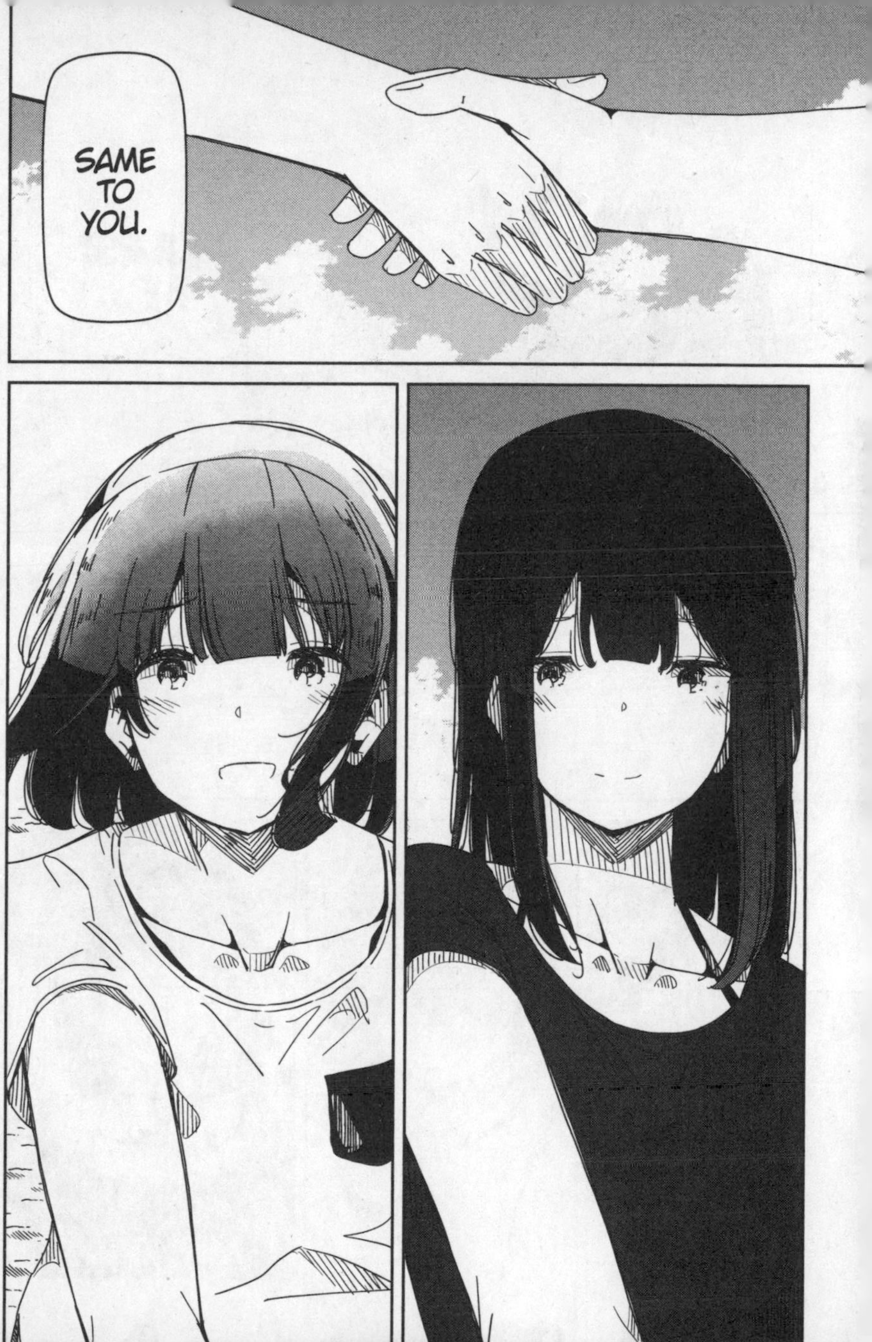
SAME TO YOU.

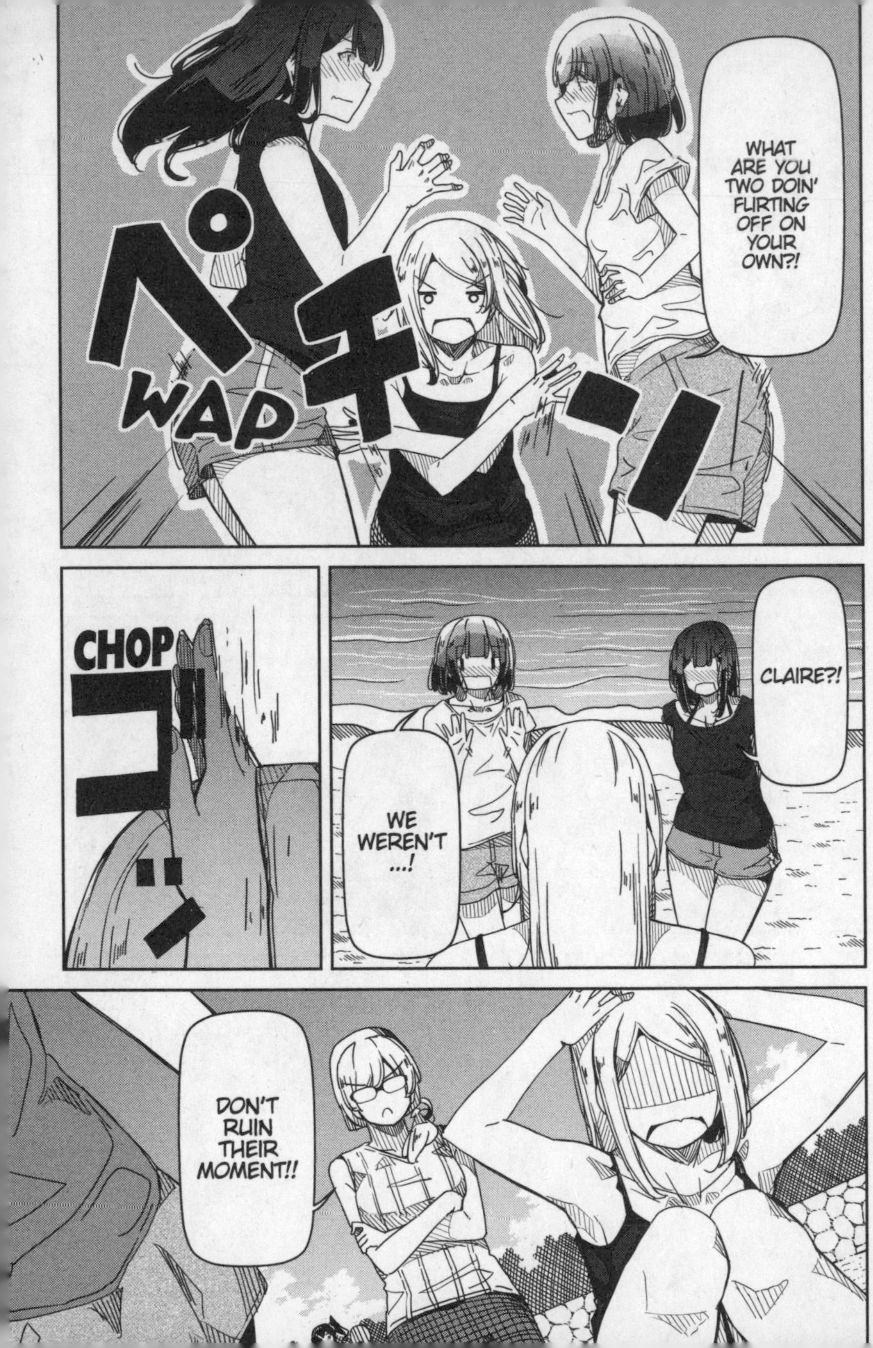
WHAT ARE YOU TWO DOIN' FLIRTING OFF ON YOUR OWN?!
WAP
CLAIRE?!
WE WEREN'T ...!
CHOP
DON'T RUIN THEIR MOMENT!!

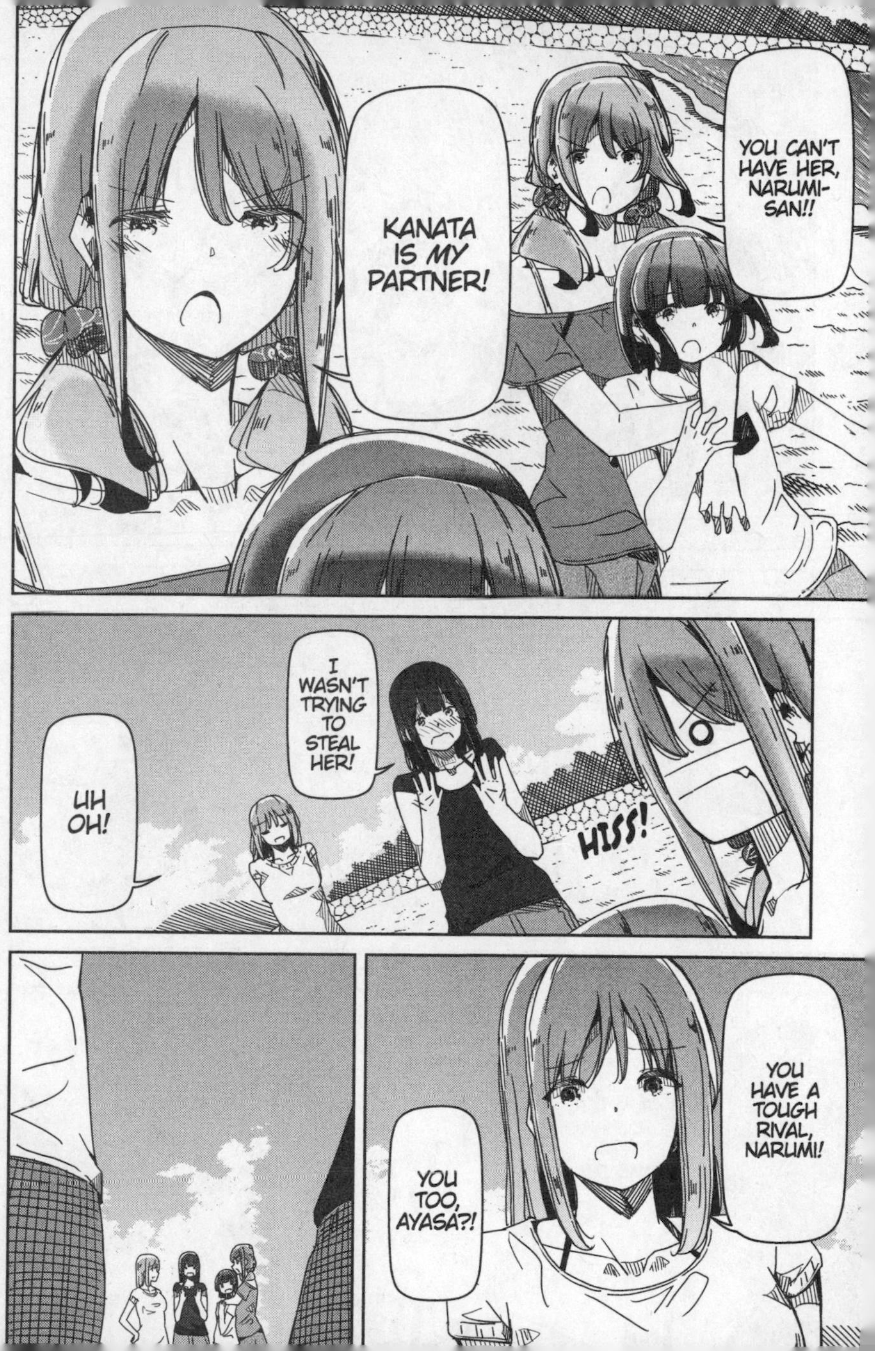
YOU CAN'T HAVE HER, NARUMI-SAN!!
KANATA IS MY PARTNER!
HISS!
I WASN'T TRYING TO STEAL HER!
UH OH!
YOU HAVE A TOUGH RIVAL, NARUMI!
YOU TOO, AYASA?!

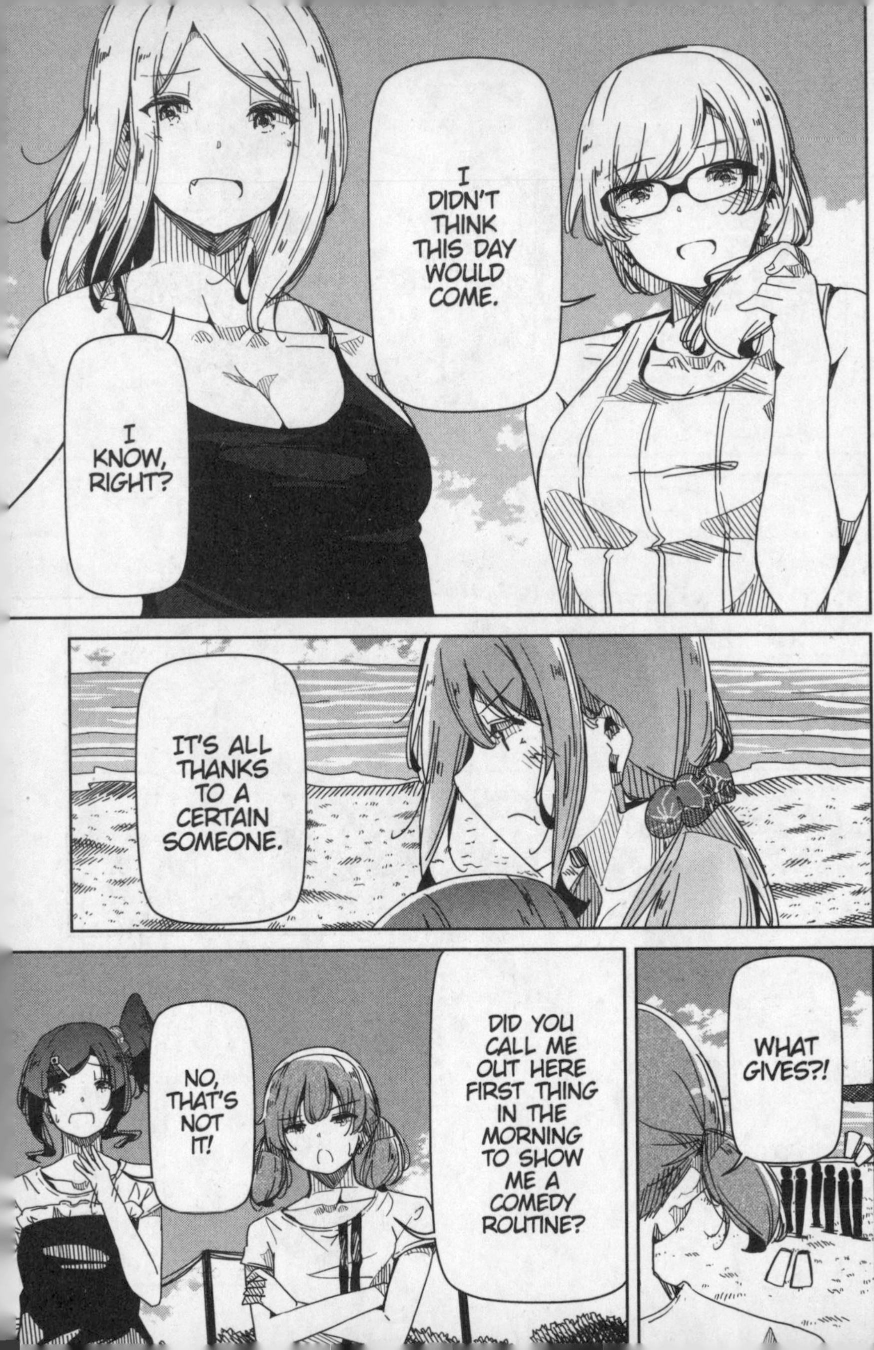
I DIDN'T THINK THIS DAY WOULD COME.
I KNOW, RIGHT?
IT'S ALL THANKS TO A CERTAIN SOMEONE.
WHAT GIVES?!
DID YOU CALL ME OUT HERE FIRST THING IN THE MORNING TO SHOW ME A COMEDY ROUTINE?
NO, THAT'S NOT IT!

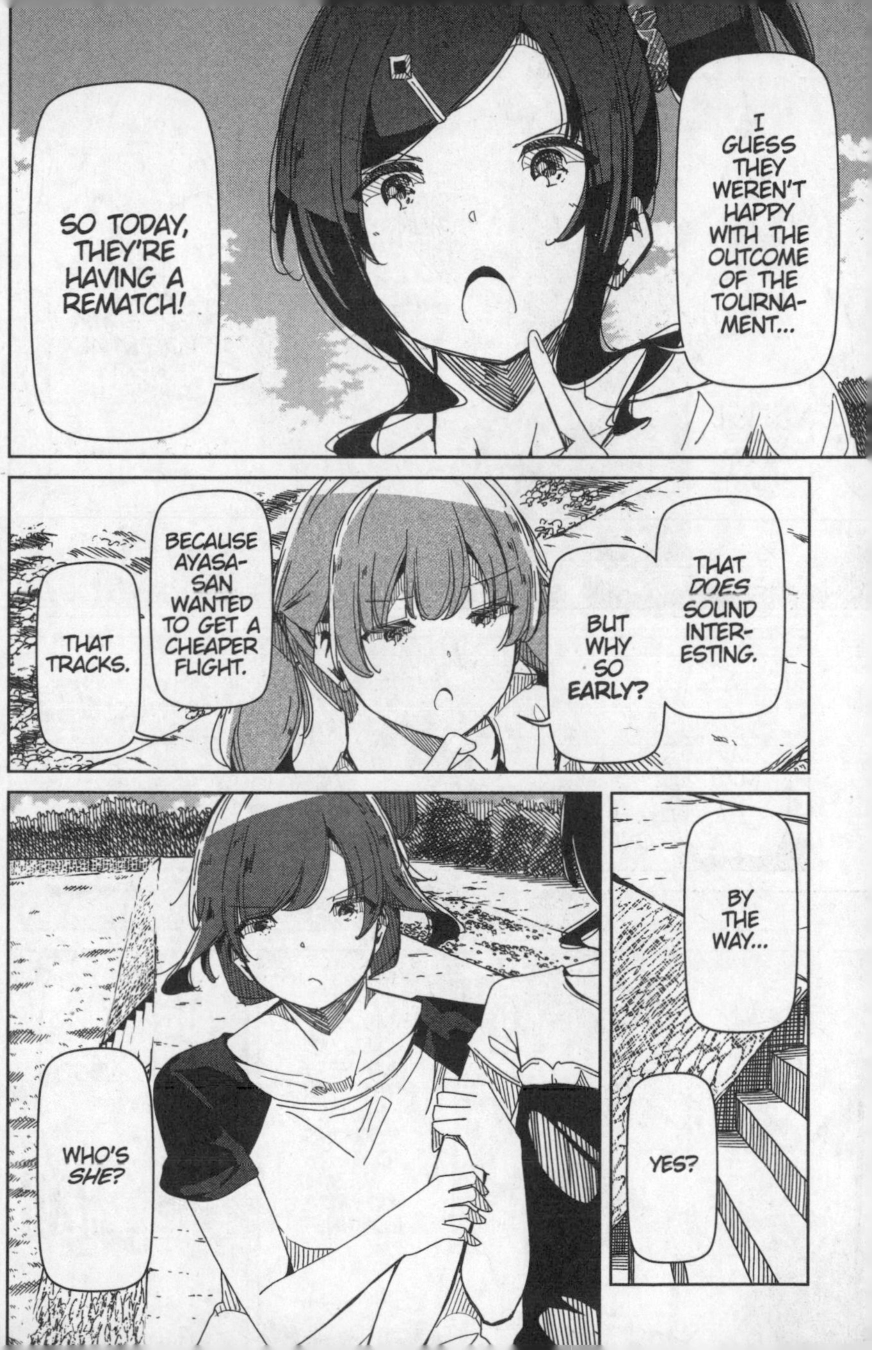
I GUESS THEY WEREN'T HAPPY WITH THE OUTCOME OF THE TOURNA-MENT...
SO TODAY, THEY'RE HAVING A REMATCH!
THAT *DOES* SOUND INTER-ESTING.
BUT WHY SO EARLY?
BECAUSE AYASA-SAN WANTED TO GET A CHEAPER FLIGHT.
THAT TRACKS.
BY THE WAY...
YES?
WHO'S *SHE*?

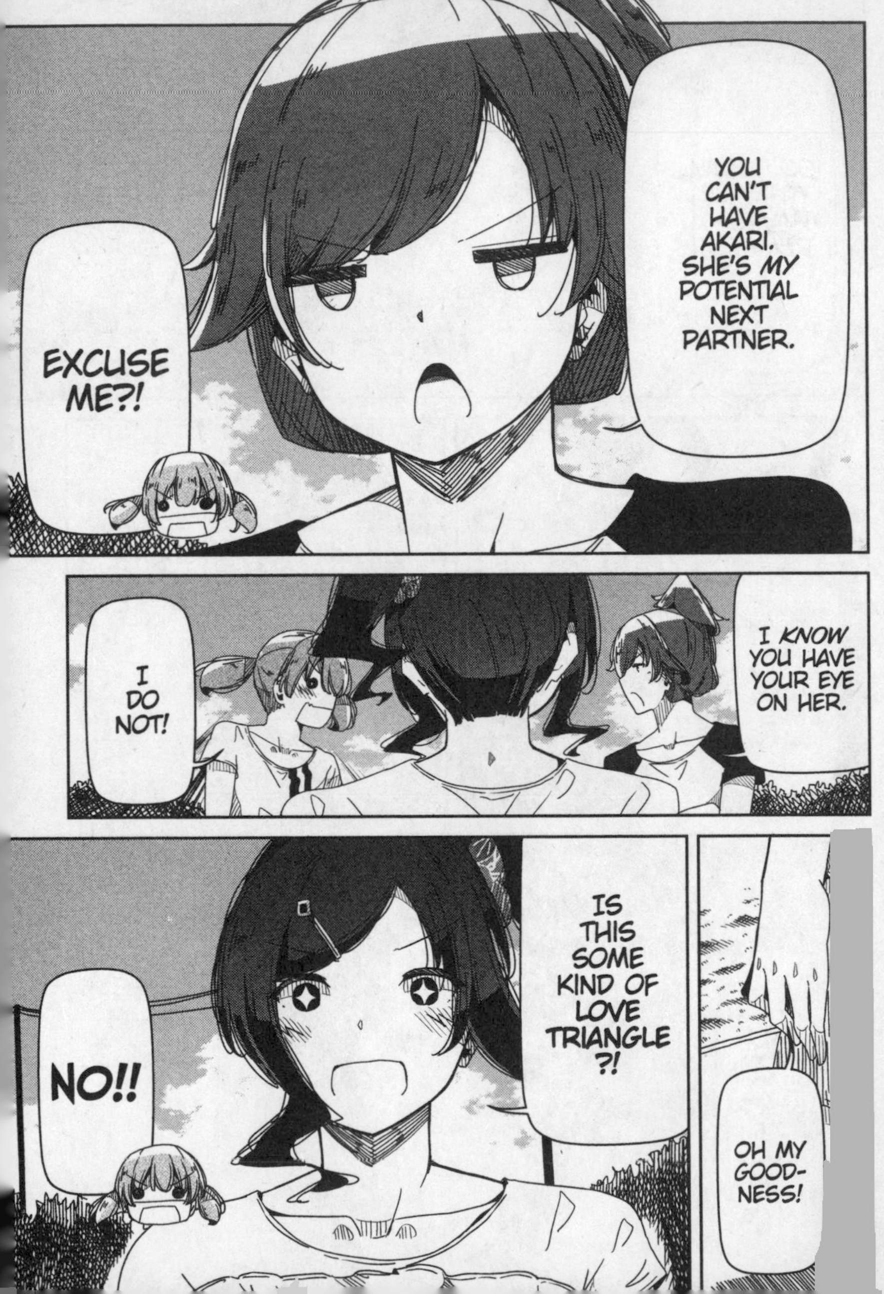
YOU CAN'T HAVE AKARI. SHE'S *MY* POTENTIAL NEXT PARTNER.
EXCUSE ME?!
I *KNOW* YOU HAVE YOUR EYE ON HER.
I DO NOT!
OH MY GOOD-NESS!
IS THIS SOME KIND OF LOVE TRIANGLE ?!
NO!!

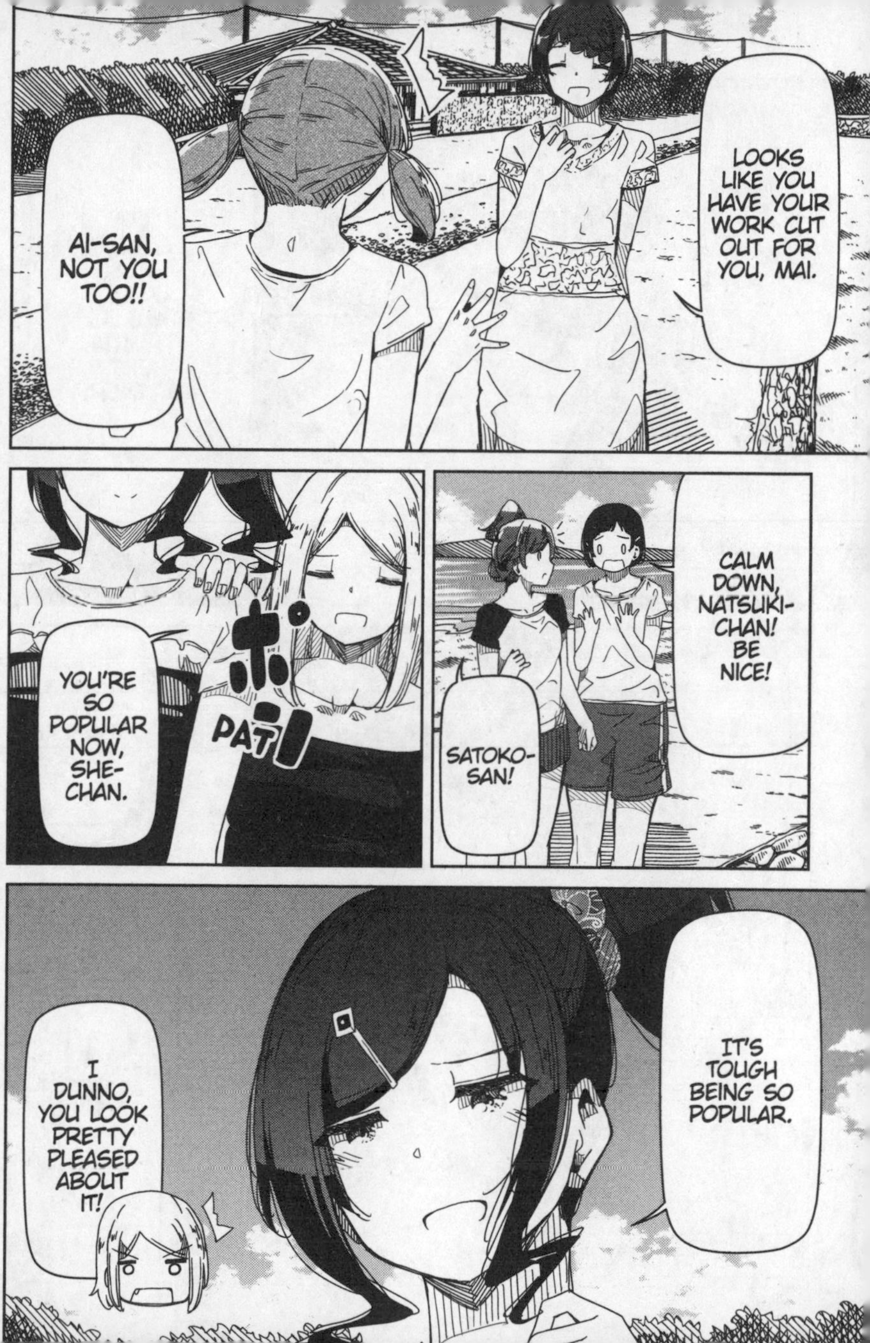
LOOKS LIKE YOU HAVE YOUR WORK CUT OUT FOR YOU, MAI.
AI-SAN, NOT YOU TOO!!
CALM DOWN, NATSUKI-CHAN! BE NICE!
SATOKO-SAN!
PAT
YOU'RE SO POPULAR NOW, SHE-CHAN.
IT'S TOUGH BEING SO POPULAR.
I DUNNO, YOU LOOK PRETTY PLEASED ABOUT IT!

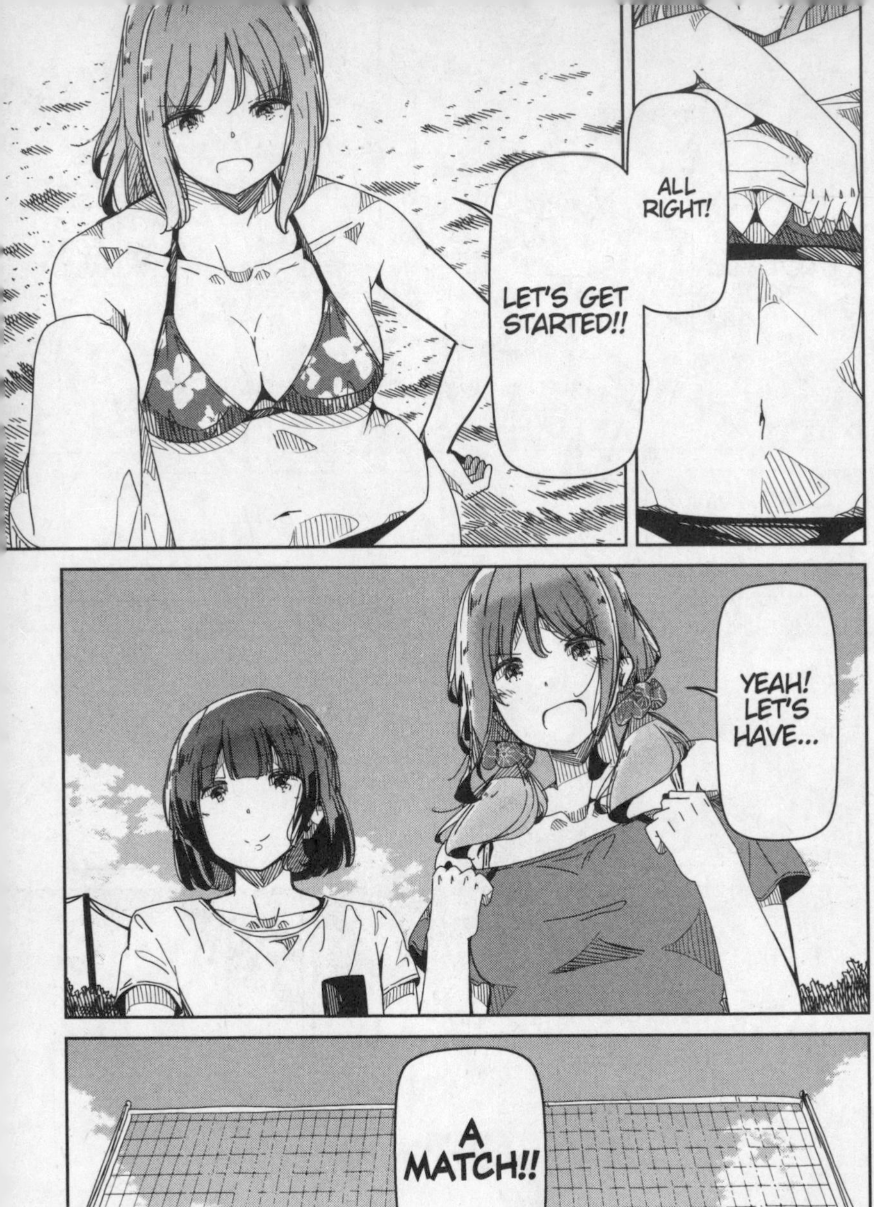
ALL RIGHT!
LET'S GET STARTED!!
YEAH! LET'S HAVE...
A MATCH!!

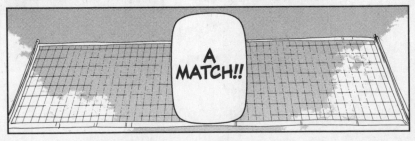

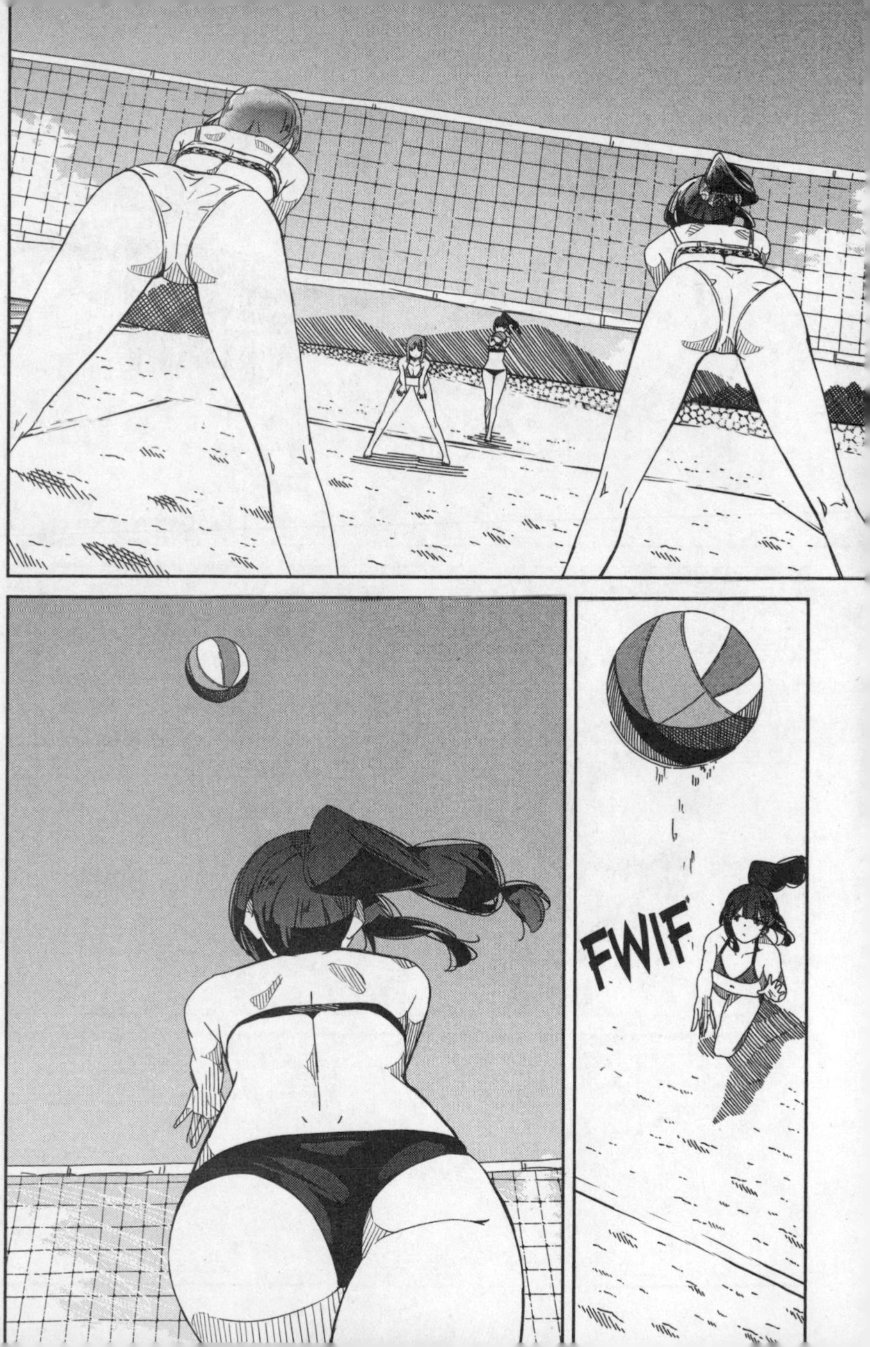
FWIF

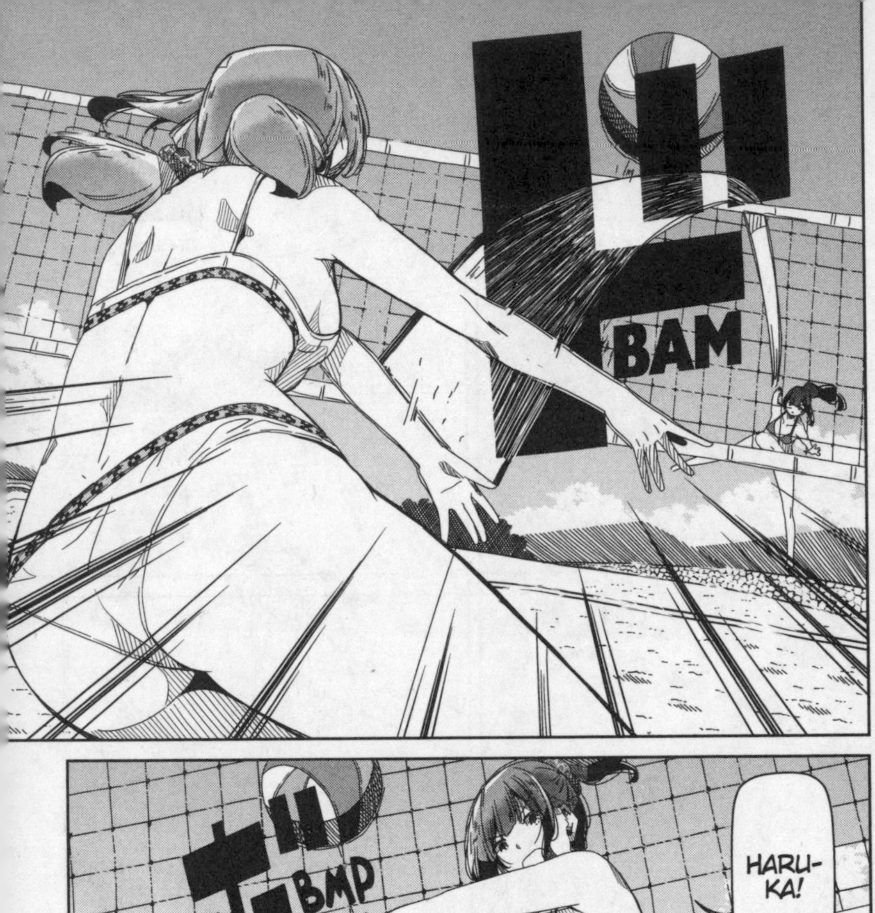
BAM
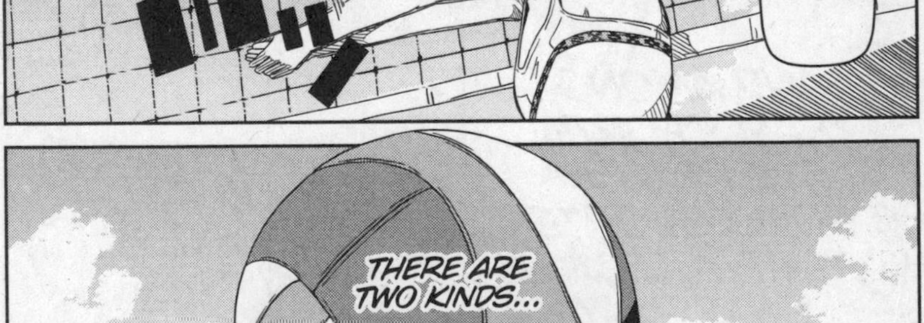
HARU-
KA!
BMP
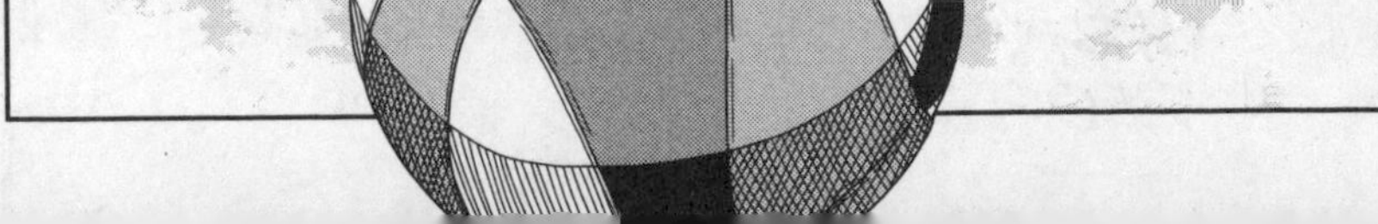
THERE ARE
TWO KINDS...

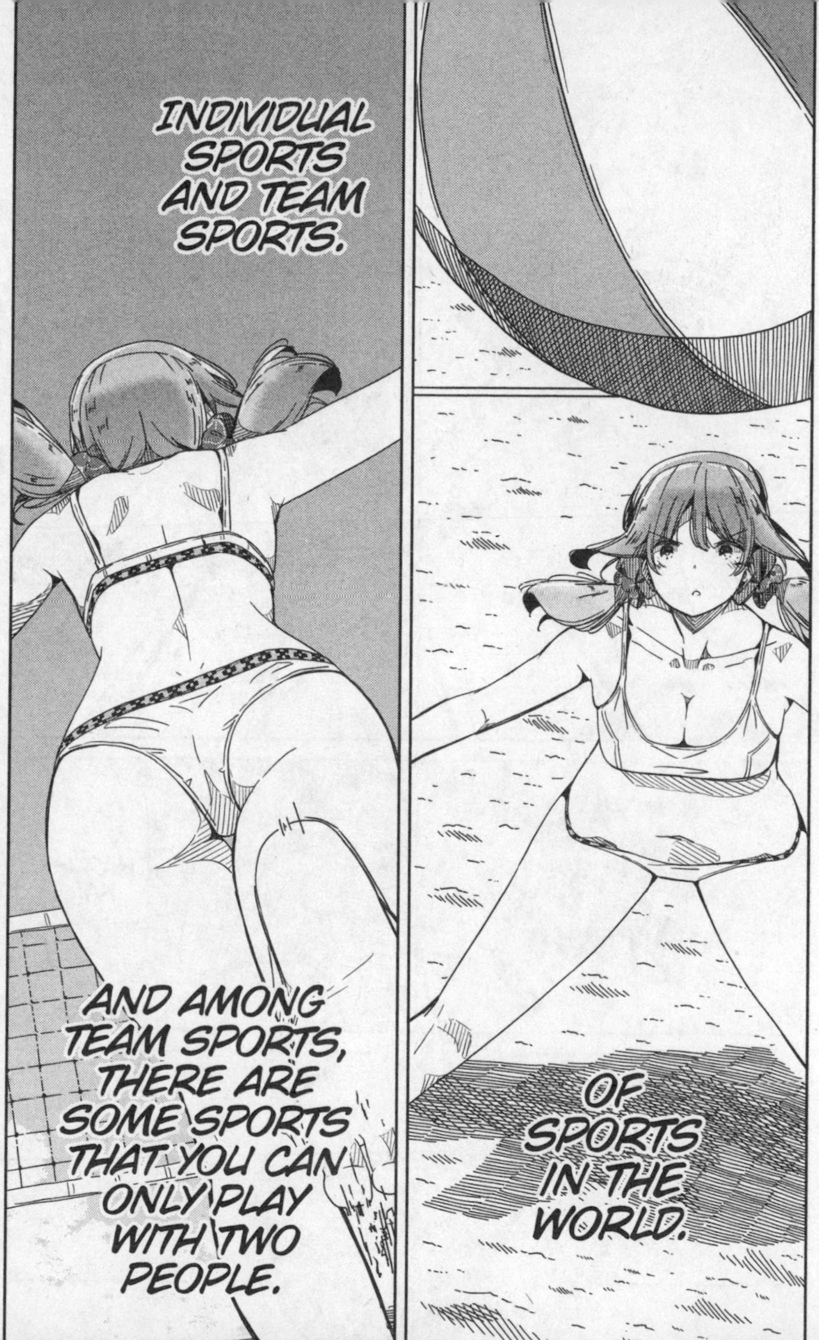
OF SPORTS IN THE WORLD.
INDIVIDUAL SPORTS AND TEAM SPORTS.
AND AMONG TEAM SPORTS, THERE ARE SOME SPORTS THAT YOU CAN ONLY PLAY WITH TWO PEOPLE.

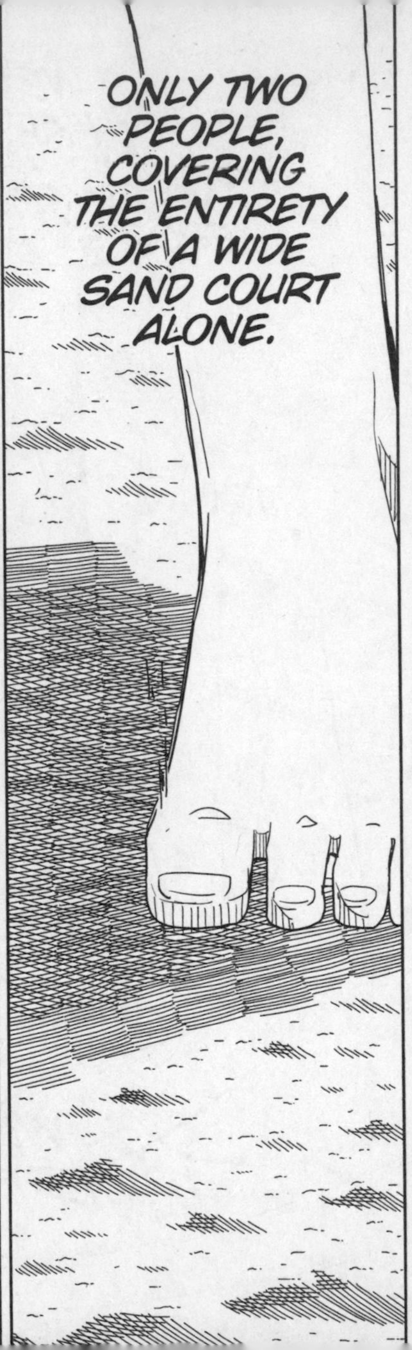
ONLY TWO PEOPLE, COVERING THE ENTIRETY OF A WIDE SAND COURT ALONE.
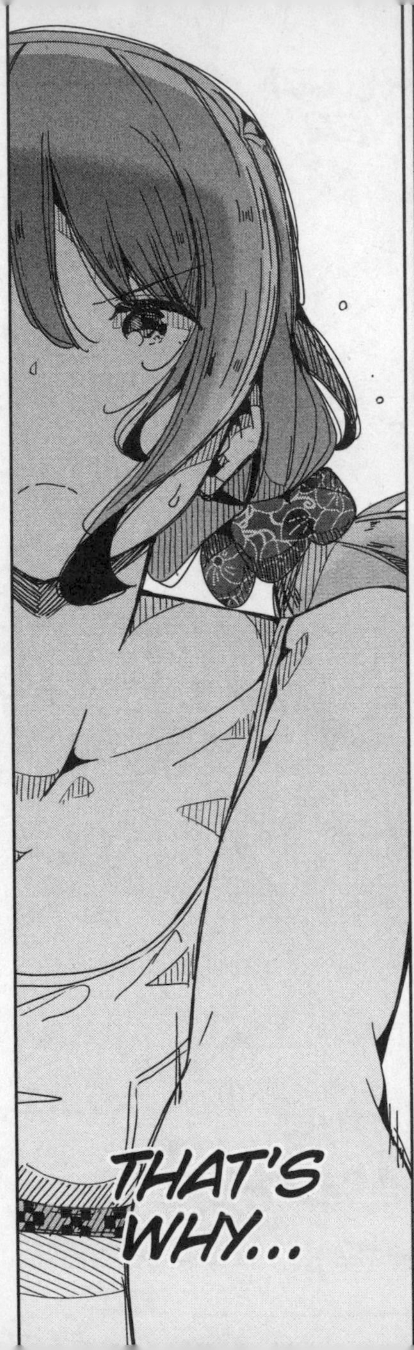
THAT'S WHY...

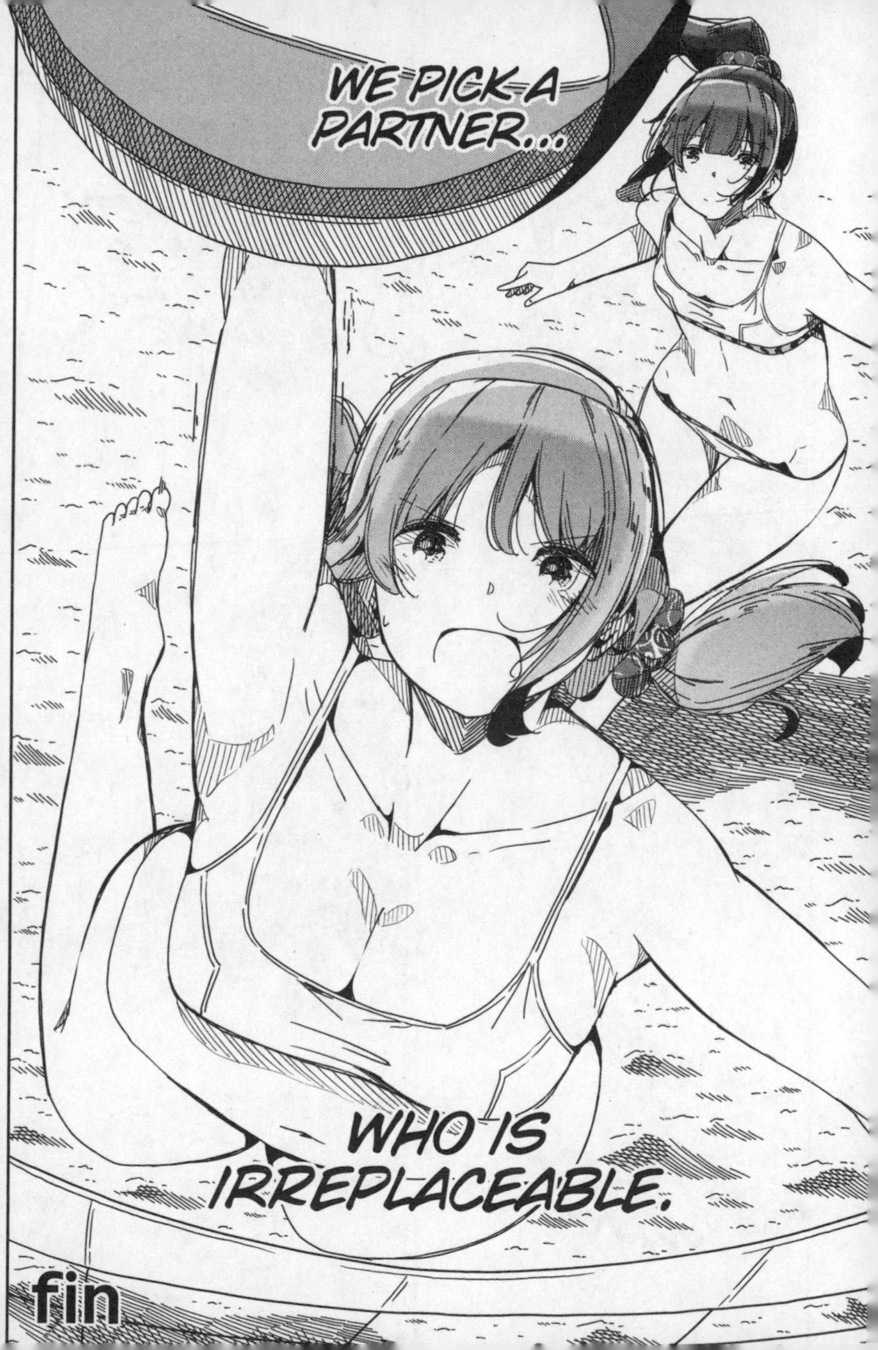
WE PICK A PARTNER...
WHO IS IRREPLACEABLE.
fin

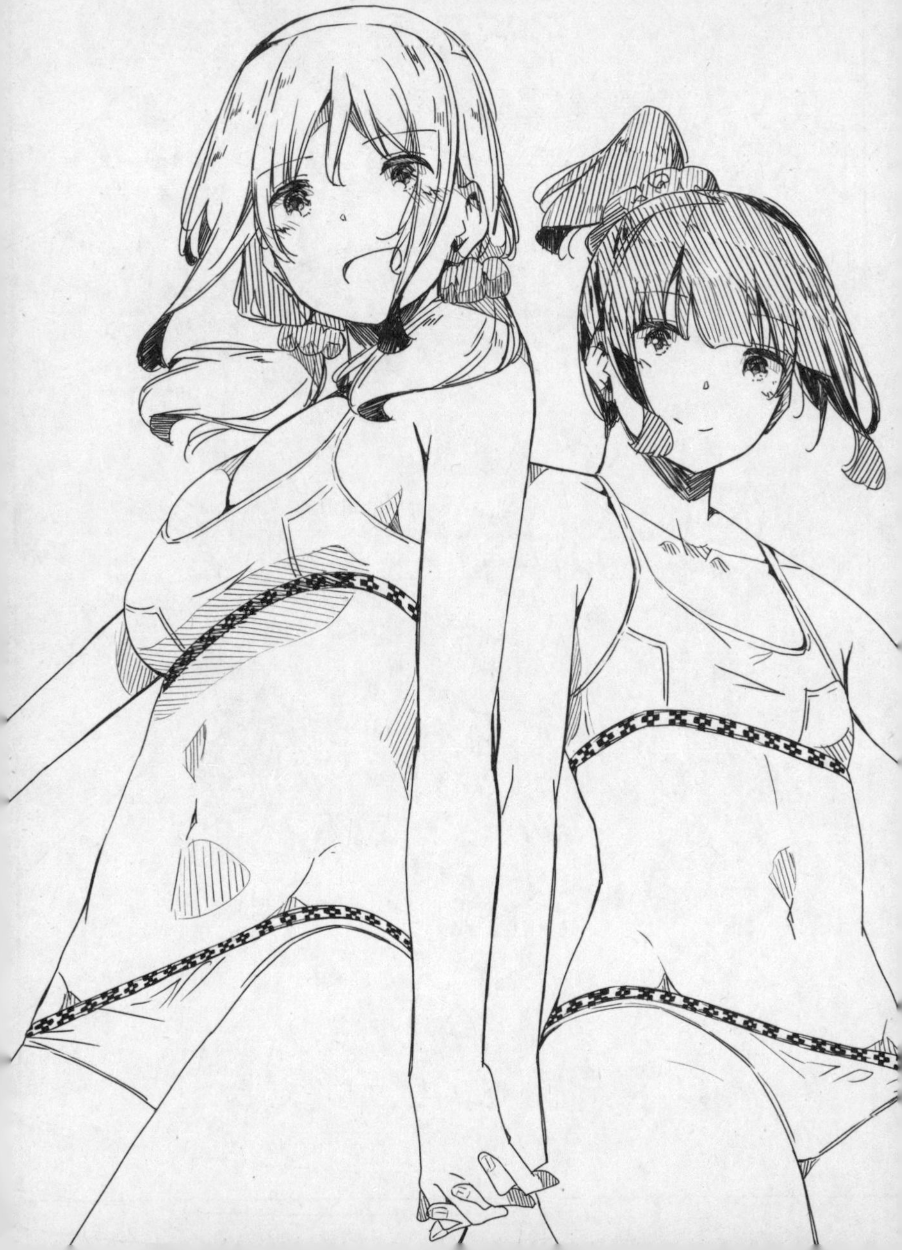

HARUKA & KANATA INITIAL DESIGNS

PONYTAIL

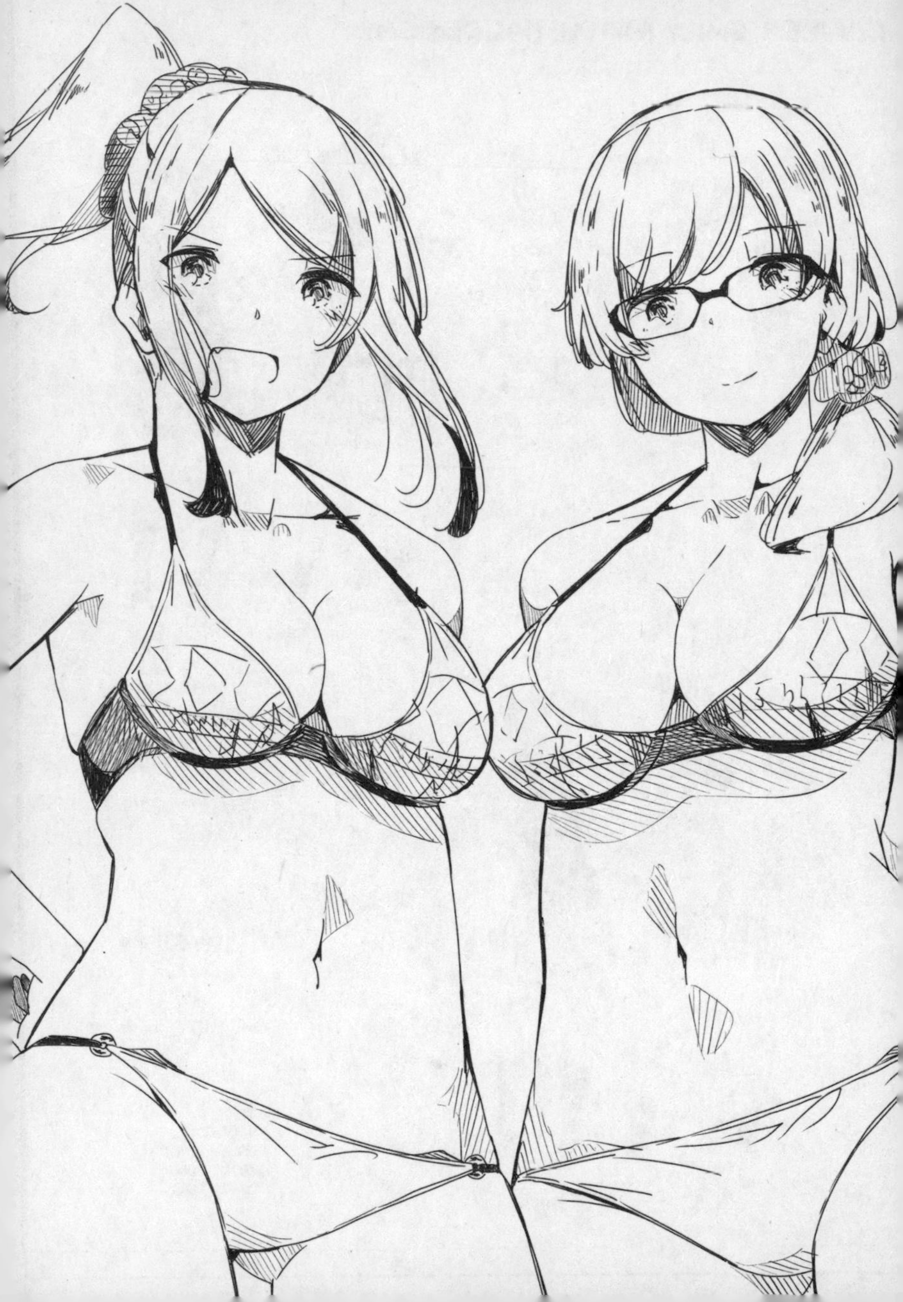

CLAIRE & EMILY INITIAL DESIGNS

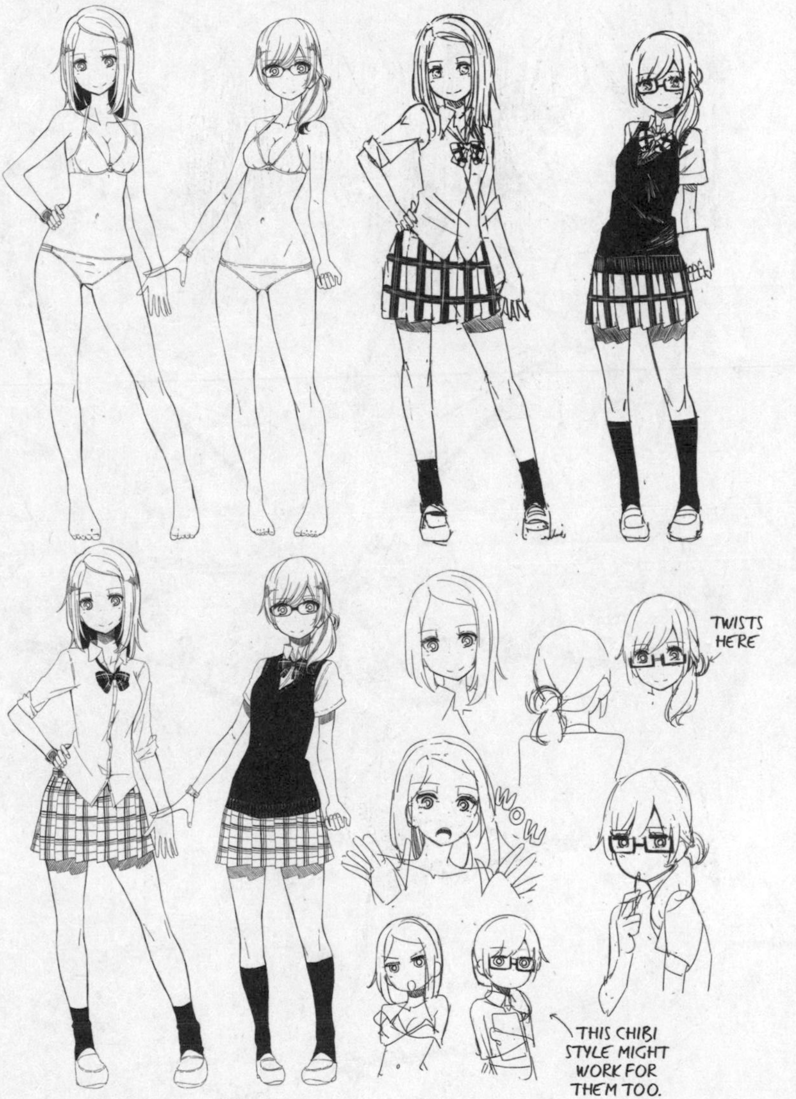
TWISTS HERE
WOW
THIS CHIBI STYLE MIGHT WORK FOR THEM TOO.

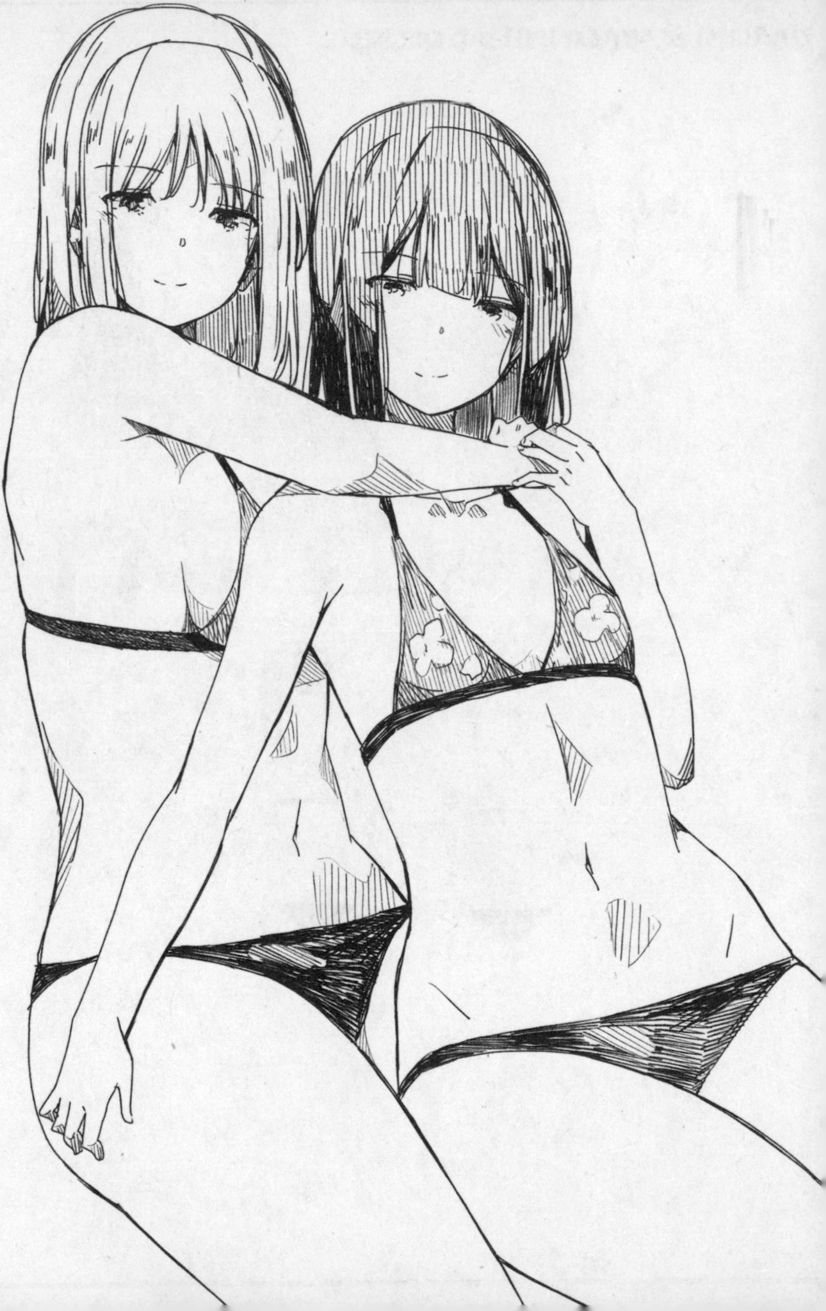

NARUMI & AYASA INITIAL DESIGNS

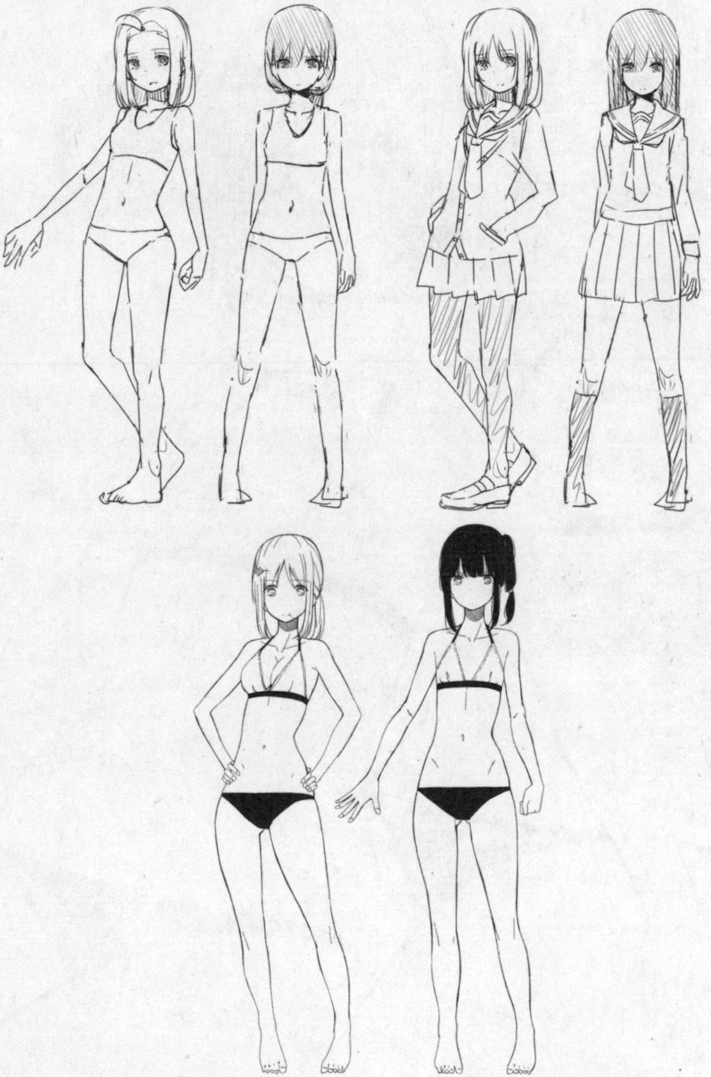

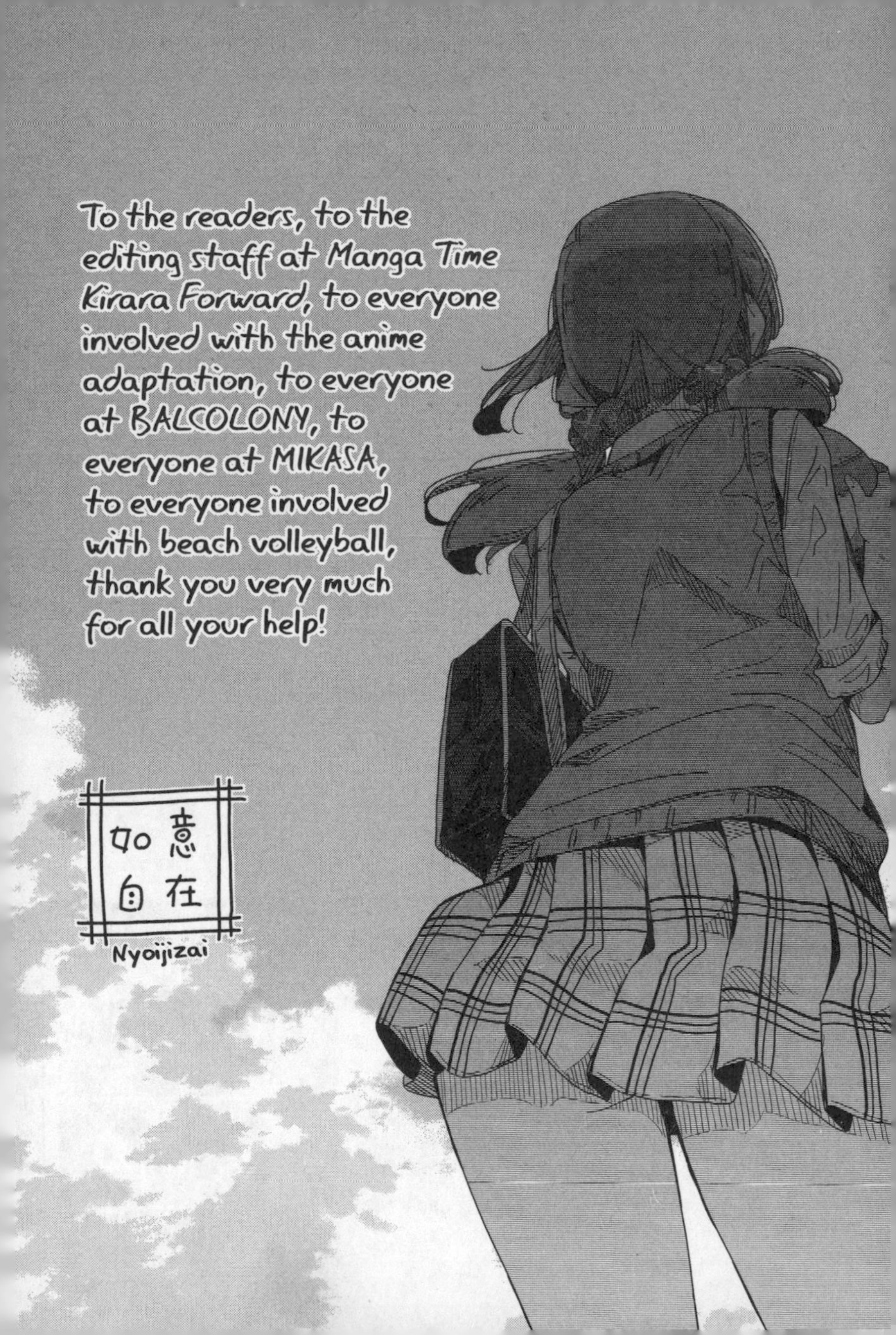
To the readers, to the editing staff at Manga Time Kirara Forward, to everyone involved with the anime adaptation, to everyone at BALCOLONY, to everyone at MIKASA, to everyone involved with beach volleyball, thank you very much for all your help!
如意自在
Nyoijizai

SEVEN SEAS ENTERTAINM

Harukana Recei

VOLUME 10 story and art by **NYOIJIZAI**

TRANSLATION
Amanda Haley

LETTERING AND RETOUCH
Ray Steeves

COVER DESIGN
Kris Aubin

PROOFREADER
Krista Grandy, B. Lillian Martin

SENIOR EDITOR
Shannon Fay

PRINT MANAGER
Rhiannon Rasmussen-Silverstein

PRODUCTION DESIGNER
Christa Miesner

PRODUCTION MANAGER
Lissa Pattillo

EDITOR-IN-CHIEF
Julie Davis

ASSOCIATE PUBLISHER
Adam Arnold

PUBLISHER
Jason DeAngelis

HARUKANARECEIVE Volume 10

Originally published in Japan in 2020 by HOUBUNSHA CO., LTD., Tokyo.
English translation rights arranged with HOUBUNSHA CO., LTD., Tokyo, through TOHAN CORPORATION, Tokyo.

Seven Seas press and purchase enquiries can be sent to Marketing Manager Lianne Sentar at press@gomanga.com. Information regarding the distribution and purchase of digital editions is available from Digital Manager CK Russell at digital@gomanga.com.

ISBN: 978-1-63858-224-3

Printed in Canada

First Printing: April 2022

10 9 8 7 6 5 4 3 2 1

FOLLOW US ONLINE: *www.sevenseasentertainment.com*

READING DIRECTIONS

This book reads from ***right to left***, Japanese style. If this is your first time reading manga, you start reading from the top right panel on each page and take it from there. If you get lost, just follow the numbered diagram here. It may seem backwards at first, but you'll get the hang of it! Have fun!!

1
2
3
4
5
6
7
8
9

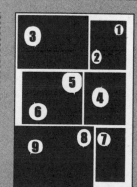